AT HOME IN EXILE

At Home in Exile

Why Diaspora Is Good for the Jews

ALAN WOLFE

BEACON PRESS, BOSTON

Beacon Press
Boston, Massachusetts
www.beacon.org

Beacon Press books
are published under the auspices of
the Unitarian Universalist Association of Congregations.

17   16   15   14   8   7   6   5   4   3   2   1

This book is printed on acid-free paper that meets the uncoated paper
ANSI/NISO specifications for permanence as revised in 1992.

Text design and composition by
Wilsted & Taylor Publishing Services

Library of Congress Cataloging-in-Publication Data

Wolfe, Alan.
At home in exile : why diaspora is good for the Jews / Alan Wolfe.
pages cm
Includes bibliographical references and index.
ISBN 978-0-8070-3313-5 (hardback) — ISBN 978-0-8070-3314-2 (ebook)
1. Jewish diaspora. 2. Zionism and Judaism. 3. Jews—Identity.
4. Jews—United States—Identity. I. Title.
DS134.W65 2014
909.04924—dc23   2014009531

For Enid

CONTENTS

INTRODUCTION

Diaspora's Destiny

I

In the years after World War II, the most important development in the more than two-thousand-year history of the Jewish people took place. I am not referring to Israel's birth in 1948, significant as that event was. I mean instead that a vibrant, successful, and above all else, secure life has, for the first time ever, become possible in states in which Jews are, and always will be, in the minority. "In the diaspora," proclaimed the *Economist* in the summer of 2012, "Jewish life has never been so free, so prosperous, so unthreatened."[1] That Jews can live among gentiles without living in fear is an epochal accomplishment, as much testimony to the perseverance of those who have made the Diaspora their home as it is to the willingness of their compatriots to overcome centuries of prejudice. Most remarkable of all, it is rarely remarked. Of course, that the Jews should live with freedom and equality, most, if alas not all, of their fellow citizens in this day and age would be the first to acknowledge, failing to appreciate how radical and unsettling their grandparents would have found such a sentiment.

It is time for the Diaspora to have its due. Living at the mercy of the majorities around them throughout history, Jews have experienced more than their fair share of discrimination and destruction, the latter as thorough and unwarranted as any group has ever faced. Nor can there be any doubt that anti-Semitism persists throughout the contemporary world and rears its ugly head all too many times. Yet lost in the tales of endless woe that Jews so frequently tell each other has been the opportunity that living in a land not their own has offered: a deep understanding of unfairness and a commitment to the absolute necessity of fighting against it. "Exile and dispersion," as David J. Goldberg, rabbi emeritus of London's Liberal Jewish Synagogue, writes of the Jews, "far from being the disasters they were invariably considered to be were in fact blessings in disguise, enabling them to escape the fate that befell other contemporary nations rooted in a single territory."[2] (In England, Liberal Judaism, to the left of American Reform, is "a kind of Jewish Unitarianism," as the historian Todd Endelman characterizes it.)[3] Now that they have become so much safer in non-Jewish lands, Diaspora Jews are in a stronger-than-ever position to transform the passion for justice that so moved the Hebrew prophets into ideals of human dignity desperately needed in an age of rising domestic inequality and overseas instability. This, unfortunately, has not been happening, at least not enough. The Jewish Defense League is a violence-prone organization rightly condemned by Jews around the world. But defensiveness is widespread among all those Diaspora Jews who remain reluctant to accept the fact that at long last they belong where they have long chosen to live.

It is not difficult to grasp why contemporary Jews have failed to appreciate the blessings that exile has conveyed to them. For the past seventy-plus years—the same years in which I, born in 1942, have been alive—Jewish life has been marked by the shift, in the course of a mere decade, from the horrors of the Holocaust to the haven offered by statehood. Both events are therefore inevitably linked, and not just because Yom HaShoah (Holocaust Memorial Day) occurs just a week before Yom Ha'atzmaut (Israeli Independence Day). It is often said that there exists within Judaism a tension between particularism and universalism, one of those dichotomies that on the one hand dramatically oversimplifies but on the other contains a great deal of truth: particularists believe that Jews should be primarily concerned with their own, while universalists insist they are under a special obligation to spread the light of reason to as many people as possible. The twin events that have dominated contemporary Jewish life created an environment especially conducive to particularism: the Holocaust, after all, singled out Jews for extermination, while Israel singled them out for expansion. Statehood promised a final solution to the Final Solution: now that they had achieved it, Jews would finally constitute a nation like the others, able to speak in its own name and defend its own interests.

Finality, alas, was not to be. Because it was built on land occupied by others, the Jewish state has been unable to satisfy the need for security that gave rise to it. Nor, despite a dynamic economy and numerous efforts at outreach, has it been able to appeal to all Jews: roughly half of world Jewry has made aliyah (ascent), the Hebrew word that characterizes the decision to leave the Diaspora for Israel. (Worse than that, at least for those who consider Israel the only appropriate home for the Jews, a significant number of Israelis in recent years have made *yeridah,* or descent into the gentile world.) As it increasingly becomes clear that the Diaspora is not a disaster and that the security offered by statehood has proven to be precarious, the lost universalism that has been so much a part of Jewish tradition may well be prepared for a comeback, and this time on firmer ground than in the past. This will be good for the Jews no matter where they live, Israel very much included. It will be just as important for the non-Jews with whom they live, Israel, again, very much included. That, in a nutshell, is what this book aims to demonstrate.

II

As important as it may be to achieve, no one should expect that a revival of diasporic universalism will prove easy. There are four intimately interconnected reasons why so many Jews are determined never to forget the events of the 1930s and 1940s, no matter the cost to the universalist element in their own tradition.

The first is the feeling, strongly believed if rarely explicitly stated, that honoring the living somehow insults the dead. Six million Jews, from this perspective, did not die so that another six million could lead the good life in New York, Toronto, London, or, God forbid, Berlin. Since Hitler was determined to kill each and every one of them, any Jew who is now alive must be so through sheer chance: by the decision of one's grandparents to leave Europe before it all began, for example, or by the fact that they boarded one train rather than another, or because they had the right connections to obtain an ever-elusive exit visa. When survival is the result of individual fortitude, pride in longevity follows. When it is a roll of the dice that determines who shall live, the winners ought to have the good sense not to brag. Every living Jew must understand that he or she is taking the place of another who never had the opportunity. Guilt that pervasive is not easily overcome. More important, at least to those who think this way, it should never be overcome. Best keep satisfaction with one's diasporic experience muted lest the ghosts of the Shoah's victims be stirred.

The never fully quarantined disease of anti-Semitism is commonly brought forward as the second reason for Jews never to succumb to any illusion of security the Diaspora seemingly offers. Hitler aimed to settle the Jewish question once and for all and, although not in the way he expected, he did; because of what he believed and managed to carry out, Jews must keep their mental suitcases constantly packed. Waiting for the next Hitler to appear requires that instances of Jew hatred, as if they had become part of a secular liturgy, be told and retold with increasing fervor. How, this responsive reading asks, can any Jew be safe in Paris when Jewish children are killed in Toulouse? British Jews can and do attend Oxford and Cambridge, but anti-Semitism in that country, now polite and respectable rather than cruel and arbitrary, is, it has been charged, as pernicious as ever. It is only a matter of time before societies long known for their record of anti-Semitism, especially those in Eastern Europe such as Hungary, Ukraine, and Russia, return to their pattern of hating the Jews, paradoxically made all that much easier because so few of them live there now. America's Jews may have it better than those in Europe, but let an economic crisis linger, and criticisms of Wall Street, which the knowing inform us are actually attacks on the Jews, will come from the angry left rather than from the nativist right. And above all else, there are the Islamic militants, whether they live in the Middle East or in the West, who, as a number of rather fervid writers cannot help but point out, have inherited the hideous Nazi obsession with the Jews and are unafraid to act upon it. Jews can never bring Hitler's victims back to life. But, the conclusion follows, they can at least avoid the mistaken optimism that condemned so many to death. Because so many were killed, everyone else must be wary.

Love for everything Israel has accomplished since its founding, third, keeps Jews in a particularist frame of mind. For those who view it as the last refuge against hatred, Israel has everything Diaspora Jewry lacks. In contrast to a long tradition of subservient court Jewry more accustomed to exercising flattery rather than power, its military makes it the dominant state in the Middle East. It is home to Jews of every conceivable variety. Because of the protection it continues to offer to Jews who remain vulnerable in Eastern European or in Arab lands, it is still the natural destination for those unwelcome in the countries in which they live. For the most religious, it is too secular and for the secular it is too religious. But its very existence demonstrates to the world that, because they have a state of their own, Jews can never again be treated as a people undeserving of the respect of others. Of course Israel needs the Diaspora, for without the support of American Jews especially, it would have too few friends in the world. Yet for all that, the notion persists that Diaspora Jews, cut off from the language, traditions, and sense of solidarity that nationhood offers, are being unfaithful to their Jewishness. Israel's strength and Jewish survival, many believe, have become one and the same. Should the day ever come when seemingly secure Diaspora Jews find themselves not so welcome at home after all, the mere existence of a Jewish state means that, unlike the last time around, they will have a place to go.

But will Israel continue to exist? The final reason so many Jews are determined never to forget the events of past decades and their relevance to the realities of today is the idea that everything the Jews have accomplished with their sovereignty is now being threatened by ever-newer enemies determined to wipe the Jewish state from the face of the earth. Statehood, to the great regret of Israel's defenders, has transferred rather than solved the problem of Jew hatred: Israel's very triumphs have led to new rounds of criticism of its policies or plans to boycott its products, and these moves, expressed in the language of support for supposedly oppressed people such as the Palestinians, are, we are told, in reality little more than expressions of age-old tropes about Jewish power. This proclivity to single out Israel for its alleged crimes, while ignoring or excusing away worse crimes of other states, offers one more argument for concluding that celebrating diasporic universalism is a bad idea. The Jewish people, always small in number and vulnerable to attack, need to present a united front to the rest of the world. Intentionally or not, a focus on diasporic success undermines that unity, for if Jews can flourish outside the Jewish state, the fundamental rationale for that state's existence is inevitably brought into question. Zionists did not build a home for some Jews so that others could treat it as a place to go on vacation. The cold, hard truth about the Diaspora is that no matter how welcoming it may seem, it will always be a second home. That is why the first home, for all its vulnerability, constitutes the last line of defense. Its Jews are willing to give up their lives so that Jews everywhere else can live.

These are all emotionally powerful matters touching on the most sensitive of subjects. Unable to ignore the Nazi years that brought such ways of thinking into being—indeed obsessed by those years to the point of reading endless books and watching nearly every new film about them—I find myself unable to dismiss such points of view out of hand. Nonetheless, they must be discussed and, when necessary, challenged. The scholar Jacob Neusner, who has argued passionately that "America is a better place to be a Jew than Jerusalem," sees in the conjunction of events that dominate the consciousness of contemporary Jewry nothing less than a new faith, which he calls the Judaism of Holocaust and Redemption.[4] But this faith, rooted in history rather than God, cannot appeal to eternal truths: the events that brought it into existence will inevitably lose their emotional power as new generations arise with new needs and interests. Already we can see signs that this is happening. According to the Pew Research Center, which published an exhaustive study of the attitudes of American Jews in 2013, 77 percent of those sixty-five or older considered remembrance of the Holocaust as an essential element of Jewish identity compared to 68 percent of those between ages eighteen and twenty-nine.[5] A similar, indeed more striking change involved Israel: 91 percent of the younger cohort say that people can be considered Jewish if they are strongly critical of Israel compared to 84 percent among the older group, and three times as many younger Jews than older ones believe that the United States is *too* supportive of Israel. Theodore Sasson of Middlebury College argues that this change does not necessarily imply decreasing support for Israel among younger Diaspora Jews so much as a change toward a more individualized, less organizationally dominated way of thinking about the relationship.[6] Yet even if he is correct, which seems unlikely given the size of the shift, there can be little doubt that the Holocaust's impact has been fading as new generations come to the fore.

One can lament all this by arguing, as one scholar of Jewish studies has, that something special will be lost if what happened to the Jews is watered down by treating Jewish suffering as a metaphor for all human suffering,[7] just as one can accuse Jews who show insufficient zeal for Zion as somehow manifesting symptoms of self-hatred. But this puts contemporary Jews in the position of making the recollection of their pain central to everything they think and do. Far better, I believe, is to face the fact that the world never stops changing while at the same time never to forget that pain and that past. For a people as for a person, living with hope means living better than living paralyzed by fear.

III

In theory, no reason prevents a Jewish state from embodying universalist values; no matter how far Israel turns to the right, as it so distressingly has in recent years, more than its share of writers and thinkers speak eloquently of human rights or find fault with their own society's chauvinism. In a world in which nation-states are primarily concerned with protecting their own, however, the Diaspora remains the place where universalistic Judaism will thrive best. Its Judaism will become more complex and vibrant as its culture intermingles with other cultures. Its religion, far from dissolving into meaningless syncretism, will be enriched by its encounter with other faiths. Its ethnicity will no longer be defined by the vulgarity of Jackie Mason, the claustrophobia of *Fiddler on the Roof*, or the determination to prevent Yiddish from breathing its last breath, but instead will be free to find new forms of expression in a world that values individual freedom more than group attachment. In one sense Jews are like everyone else: they must manage to find ways to be true to their heritage in an ever-changing world. In another sense they are relatively unique: their character as a diasporic people gives them a powerful advantage for meeting that challenge, even if their current inclination is not to use it.

Because I speak favorably about the Diaspora, no one should accuse me, or so I hope, of being a "diasporist." Readers of Philip Roth will know that I am referring to *Operation Shylock*, in which a Newark-born Jewish novelist named Philip Roth finds himself distressed by another man using the same name, and even wearing the same clothes, who advocates "a program that seeks to resettle all Israeli Jews of European origin back in those countries where they or their families were residents before the outbreak of the Second World War and thereby to avert a 'second Holocaust,'" this one at the hands of the Arabs.[8] Roth meant diasporism to be absurd, and it indeed is; leaving Tel Aviv for Krakow would benefit the residents of neither (although this did not prevent the Israeli Dutch avant-garde artist Yael Bartana from imaginatively exploring the same ground in *And Europe Will Be*

Stunned, a three-part video in which a Jewish resistance movement in Poland advocates reverse Zionism in order to bring pluralism back to that country).

It is more important what Jews think than where they live: Just as Israel remains the home of at least some Jewish universalists, the Diaspora has more than its share of narrow particularists. At one point in *Operation Shylock,* Roth the novelist is saved from a mob outside Ramallah by an Israeli lieutenant, Gal Metzler, who, as it happens, had just been reading one of his novels. They get into a discussion—*Operation Shylock,* like so much of Roth, is one long discussion after another—and Metzler tells him that "the Diaspora is the normal condition and Zionism is the abnormality," which, to him, means that only Diaspora Jews can be authentic ones.[9] Roth was no doubt playing on writers such as A. B. Yehoshua—we will meet him in the chapter that follows—who insist that only in Israel can Jews lead authentic lives. I disagree with both; if by authentic we mean being shaped by one tradition while gaining respect for others, Jews can lead that sort of life anywhere.

Unlike those who see threats to Jewish continuity from both anti-Semitism and assimilation, I believe that Judaism, which has been around so long, is not going away anytime soon. The crucial question is what kind of Judaism it will be: open and inquiring or defensive and insecure. No one can know the answer to that question; so much happened to the Jews in the twentieth century that presuming to predict what will happen to them in the remainder of the twenty-first is beyond anyone's capacity. But just as Israel is a fact of life, and, in my opinion, has every right to exist (although I hope in a humane way rather than the one its current direction indicates), the Diaspora also is here to stay, and with it the universalism that was so much part of its history. Now that the events of the 1930s and 1940s are beginning to lose their hold on the consciousness of younger generations, Jews in both Israel and the Diaspora need each other more than ever. Their relationship will be best served if one side drops its contempt and the other awakens its conscience.

CHAPTER 1

We'll Rot till We Stink

I

Chaim Weizmann (1874–1952), the distinguished chemist, respected Zionist, and future first president of Israel, was not pleased. "I was astonished to hear a few months ago," he told a Tel Aviv meeting in 1947, "that someone wants to establish a Jewish university in America. I raise my voice in warning: Do not waste the strength of the Jewish people. There is no substitute for Zion."[1] Nearly a half century earlier, Weizmann had begun to develop plans for a university in Palestine;[2] proud of his success—the Hebrew University of Jerusalem is undoubtedly one of Zionism's greatest accomplishments—he may well have viewed the American effort as unwelcome competition. Such was the conclusion of one of the most learned Jewish scholars of his era, the Hebraist Simon Rawidowicz (1897–1957), born in a town in Lithuania then part of Russia but living in England. What a shame it would be, Rawidowicz wrote in protest, if the Zionist pioneers viewed the Diaspora only as a source of fund-raising rather than as a worthwhile place of learning.

Weizmann's plea fell on deaf ears; one year after he gave his talk, Brandeis University came into existence—and soon thereafter hired Rawidowicz, who had been turned down for a position at the Hebrew

University, to build its graduate program in New Eastern and Judaic Studies. Still, in dismissing the idea of a Jewish university outside Palestine, Weizmann was reflecting a point of view that had become deeply entrenched in the Zionist view of the world. This was called *shlilat ha'golah*, or "negation of the Diaspora." Hebrew has two cognate words for those who live outside the Jewish state, *golah*, usually translated as "dispersion," and *galut*, meaning "exile." For Weizmann this was a distinction without a difference: a Jewish university ought not to be built in the United States, he believed, because Jewish life in any society but Israel was too impoverished to sustain it. "The spiritual centers of Jewry have been destroyed," as he put the matter in his 1947 talk. "The source from which the Diaspora drew is weakened and we must create the center here in order to educate Jews."[3]

More than any other idea associated with the Zionist movement, Diaspora negation poses as clearly as possible the question of just what it means to be a Jew in the contemporary world. Classical Zionists insisted that anything necessary to arouse the Jewish people from their torpor, to raise their sights and appeal to their pride, no matter how harshly expressed, was a necessary step on the road to statehood—and therefore crucial to Jewish survival. With the arrival of the twin cataclysmic twentieth-century events that have done so much to shape contemporary Jewish consciousness, the Holocaust followed by the founding of Israel, such a position seemed to justify itself: if Jews were indeed facing extermination, the choice to live in exile could only be described as a horrible miscalculation, and the opportunity to live in their own state offered a chance not to be missed.

Although the twentieth century teaches the dangers of statelessness, however, it also demonstrates the blinders of nationalism. Nationalists everywhere have an inclination to romanticize their own and condemn their enemies. Jewish nationalism added its own wrinkle: aspiring to create a state out of people scattered all over the world, Zionism cast aspersions on those who were still part of the nation so long as they were reluctant to become part of the state. The inevitable question raised by persistent efforts to offend those who live outside the Jewish state, down to their reiterations at the present time, is whether a deep love of the Jewish people requires hostility toward so many of the individual Jews who compose it. More than a century of argument that the Diaspora is the wrong place for Jews to live, after all, has not stopped millions of Jews from still doing so. If they are making a serious mistake, they should by all means be subject to criticism. But if the Diaspora is neither so fearful nor so harmful as its detractors insist, it is possible and desirable for Jews to live as a majority in a Jewish state and take pride in their people that way—or to live as a minority somewhere else and take pride in their people in another way. Indeed, should the Jewish state be taking steps that undermine its viability, as many believe to be happening in this era of illegal settlements and right-wing intransigence, the best thing Jews can do to further the survival of the Jewish state is to remain outside Israel and keep the tradition of diasporic universalism as vibrant as possible.

II

Of all the adherents to *shlilat ha'golah*, the best known is Chaim Nachman Bialik (1873–1934), Israel's national poet. In "Return," written in 1896, a Jewish youth comes back to the village of his birth and is shocked by what he finds:

> Once more. Look: a spent old scarecrow
> shriveled face
> straw-dry shadow
> swaying like a leaf
> bending and swaying over books.
> . . .
> There's the household cat
> has not moved since I left,
> still dreaming by the stove
> playing cat and mouse
> in his dream.
> . . .

You've not changed:
All old as the hills.
Nothing new.
I'll join you, old cronies!
Together we'll rot till we stink.[4]

Bialik had reason for his concern: he was preoccupied by the hostility shown by the tsarist authorities toward the Jews of Russia and Ukraine; and he was convinced of the Jews' passivity in response. (His powerful poem "In the City of Slaughter" was written in response to the 1903 Kishinev pogrom.) In truth, the Jews of the Pale were not nearly as resigned to their fate as Bialik suggested, not even during Kishinev, where resistance did in fact take place.[5] Nonetheless, his message could not have been clearer: the only future for the Jews in the lands in which most of them were born was inevitably going to be a decrepit one.

Bialik was joined by a host of like-minded others. Joseph Chaim Brenner (1881–1921), a short story writer who was later murdered at the hands of an Arab mob in the city of Jaffe, and who spoke of Diaspora Jews as "gypsies and filthy dogs," often wins the contest as the most extreme: "No other Jewish writer has ever portrayed in such cruel terms his fellow Jews," writes the historian Walter Laqueur, "the fools and the brutes, the dirty *schnorrers*,* or the decay of a people which had lost all the attributes of normal existence."[6] In truth, however, the contest was wide open. Aaron David Gordon (1856–1922), an early theorist of Labor Zionism, whose organic version of nationalism was strongly shaped by German romantic thinkers, wrote of the "parasitism of a fundamentally useless people" that "was broken and crushed . . . sick and diseased in body and soul."[7] Jacob Klatzkin (1882–1948), a translator, philosopher, and editor, like Bialik believed that the Jews "would rot away" if they continued to live in exile,[8] a condition he defined as "nothing more than a life of deterioration and degeneration, a disgrace to the nation and a disgrace to the individual,

*Translation: Beggar, sponger.

a life of pointless struggle and futile suffering, of ambivalence, confusion, and eternal impotence."[9] The Hebrew essayist Micah Joseph
Berdichevsky (1865–1921) dismissed those "who were not a nation, not
a people, not human."[10] And then there was the literary critic Isidor
Eliashev (1873–1924), who wrote that the typical Eastern European
Jew "repels every healthy man. . . . They live like a worm reared in the
gutter of a roof which then falls off the roof into a street-drain, but
perforce then acclimatizes itself to its new environment."[11]

Although the brutal conditions in the Pale may have given these
writers their bitter tone, their views were different only in degree from
those who characterized the more assimilated and better educated
Jews of Western Europe in equally harsh terms. Heinrich Graetz
(1817–1891), the first modern historian of the Jewish people, predated
writers such as Bialik and Brenner and in that sense does not belong
with those committed to *shlilat ha'golah*. At the same time, he also
provides a vivid example of just how far Jews could go in condemning others of their own faith. Because Jews were doomed never to
be fully accepted by their Christian hosts, as Graetz filled his many
volumes documenting, it stood to reason that any Jew who strove for
such acceptance must have been misguided, his mind poisoned by the
temptation of living with Christians all around him. Graetz found
a prototype for this dangerous form of assimilation in the reformer
David Friedländer (1750–1834), son-in-law of a leading Berlin banker
and widely viewed as a leader of the Jewish Enlightenment. Friedländer had unsuccessfully proposed a "dry baptism" in which Jews
would be allowed to join the Lutheran Church, although without sub-
scribing to the divinity of Jesus Christ, and for this apostasy Graetz
overlooked all his subsequent work on behalf of Jewish emancipation
to label him what today would be called self-hating. "Neither Jewish
antiquity, nor Hebrew poetry, nor family ties, had power to keep him
loyal to his banner, even with half-hearted devotion" the historian
wrote. Taking no pains to conceal his contempt, Graetz characterized
Friedländer and his friends as "apes" who "deplored the decay of morality among the Jews, without noticing that their own shallow desire for
enlightenment had contributed to it."[12]

As we might expect from his fears about the creation of a Jewish university in America, Chaim Weizmann was one of those who
walked in the shadow of Graetz. An Eastern European by origin—he
had been born in Motal in Byelorussia—Weizmann had moved to
Germany to pursue his education, but hardly grateful for the opportunities offered him, he characterized the headmaster of his school
as a "fatuous German of the Mosaic persuasion . . . , an intellectual
coward and a toady."[13] The leaders of the major German Jewish bank-
ing families, descendants of those who had made the world of David
Friedländer possible, fared little better. The Warburgs, the Ballins,
the Arnholds, and their ilk were, he charged, "more German than the
Germans," and because they were so desperate to assimilate, "slaves in
the midst of freedom." It did not matter to Weizmann that the leaders of the German Jewish community, as the Oxford historian Peter
Pulzer puts it, "were liberal in the broad sense that they addressed,
and spoke for, the urban bourgeoisie, that they favoured trade and
industry over agriculture and an extension of parliamentary against
executive power liberals who used their influence to soften the reactionary policies of the emperor Wilhelm II."[14] To Weizmann they
were Jews who do not give their all to Zion and for that reason not
to be fully trusted.

Neither Graetz nor Weizmann, it is important to note, were casting their eyes on those too poor and oppressed to know what was in
their best interest; elite Jews in nineteenth and early twentieth century Germany were at the opposite end of the social scale from the
poverty-stricken occupants of the shtetl. Yet both men found bankers
and intellectuals as repulsive as Bialik found the spent scarecrows of
the Pale. One group might be Orthodox, traditional, and subjects of
an authoritarian tsar and the other modern, assimilated, and liberal in
outlook. But they were equally viewed as tainted by the conditions of
diasporic life. Jews needed to be in touch with their own history or to
yearn for their own territory. If they ignored the lessons of their past
or stopped dreaming of the next year in Jerusalem, and the Diaspora
encouraged them in both inclinations, something was fundamentally
wrong with them.

As I pointed out in my introduction, Jews have long viewed themselves as divided between universalists who, by generalizing from the problems faced by the Jews, call attention to the problems faced by all people, and particularists, who believe that Jews need to be concerned only with the needs of other Jews. In its most extreme forms, *shlilat ha'golah* added a third disposition to these two. I will call this approach *selectivism*. Those who expressed such contempt toward the Diaspora, preoccupied with matters entirely Jewish, were by definition not universalists speaking on behalf of humankind in general. But nor were they defending the particular interests of the Jewish people as a whole; their concern instead was with a select group of them, those who were viewed as secure in their Jewish identity, for example, or those who understood their oppression and were prepared to rebel against it. For universalists who viewed particularism as a step down from cosmopolitanism, selectivism was a step down from particularism: The circle of concern was narrowed from all humanity, to all Jews, and finally only to those Jews deemed worthy of the name. Just being born of a Jewish mother meant little to a selectivist. One must transform one's Judaism into something strong and heroic to be truly special.

The most pronounced selectivist produced by the Zionist movement was Vladimir (or Ze'ev) Jabotinsky (1880–1940), the militant advocate of Jewish self-defense. Long before there was any prospect of creating a Jewish state, Jabotinsky had already begun to reflect on what kind of people it would require. In a 1905 obituary for Theodor Herzl (1860–1904), the great Zionist popularizer, Jabotinsky drew a contrast between the "Yid," the oppressed Jew of the Diaspora, and the "Hebrew," the new man who would no longer be unashamed of his race:

> Our starting point is to take the typical Yid of today and to imagine his diametrical opposite. . . . Because the Yid is ugly, sickly, and lacks decorum, we shall endow the ideal image of the Hebrew with masculine beauty. The Yid is trodden upon and easily frightened and, therefore, the Hebrew ought to be proud and independent. The Yid is despised by all and, therefore,

the Hebrew ought to charm all. The Yid has accepted submission and, therefore, the Hebrew ought to learn how to com-
mand. The Yid wants to conceal his identity from strangers
and, therefore, the Hebrew should look the world straight in
the eye and declare: "I am a Hebrew!"[15]

Because Jabotinsky was so distinctly a man of the political right, one
can be forgiven for believing that the "Yids" he believed unworthy of
full membership in the Jewish state were secular liberals. In reality,
however, Jabotinsky himself, while no liberal, was resolutely secular:
"It is difficult to discern the presence of any element in the Jabotinsky
makeup—psychological, emotional, or cultural—that had its source
in Jewish religion," as Israeli historian Anita Shapira describes his outlook on the world.[16] This helps explain why he was such an opponent
of those Orthodox Jews who, as he put the matter in a 1919 essay, "do
not remove the rust of exile from themselves and refuse to shave their
beard and sidelocks."[17] It was not faith that made one a Hebrew but
pride; the ultra-Orthodox had too much of the former and too little
of the latter.

As Jabotinsky's remarks suggest, selectivism is not pretty. For one
thing, it has, as its name implies, strong Darwinian overtones: the
fittest Jews would survive, but the fate of the weaker ones, assuming
one believed in God, would lay in his hands. Selectivism is also inher-
ently inegalitarian: Jews may be better than gentiles, but some Jews
were better than other Jews. It grows out of a Hobbesian view of the
world as so engaged in constant struggle that Jews must renounce
the idealistic, even the messianic, side of the tradition to better arm
themselves against their ever-present enemies. In at least one important way, selectivism is not even very Jewish, for it replaces the idea
of a chosen people with the notion that no matter how many of the
Jews God may have chosen, far fewer will be selected to take on the
difficult but necessary task of Jewish self-defense.

Despite all this, selectivism remained an undercurrent in Zionist
thought until relatively recent times, adding a dark and unpleasant
hue to the initial Zionist response to the Holocaust and retaining an

abiding attraction among all too many prominent Israeli leaders in the early years of statehood. Ultimately selectivism would prove itself so alien to Jewish values that it would lose its appeal, upgrading itself, so to speak, into the particularism out of which it grew. Still, we need to revisit the time in which selectivism dominated Zionist ideas about the Diaspora, not out of fear that history will repeat itself but in order to understand why, for all the benefits nationalism offers a people in the form of solidarity and identity, it can come with considerable costs in the form of myopia and internecine bickering. In that regard, Jewish nationalism, especially in its most extreme forms, is no different from any other.

III

Negation of the Diaspora was born in the last decades of the nineteenth century and the first decades of the twentieth. No one at the time could have known that the Russian pogroms, which had convinced so many Zionist activists of the hopelessness of diasporic life, would prove to be a relatively minor matter compared to the Holocaust that lay around the corner: forty-nine Jews were killed in the Kishinev pogrom of 1903, another nineteen in a similar attack two years later. Nor was it clear that the first intrepid adventurers who had moved to Palestine would eventually be followed by millions and result in statehood. If anything, Herzl, assimilated, liberal, and secular, was willing to consider Uganda and not the Holy Land as a (temporary) home for those threatened by the pogroms. (The Uganda option, first discussed in 1903, was officially rejected by the Seventh Zionist Congress in 1905.) For those most deeply involved in the politics of Zionism, the Diaspora was dangerous and a Jewish state a necessity, but the danger was limited and the state mostly a distant promise.

This would all change as the full dimension of the horror launched by Hitler in the 1930s became apparent. Given that Jews were being killed in one part of the world while creating a potential safe haven in another, a linkage between these two events was inevitable. But the unpleasant way in which they became linked was not inevitable at all.

As the Israeli writer Tom Segev shows in painful detail in his book *The Seventh Million*, Zionists did not rise up in sympathy with the Holocaust's victims and offer them immediate welcome in the Holy Land. In part their reasons for not doing so were overridingly practical: the *yishuv*, as the pre-state Jewish community in Palestine was called, lacked the capacity to absorb newcomers, especially those so infirm or dependent that they would drain whatever small resources it possessed. When the dominant need was for farmers, the new society in the making had little use for urban dwellers, as so many European Jews had become. Modern Hebrew was the language of daily life, not Yiddish, Polish, or Hungarian. Immigration to Palestine, in any case, was restricted by the British, who exercised political control over the region at that time. A certain amount of selectivity in who would be allowed to come to Palestine was inevitable.

Still, practical reasons for selectivity were not the only reasons. "The expression 'diasporic Jew,'" as Shapira put it, "transmitted a whole complex of features that were regarded as objectionable in the eyes of Palestinian Jewish youth: distance and alienation from labor and nature and, most particularly, weakness and lack of physical abilities. It symbolized everything that youth in Palestine did not want or need to be."[18] Why not, then, hold out the prospect of home only to those considered capable of the hard toil of state building while denying it to those deemed otherwise? "In days of shortages and unemployment, this material will cause us many problems," wrote Yitzhak Gruenbaum (1879–1970) in 1935, two years after he had made his own aliyah. (In Poland, Gruenbaum was an editor, politician, and leading Zionist activist; in the new state, he was the first interior minister.) "We must be allowed to choose from among the refugees those worthy of immigration and not accept them all."[19] Eight years later, after the full dimensions of the tragedy had become apparent, Apolinari Maximillian Hartglass (1883–1953), the coordinator of a committee established to consider the issue of Jewish rescue and who in the early 1930s had assumed Gruenbaum's seat in the *sejm*, or Polish parliament, wrote a five-page memo extensively quoted by Segev. On the one hand, it reads as an exercise in moral reasoning and on the other a rationale for triage:

Whom to save? . . . Should we help everyone in need, without regard to the quality of the people? Should we not give this activity a Zionist-national character and try foremost to save those who can be of use to the Land of Israel and to Jewry? I understand that it seems cruel to put the question in this form, but unfortunately we must state that if we are able to save only 10,000 people from among 50,000 who can contribute to building the country and to the national revival of the people, as against saving a million Jews who will be a burden, or at best an apathetic element, we must restrain ourselves and save the 10,000 that can be saved from among the 50,000—despite the accusations and pleas of the million.

So many Jews from so many parts of the world needed a safe haven, and so few could be admitted, that charges of discrimination filled the *yishuv*'s air: why should Germans be given preference over us, Russians asked, while Poles suggested that the Jews in their country were treated worse than in any other. The key to understanding immigration, however, had little to do with national origins and much to do with fitness for the task of statehood. Jews, as always, were divided on the issue of selectivity. As Segev points out, many Jews in Palestine, committed to ideas of national solidarity, wanted to do everything in their power to help all those in danger. "But," Segev continues, "there was at the same time a strong countertendency to 'negate the Exile.' . . . The years of the Holocaust was the coming of age of the second and even the third generation of young people who had been educated in this spirit, raised to be 'proud and generous, and cruel,' as Jabotinsky put it." Only this pervasive distrust of diasporic life can explain why the immediate connection between the Holocaust and Zionism was delayed, instrumental, and cold-blooded rather than instinctive, humanitarian, and idealistic. "The old Zionist credo denouncing the galut passivity," notes Amnon Rubinstein, former dean of the Tel Aviv Law School, "was instinctively applied to a situation that lies beyond human experience, to which there is no moral guide and in which standard criteria of honor and courage are not applicable."[20]

Unlike Jabotinsky, David Ben-Gurion (1886–1973), later to become Israel's first prime minister, had his roots in the socialist tradition; his ideology and Jabotinsky's were in constant conflict. In theory, Labor Zionism grew from universalistic roots; influenced in part by Marxism, Labor Zionists convinced themselves that the workers of both the Jewish and the Arab worlds in the Middle East would eventually unite. But in practice, Labor Zionists were just as likely to view the Jews of Diaspora as decadent as those of a more militant bent. In 1917, for example, Ben-Gurion expressed his version of selectivism this way: "Anything which is great and important enough for our present road, we shall carry with us; anything which is small, rotten, and smacks of galut we shall throw away so that it will disappear with the bad heritage of the dead past, so that this past will not cast its shadow over our new soul and will not desecrate the sanctity of our redemption." No wonder that when it came to the Diaspora, these two men, for all their political disagreements, were on the same page. "Both Ben-Gurion and Jabotinsky, incorrigible opponents" writes Rubinstein, "denied the legitimacy of Jewish history in galut." As the Israeli historian Zeev Sternhell comments, "A hatred of the diaspora and a rejection of Jewish life there were a kind of methodological necessity for Zionism."[21]

No figure would prove more important in building the Jewish state than Ben-Gurion, whose overriding commitment was to *mamlachtiut*, a Hebrew term referring to the primacy of the state over civil society.[22] With that commitment firmly in place, it was inevitable that as the full dimensions of the Holocaust became known, Ben-Gurion would view it through the eyes of the state he was in the process of building. "The extermination of European Jewry is a catastrophe for Zionism" he told the Jewish Agency, the organization with primary responsibility for bringing Jews to Israel, in 1943, because "there won't be anyone to build the country with."[23] That the Holocaust would be a disaster for all Jews and not just for the Zionist project did not occur to him, because he believed that the latter subsumed the former. That it was a catastrophe for the human race was too universalistic a sentiment for him even to contemplate.

If those responsible for building the new state showed any emotions toward victims of the Holocaust, they tended to be negative ones: having survived by acts of their own volition, they were not very warm to those who had stayed behind. "Among Jews," writes the British American historian Bernard Wasserstein about this period, "there was a widespread if seldom explicitly voiced suspicion that those who survived against overwhelming odds must have done so by ignoble or corrupt means."[24] The term popular in Zionist circles to describe Jews blown from one place to another by the tragedies of the 1930s and 1940s—*human dust*—was not meant as a compliment.[25] (That the same term would eventually be used against Jews from Arab lands, and then against Arabs in general, testifies to just how negative it was meant to be when applied to Jews from Europe.) But *dust* would prove to be a sensitive term when compared to the ultimate insult. "At some point," Segev notes, "the word sabon, 'soap,' came to be used to refer to Holocaust survivors."[26] Yoel Palgi, who had seen the destruction firsthand as a parachutist in Hungary, was shocked on his return home in 1945: "There is a kind of general agreement that the Holocaust dead were worthless people. Unconsciously, we have accepted the Nazi view that the Jews were subhuman."

Selectivism of this sort persisted into the first years of Israeli statehood. Victims of the Shoah who had found their way to Israel brought with them an intense hatred of everything German. But to Ben-Gurion, economic and financial realities made cooperation with Germany necessary, both for the funds that would accompany restitution and for the solidification of a Cold War alliance with the United States. One Lithuanian Jew who had lost his family in the Holocaust, Meir (Mark) Dworzecki (1908–1974), had been taken prisoner by the Germans while serving in the Polish Army. He escaped and fled to the Vilna ghetto, where he worked as a physician before being sent to a series of Estonian concentration camps. He managed to survive and upon arriving in Israel made his feelings clear; when it came to the Germans, he wanted "to spit in their faces." Ben-Gurion, in Segev's words, "answered with a blunt and revealing outburst. You have a ghetto mentality, he said to the opponents of restitution, adding that sovereign nations deal in security, economic strength, and the well-being of their peoples but do not 'spit on anyone.'"[27] The one thing Israeli leaders knew is that they had put any kind of ghetto mentality behind them. The sooner Israel's immigrants did the same, no matter how courageous they had been in those ghettos, the better off all Jews would be. As a state, Israel needed to think big. It had no room for those unable to escape the ghetto who still thought small. If that meant not only indifference to those who had been Hitler's victims but also a not very well disguised form of contempt, then so be it. The realities of statehood demanded no less.

IV

Negation of the Diaspora, at least in such extreme form, could not last forever. The first chink in the armor took place in 1949 after Ben-Gurion spoke to a labor delegation (American Histadrut) that was visiting Israel. "BEN GURION URGES U.S. PARENTS TO SEND THEIR CHILDREN TO ISRAEL FOR PERMANENT SETTLEMENT," blared the headline of the Jewish Telegraph Agency's account of what he said to the delegation.[28] Ben-Gurion's remarks did not sit well with the leaders of a number of American Jewish organizations, especially the American Jewish Committee. Founded in 1906 in response to the Russian pogroms, the AJC was led primarily by German Jews, such as its long-term president Louis Marshall (1856–1929), who worried that an influx of Jewish immigrants from the Pale would harm their privileged positions in American life.[29] Still, for all its shortcomings, the AJC was universalist in outlook; its two most prominent leaders at the time Ben-Gurion made his comments, Jacob Blaustein (1892–1970) and Judge Joseph M. Proskauer (1877–1971), would become known for their work on behalf of the United Nations and campaigns to protect international human rights.

As a universalist organization, the AJC in the years immediately after World War II was ambivalent about Zionism. While sympathetic to the idea of a Jewish homeland, it was also concerned that excessive nationalism would undermine its equally strong commitment to the idea that American Jews, having made the United States their home, should continue to live there. Blaustein, the AJC's then president, who had just been to Israel and had seen Ben-Gurion, was livid when he learned of the prime minister's 1949 comments. The AJC was especially concerned that Ben-Gurion's desire to turn American Jewish children into Israelis—the prime minister had gone so far as to say that Israel was intent on doing so even if their American parents refused to cooperate—would lend support to the American Council for Judaism, an organization established in 1942 not to soften Jewish nationalism, as the AJC hoped to do, but to oppose it root and branch. Ben-Gurion was a successful politician in Israel but his approach to the Diaspora threatened chaos, an especially ominous development given how obviously dependent the new state would be on the financial support of American Jews. A political realist as well as a committed Zionist, Ben-Gurion quickly came to understand the importance of American support and the need to win it. In the aftermath of the 1949 brouhaha, he engaged in a series of letters with Blaustein that resulted in an accord between the two leaders. Meeting Blaustein and the AJC more than halfway, Ben-Gurion agreed that "the Jews of the United States, as a community and as individuals, have only one political attachment and that is to the United States of America. They owe no political allegiance to Israel." We welcome American Jews, the agreement continued, "but the decision as to whether they wish to come—permanently or temporarily—rests with the free discretion of each American Jew himself."[30] As the historian and essayist Charles Liebman points out, Ben-Gurion's silence on the question of Diaspora negation, as well as his willingness to sign off on a neutral term such as *immigration* rather than the emotionally charged word *aliyah*, "must have been degrading to a man who had so many times spoken of *aliya* as Jewish self-fulfillment and who had referred to the day of his own arrival in the country as a day of rebirth."[31]

Ben-Gurion's acceptance of the agreement with Blaustein would have been degrading if he had meant it. But the agreement proved to be without impact, in part because Ben-Gurion's commitment to Diaspora negation was too deep to be moderated. One thing, however,

did change in the years after their agreement was reached: explicit selectivism dropped out of the picture. This happened for many reasons,
but the most important one had everything to do with the most dramatic event in the first decades of Israel's history: the capture of Adolf
Eichmann in Buenos Aires and his subsequent trial in Jerusalem.

On one level the Eichmann trial served to confirm what many Israelis took to be the essential truth of Diaspora negation. Ben-Gurion
spoke for them, especially those whose roots in the country predated
statehood, when he commented that Eichmann's testimony proved
"the profound tragedy of exile, of dependence on alien mercies, of
abandonment to the evil and willful impulse of tyrants."[32] When told
by leaders of the AJC that the Eichmann trial ought to emphasize the
suffering of all under the Nazis and not just those of his own people,
Ben-Gurion could barely control his rage. The "Judaism of Jews in the
United States is losing all meaning and only a blind man can fail to
see the day of its extinction," he responded at a meeting of the World
Zionist Congress. The future for Jews in exile was "the kiss of death
and the slow . . . decline into the abyss of assimilation." Extinction, assimilation—to Ben-Gurion in his more intemperate moments, which
were many, they were the same.

Still the Eichmann trial brought human faces to the Holocaust:
Israelis were presented with stories of suffering too overwhelming
to be explained away by any notion of diasporic degeneracy. As no
one had done before, Eichmann demonstrated how little a role selectivism had played for the Nazis: because they were so indiscriminate
in their hatred of Jews, killing everyone with no thought about who
might be the better Jews among them, it no longer made sense for Jews
to differentiate among themselves. As a result of the trial, the historian
Deborah Lipstadt points out, "Israelis increasingly recognized that
the distinction between Jews in the Diaspora and those in Israel was
not 'moral or qualitative,' but a matter of 'chronological accident.'"[33]
Even Ben-Gurion, for all his hostility toward exile, understood how
the Eichmann trial changed the way Jews should talk about each
other. Once again responding to American critics, he reversed course:
instead of arguing that Israel could accept only some of the Holo-

caust's victims, he insisted that only Israel could speak in the name of *all* of them. "The Jewish state (which is called Israel)," he wrote to Proskauer, then honorary president of the AJC, "is the heir of the six million who were murdered, the only heir for these millions.... If they had lived, the great majority of them would have come to Israel. The only historic prosecuting attorney for these millions is Israel."[34] Ben-Gurion's position had more to do with fantasy than reality—had the six million managed to live, who knows where they would have chosen to go?—but it is out of such mythical thinking that nationalism is formulated. If making distinctions between Jews once fulfilled the need of *mamlachtiut*, now emphasizing their similarities served the same goal. With the Eichmann trial, selectivism finally rose to the level of particularism.

Besides the Eichmann trial, another reason for the passing of selectivism can be offered. As the Berlin-based assimilated Jewish sociologist Georg Simmel (1858–1918) had once pointed out, conflict is as necessary as consensus if a society is going to find means of reproducing itself. (The son of a wealthy chocolate manufacturer who died young, Simmel was adopted and raised by the music publisher Julius Friedländer, grandson of David;[35] thanks in large part to another Berlin-born Jew, Ludwig Cohen, who, under his new name of Louis Coser would become a prominent American sociologist, Simmel's ideas became part of the standard sociological curriculum.) Simmel's insight proved to be the case with Israel. After the 1967 war broke out, conflict with their enemies helped Israelis overcome their differences. Arabs unified Jews in ways Jews were never able to do by themselves.

A third factor that made overt selectivism a thing of the past was that a more mature Israel was in a much better position than the generation of Ben-Gurion to look openly and honestly at its own history. The 1991 publication of the original Hebrew version of Segev's *Seventh Million* provided evidence for that conclusion. Although strongly criticized in Zionist quarters, Segev's book nonetheless brought to light an unpleasant reality and in that sense helped Israel heal some of its early wounds. As if to bring to a close the period in which Israeli Jews treated European victims of the Holocaust with disdain, the words "those who went like sheep to the slaughterhouse" were, with the strong support of former speaker of the Knesset Dov Shilansky (1924–2010), himself a Holocaust survivor, deleted from the prayer serving to memorialize them in 1995.[36] Israel was a Jewish state founded by nationalists and was therefore never likely to be attracted to full-throated universalism. But the reflections prompted by Segev's book and Shilansky's determination suggested that its particularism would no longer be accompanied by a language adhering to the proposition that not all Jews were worthy of the protection other Jews had already obtained. As the twentieth century came to an end, so did the idea, shared by Zionists as different from each as Jabotinsky and Ben-Gurion, that among Jews only the strongest can and do survive. This did not, however, mean that less harsh ways of negating the Diaspora died as well. *Shlilat ha'golah* would continue into the new century, even if in modified form.

V

Whatever can be said of Jews who live outside Israel today, they are neither the fearful subjects of a hateful tsar nor Germans so tempted by assimilation that they write letters seeking admission to Christian churches. The Jews of the Pale, whose passivity so alienated the early twentieth-century advocates of *shlilat ha'golah*, are gone, either murdered by the Nazis or able to find their way, for the most part, to Israel, the United States, and France. A number of the descendants of prominent German Jewish families also came to America, and the Reform synagogues they attended were, at least for a time, not very receptive to Zionism, but today's equivalent of a David Friedländer, a Jew successful on Wall Street, would most likely be a major contributor to Jewish causes. The Diaspora has changed, dramatically so, from what it was when political Zionism made hostility toward those who remained behind so central to its worldview.

Israel has changed, equally as dramatically, since its founding in 1948. Israel's current Jewish population is just under six million, making it larger than Serbia, Denmark, and Ireland, and when it reaches that mark, not only will the symbolism be significant but it will also suggest just how far, and in so little time, the embattled *yishuv* has become a full-fledged state. Given continued Arab hostility and Iranian nuclear ambitions, whether Israel has achieved sufficient national security is subject to extensive debate, but no one can deny that it is the major military power in its region. Economically, Israel's performance has been stunning; it is among the world's leaders in electronics and medical innovation. For all its internal divisions and contentious political culture, it remains the most vibrant democracy in the Middle East. The success of Israel is as difficult to deny as the success of the Diaspora. If the latter makes it illusionary to claim that the Diaspora is hopeless, the former makes it unnecessary: It is one thing to engage in Diaspora negation when building a state whose future is precarious, but another thing to disparage the Diaspora when that state has become well established and presumably secure in its identity. Zionism has not realized all its goals, but it has achieved enough of them to conclude that, as nationalist movements go, it has been one of the world's most successful.

Despite these changes, negations of the Diaspora continue to find expression in one outlet or another. The *Jerusalem Post*, a right-leaning English-language newspaper, is particularly given to publishing the thoughts of those persuaded of the evils of diasporic life. The English-born Canadian Barbara Amiel, Lady Black of Crossharbour and wife of media baron and convicted felon Conrad Black, is among them. Israel may have been created to offer Jews protection, she wrote in February 2001, but now Jews, and especially the Israelis among them, are singled out for hatred much as they were during the Nazi era. When anti-Semitism is so widespread, Diaspora Jews are foolish if they believe that their hosts will protect them. "Jews have survived more than 2,000 years in the single, unshakeable belief that one day their dislocation would end with their return to the Promised Land. This is the central underpinning of Judaism. . . . Without the possibility of Israel, Judaism becomes pointless."[37] Five years later Joshua Adler, a rabbi and former US Army chaplain who had made aliyah in 1972, took to the pages of the same newspaper in much the same fashion in an article called, simply, "Negate the Diaspora." Jews are threatened by enemies such as Iran's Mahmoud Ahmadinejad, he wrote, and his hope was that "our example of living Zionism will inspire many thousands of Jews in America and elsewhere to join us here in the land of our forefathers."[38] Negation of the Diaspora is a spring that constantly bubbles to the Israeli surface, as if necessary to replenish the land that is Zion.

Short op-eds are not the best places to develop long arguments. A more eloquent case for the relevance of Diaspora negation to contemporary conditions was made by the New York–born writer and translator Hillel Halkin, who published a series of letters to an American Jewish friend in 1977. Israel, he wrote his friend, is under constant threat from the Arabs just as Jews were once under constant attack from Christians. But Halkin's arguments moved far beyond that oft-repeated point. The Diaspora may seem attractive, but Jewish life there—"a smattering of Yiddish or Hebrew remembered from childhood, a nostalgia for a parental home in which Jewish customs were still kept, the occasional observance of an isolated Jewish ritual, the exclusion of certain nonkosher foods from an otherwise nonkosher kitchen, a genuine identification with the Jewish people combined with a genuine ignorance of its past history and present condition"— is not much to brag about. Is it any wonder, Halkin therefore concluded, "that the same classical Zionist beliefs that justified modern Jewish settlement in Palestine, and that justified the establishment of a Jewish state, justify the country to this day"?[39] It all comes down to an inescapable syllogism: Jews ought to lead Jewish lives; Jewish lives are best led in a Jewish state; therefore committed Jews should live in Israel. Six years of his own life there had convinced him that his choice was the right one, in large part because "Jewish life in the Diaspora is doomed."

Halkin's case is passionate but not persuasive. The problem he faces is the same one that all contemporary Diaspora negators must confront: for all the talk of nasty Arabs, seductive assimilation, and unrelenting Jew hatred, diasporic Jewish life has improved in undeniable ways since the classical Zionists expressed their thoughts at the end of the nineteenth century. This, I believe, explains why even as learned a figure as Halkin, although he evokes the idea of an unchanged Jewish world, ultimately grounds the case for Zion not on ideological commitments to such large-scale projects as nationalism or socialism, which the founding generation did, but on a post-1960s personal quest for individual fulfillment. In defense of the Diaspora, Halkin's friend pointed to the creativity of so many of its great writers and artists. Halkin is not impressed; American Jewish literature, he writes, is "neither very American, nor very Jewish, nor very good." His major complaint comes down to one of belonging. Should Jews revel in alienation and marginalization, the qualities often held to produce great works of art? Halkin answers with a resounding no. Far better, in his view, for Jews to have "a culture and an inner world of our own." In another letter, Halkin writes that "it would be untrue to declare that I see nothing of myself reflected in the counter-culture." Very much a product of the time in which they were written, his letters represent Zionism as therapy: the Diaspora must be negated because we all need to put behind us the childish ideas that prevent us from leading truly authentic lives.

The notion that Diaspora negation has left the terrain of politics for the realm of psychology was given further confirmation by the thoughts of the prominent Israeli novelist A. B. Yehoshua. In May 2006 Yehoshua told a distinguished audience at the Library of Congress in Washington, DC, that they were merely "playing with Jewishness." "If . . . in 100 years Israel will exist, and I will come to the Diaspora [and] there will not be . . . [any] Jews, I would say it's normal," he declared. "I will not cry for it. I . . . will not have [and] cannot keep my identity outside Israel. . . . [Being] Israeli is my skin, it's not my jacket. You are changing jackets."[40] Yehoshua spoke in the angry tone of classical Diaspora negation. But like Halkin's, the content of his argument could not be more different than the militant comments of the late nineteenth-century Zionists from the Pale. For them, Diaspora Jews were struggling to live, not playing with life; Jewish identity was not a matter of what was in one's skin but of having any skin at all. For Yehoshua, by contrast, it is all about lifestyle. In subsequent remarks published in the newspaper *Ha'aretz* designed to clarify the points he had tried to make at the Library of Congress, and in particular to deny (unconvincingly) that his intent was to negate the Diaspora, he wrote that for an American "his Jewishness is voluntary and deliberate, and he may calibrate its pitch in accordance with his needs."[41] Jews in Israel, by contrast, because their lives are shaped by living in an all-absorbing Jewish world, have an identity that is "immeasurably fuller and broader and more meaningful than the Jewishness of an American Jew." A touch of selectivism is present in all this, for once again, Diaspora Jews are held to be inferior to those fortunate enough to live in a Jewish state. But the terms of the selection process are considerably softened from the time of Jabotinsky and Ben-Gurion. There is no talk here of "human dust" or "soap." Become an Israeli and you are complete. Live elsewhere and you are partial.

A number of voices, Israeli and American, liberal and conservative, secular and religious, rose up in protest against Yehoshua's tirade, and their defense of the Diaspora can be cited as evidence that what was once a central tenet of Zionist thought had become an unwelcome remnant. Yet it is also possible to conclude from the controversy that Diaspora negation, rather than having been repudiated, had merely been driven underground. Halkin, who was at the Library of Congress speaking on another panel, suggested as much: "I can remember a national convention of rabbis—it was in Washington too, I believe—that I was invited to address some time in the late 1970s or early '80s," he said in response to Yehoshua. "I was playing the role of the fire-eating Zionist to the hilt. The rabbis wanted me to talk about Israel-Diaspora relations? Well, then, I would tell them what I thought. I thought every self-respecting Diaspora Jew belonged in Israel, and that American Jewry should liquidate itself as soon as possible by moving there en masse." But, Halkin went on, he does not do that kind of thing anymore. "The rabbis, needless to say, were ... offended. ... And because I don't really enjoy giving offense, I've stopped talking that way to American Jews."[42]

Whatever Halkin's preference, Yehoshua's is otherwise: controversy is his forte, and he cannot stop repeating his critique. Two years after his talk in Washington, while speaking at the invitation of his Parisian publisher, he made the identical distinction between complete and partial Jews, this time including the French in the latter category.[43] Four years after that, he once again used the same terminology to characterize American Jews at the HaKatedra Strategic Friday lecture series, held at Tel Aviv's Eretz Israel Museum in March 2012. What is striking about all this is not Yehoshua's inability to stop talking about the dangers of the Diaspora; it is his just as frequent attempts to cast the whole issue as a matter of choice. Since no choice, in his view, could be more inauthentic than the one of Israelis who already live in the Jewish state to move elsewhere, in his Tel Aviv lecture he reserved special scorn for them: "There are about 500,000 Israelis abroad who can easily glide into their Israeliness, which they consider only citizenship and not identity. There is nearly no home without a convertible outside. I know these homes, who are well off. Why? Because they cannot find jobs here? The Swedes, too, don't have work in high technology like they would want, but you will not see so many Swedes in the United States."[44] Bialik had condemned his fellow Jews because they never change. Yehoshua condemns them because they change too much. The former wanted Jews to leave where they were. The latter, at least with respect to Israelis, wants them to stay where they are. Those who negate the Diaspora like to argue that with respect to Zionism, nothing much is different. The very nature of their arguments tell us that much is different indeed.

It is not only Yehoshua who cannot stop talking about Diaspora negation. As his Tel Aviv lecture suggests, no change in Zionism's relationship with the Diaspora is more emotionally sensitive than the presence of Israelis within it; who among the early advocates of *shlilat ha'golah* could have imagined a situation in which those fortunate enough already to live in the Jewish homeland would pack their suitcases to move back into the Christian wilderness? Worried that such movement had become all too common, the Netanyahu government, as if unconsciously echoing Ben-Gurion's 1949 threat to turn American children into Israelis, in 2011 developed an advertising campaign suggesting that in the Diaspora, Israeli Jews will forget the lessons of the Holocaust or sit by helplessly as their children get lost to Christmas. The overwhelmingly negative reaction to the message led the government to remove the ads from the airwaves. But the whole incident can be taken as an indication that the negation of the Diaspora is not only still a feature of Israeli public life but has also been officially sponsored by the Israeli state.

The Diaspora negation of Halkin and Yehoshua comes nowhere close to the offensive language used by Jabotinsky in drawing a contrast between the Hebrew and the Yid. Yet while there is little to say in defense of the extreme forms of Diaspora negation associated with Jabotinsky, even critics of his position can appreciate that he was wrestling with the most serious of matters. Jewish life, especially in the Pale, was as difficult as it was dangerous. The decision to move to Palestine required onerous and unfamiliar work in the harshest of possible conditions. No one knew whether such early efforts would actually result in the creation of a Jewish state. Diaspora negation turned its back on the Jewish tradition of universalism and in that sense represented a setback for the values of the Jewish Enlightenment. But it was a product of a time and a place in which tough decisions had to be made. The classic Diaspora negators are best viewed as tragic figures, narrowly focused human beings who nonetheless believed themselves carrying out great deeds.

The same is no longer true of the generation of Halkin and Yehoshua. One of the most famous sentences written by another assimilated German Jew, Karl Marx, is that history does repeat itself, the first time as tragedy, the second as farce.[45] (In one of history's more improbable encounters, Marx, the communist and occasional anti-Semite, met the Jewish nationalist historian Heinrich Graetz at the baths in Carlsbad, now located in the Czech Republic, and the two of them later engaged in an affectionate correspondence, complete with exchanges of photos.)[46] Marx's epigram is the first thing that comes to mind in pondering the Diaspora negation of today, especially when watching the comically inept ads directed at Israelis living abroad. Jews have choices and not all of them choose Zion. One response would be to accept this as a fact of life, find value in all the choices made, and be grateful that a people once so lacking in choices that they were helpless against destruction have available to them so many options. Contemporary negators of the Diaspora cannot do this, for they treat Jews who have not joined them in Zion with condescension, even if their condescension stops short of contempt. It is as if all those who engage in Diaspora negation at the present time know that, despite their best efforts, the Diaspora Jews they hope to reach, including those from Israel, are not going to be convinced by their arguments. Defensiveness runs like a silk thread through their efforts. They are not calling people to action so much as calling them out.

All this explains why we are now dealing with performance as much as politics. Of all contemporary Diaspora negators, Yehoshua is the one who performs with the greatest flair. As Yehuda Kurtzer, president of the Shalom Hartman Institute of North America, an organization dedicated to advancing Jewish learning, has suggested, the vision of Israel Yehoshua holds out to his non-Israeli audiences— "Street signs in Hebrew! Shabbat is a day of the week! Kosher Mc- Donald's!"—corresponds to the Disneyland version of the Jewish state so many Americans find attractive.[47] People go to hear him for the same reason they attend the theatre. They know the lines will be brilliant and the metaphors arresting. They are impressed by the passion with which they are delivered. The subject will be a timeless one dealing with profound dilemmas of the human condition. They will be moved. But they will not be moved to do anything significant. The Diaspora is their home. The person telling them it should not be speaks like family. But he most resembles the cantankerous uncle who does not fully grasp the complexities of life in the modern world. Best applaud, come back again if need be, and then get back to reality.

VI

Jonathan Woocher, a Jewish educator, wrote a book in the 1980s in which he attempted to delineate the shared values that helped members of the American Jewish community understand their role and sense of purpose. One of the most important of those values, Woocher claimed, was an insistence on the importance of both the Diaspora and the Jewish state, "a partnership of equals," as one Jewish official put it, "who seek practical ways to work with, and relate to, and understand, each other. A partnership that pools its talent, and strives to improve the quality of life of both partners, with a full and total commitment to the viability of Jewish life in Israel, and of Jewish life in North America." American Jews would support Israel strongly, from this perspective, but they would be under no obligation to make aliyah. In this sense, what Woocher calls the civil religion of American Jews while supporting Zionism was also an alternative to it, and especially to its repeated expressions of Diaspora negation. "The nation of Israel and the people of Israel—the Jewish people—depend on each other and need each other," another official declared. "It takes the combined strength of the Jews in the Diaspora and the Jews of Israel to insure the destiny of the Jewish people."[48]

Although Woocher argued that such shared values were already in existence at the time he wrote his book, this one key component— the idea of an equal partnership between the Jewish state and the Diaspora—was not. Israelis, for one thing, did not agree with such sentiment: According to a survey taken in 2000, 69 percent of Israeli Jews felt that Diaspora Jewry and Israeli Jewry were different peoples, and the percentage of those who believed that the two peoples had a common fate was declining.[49] American Jews as well, especially those in charge of major Jewish organizations, did not accept the idea of a common partnership, because for them Israelis remained the senior partners on any question involving world Jewry. Woocher all but acknowledged as much, if indirectly. "It has been said," he wrote, "that American Judaism recognizes only one heresy, which subjects the perpetuator to immediate excommunication: denial of support to the state of Israel."[50] For that reason, American Jews, far from being equal partners, were, with respect to the Jewish state, cheerleaders. Partners disagree, at least at crucial moments. But in the United States disagreement with Israel was considered unwise when Israel's very existence seemed threatened. "We want you to disagree with us," Yossi Beilin, a prominent Israeli dove, told a meeting of influential American Jews in 1992. "We can't do that," replied Ruth Popkin, who was then head of the Jewish National Fund. "Our job here is to defend you."[51]

Woocher's depiction of the shared concerns of American Jews may not have been quite accurate when he wrote it, but it is becoming true now as more and more Americans are taking Beilin's advice and disagreeing with the policies of the Israeli government. As they do, they are bringing into being the idea of a full partnership between Jews in America and Jews in Israel that Jewish religious leaders mistakenly believed was already in place decades ago. Diaspora Jews who rally around the Jewish state are in essence confessing that they feel so unequal compared to Jews in Israel that they are unable to offer the criticism they need; they may be full citizens of the countries in which they live, but they feel they are second-class citizens when it comes to world Jewry. Those who do offer such criticism, by contrast, have rejected once and for all the notion that Jews who live in the Diaspora will inevitably be weak and ashamed; in ways Jabotinsky would never have predicted, *they* are the ones proud to stand on their own two feet and call things as they see them. In an interview with Noa Levanon, an editor at *Ynet*, an Israeli website, Alvin Rosenfeld, a professor of Jewish studies at Indiana University, argued that progressive Jewish critics of Israel "feel the need to negate Israel in order to validate a newly affirmed Diaspora identity, similar to the rejection of the Diaspora in Israel, especially during the nation's early years."[52] In actuality, however, such critics are negating neither the Diaspora nor Israel but trying to bring the tradition of negating one or the other to an end.

VII

How will we know when the end of Diaspora negation has finally been reached? One possibility suggests itself: when Jews recognize that their Diaspora is more like others rather than unique unto itself. There are, after all, many Diasporas in the world, and none of them have been accompanied by anything like the hostility to those who live outside the home country quite comparable to *shlilat ha'golah*.

Consider, for example, India, a state created just one year before Israel. The Indian diaspora is, after China's, the second largest in the world. Yet unlike among the more militant Zionists, one does not hear many cries of anguish from Indians, including the nationalists among them, that those who live abroad lead partial lives. On the contrary, the novels written by Indians in Canada, the United Kingdom, and the United States go a long way toward defining contemporary Indian identity. Then there are the Irish, who, like the Israelis, suffered under British colonialism: nineteenth-century Irish nationalists did not look upon their countrymen in Boston or Liverpool as unworthy but viewed them as allies in their struggle, and the descendants of those who fled the old country have thereby been spared pathetic pleas to come back. The same is true among the Greeks, Lebanese, Armenians, Ethiopians, and a wide variety of other national groups whose members are scattered around the world. Financial dependency, ethnic pride, a shared sense of distinctiveness—these tend to be unifying, not divisive, features. Disagreements and disappointments exist and jokes representing a certain hurt are told. But few are the condemnations of others as rotting until they stink because they live in one place rather than another. Only the Jews, among all these diasporas, have such a pronounced history of so strongly disparaging those who chose to live somewhere else.[53]

The lesson, I hope, is clear. There are many ways to be Jewish. The notion that there ought to be a contest for the worst way, and that the prize should go to those who live among non-Jews, seems increasingly perverse. Negation of the Diaspora may have been crucial to the building of a new state, at least in the eyes of the state builders themselves. Now built, that state now wants nothing more than to be accepted as normal; like every other state, Israel ought not to be condemned, most of its citizens believe, for taking steps to provide for its own security. But Israel can never be a normal state when it continues to manifest the insecurities inherent in the concept of Diaspora negation: All those who proclaim that Jewish life outside Israel is unworthy are in essence proclaiming that Israelis are in fact different from everyone else.

Zionism's suspicion toward the *galut* is especially odd given that Zionism itself was born there; without exile, there could never have existed such a passionate and intense longing for statehood. It is for this reason that it seems appropriate, if not inevitable, that Zionism's survival will increasingly depend on the very conditions that created it. Exile is not the enemy of the Jewish state; isolation is. Now more than ever Israel needs the universalism that isolationism abhors. It is one thing for Jews to turn their backs against the whole world. It is even more problematic to spurn those proud to be Jewish but also happy to be citizens of the countries in which they were born. As memories of the events of the 1930s and 1940s fade, so, one hopes, will Diaspora negation. Only then will Jews be in a position to recognize not only what they have in common with the rest of humanity but also what they have in common with each other.

CHAPTER 2

Defenders of Diaspora

I

The state of Israel has never suffered for want of critics. Among them have been some of the best-known figures of the twentieth century, including Hannah Arendt, Martin Buber, and Albert Einstein, all of whom understood the dangers of excessive Jewish nationalism and warned about the need to make some accommodation with the Arabs who already lived on the land the new state claimed for itself. Yet for a variety of reasons—Arendt's arrogance, Buber's mysticism, and Einstein's idealism are the ones most commonly cited—their views on the question of Zion have generally been dismissed, especially by Zionists themselves. Just because they were brilliant in one area of inquiry, it has been said of them, does not mean their views can be trusted on all of them.

In this chapter I want to concentrate on a trio of lesser-known figures whose views must be taken into account if the question of where Jews are best off living is to be adequately assessed. One of them, Simon Rawidowicz, the scholar of Hebrew who objected to the idea that only in Israel could a Jewish university thrive, was introduced in the previous chapter. He will be joined in this one by Simon Dubnow and Ahad Ha'am. My attention is drawn to these three men not because I think they were more perspicacious than their more famous colleagues; on some issues, as we will see, they were plainly wrong. It is not what they said about the Jewish state that makes them important but what they said about Jews living elsewhere: all three refused to give unconditional support to the idea of Diaspora negation. Their views on the complications of Jewish statehood meant that they were left behind as the engine of political Zionism picked up steam. For that very reason, their writings have taken on a prophetic tone at the present time when Israel has become increasingly unsure of what direction it ought to take.

Dubnow, Ha'am, and Rawidowicz were all transitional figures. Their personal lives, for one thing, encapsulated in a matter of decades the transition from tradition to modernity: born in the Eastern European Pale, they would wind up living in such cosmopolitan urban centers as Berlin, London, and Chicago. Their ideas were similarly caught between two different worlds: particularists in the sense that they were steeped in Jewish history and culture, they drew from their backgrounds universal lessons that could be applied to any people wrestling with questions of identity and meaning. Despite having had their share of Orthodox rabbis in their family histories, they were either secular in outlook, strongly influenced by liberal political philosophers such as John Stuart Mill and Herbert Spencer, or committed to furthering human rights. Most important, diasporic life, each of them believed, for all the horrors of the pogroms and the indignities of discrimination, had its special strengths: an appreciation of the capacity to survive under hostile conditions; a concern with political and civic rights important to those who are in the minority; a flowering of multiple ways of life in the absence of state-enforced conformity; and the advantages of what today we might call globalization. Let there be a Jewish state, they all, with differing amounts of enthusiasm, concluded. But Diaspora, even when problematic, was not equivalent to disaster. If statehood resulted in a loss of the insight that Jews were a special people because for so long they had found ways to make do without a state of their own, the costs of that loss would be impossible to calculate.

II

Over the course of two days—November 30 and December 8, 1941—the Germans, who had occupied Latvia the previous July, rounded up some twenty-four thousand of the Jews of Riga, the capital of the country, and sent them to a nearby forest to be executed. Simon Dubnow (1860–1941), who had succeeded Heinrich Graetz as the foremost historian of the Jewish people, was, at eighty-one, too frail to board the bus with sufficient promptness; he was shot and killed by one of the accompanying Latvian guards.[1]

The city and the man quickly became the equivalent of legal exhibits in the case against the Diaspora. A Baltic seaport open to the world, Riga has always had more in common with Berlin to the West than Moscow to the East. Although it had a large Yiddish-speaking community of working-class and poor Jews, it also lacked a historical ghetto and, among its more prosperous Jews, contained a significant number of those who were successful in business, the professions, and ideas; the philosophers Yeshayahu Leibowitz (1903–1994) and Isaiah Berlin (1909–1997), among the greatest of twentieth-century Jewish thinkers, for example, both grew up there. (Leibowitz and Berlin not only have the same first name—Yeshayahu is Hebrew for Isaiah—they also shared a teacher who frequently compared the younger man unfavorably with the older one.)[2] The vibrancy of Riga's middle-class Jewish life is not something to be gleaned only from books: YouTube contains a nine-minute film clip from 1939, just before tragedy struck, showing Riga Jews, along with those from two other cities in the region, dressed in all their finery promenading through the streets, as popular music from the time plays in the background.[3] As was said of the equally assimilated Jews of Germany, if Jews were not safe in Riga, they could not be safe anywhere.

Dubnow, in turn, was a Diaspora unto himself; born in Mstislavl in Belorussia, he had lived in St. Petersburg, Odessa, Kovno (also called Kaunas, in central Lithuania), and Berlin. Even after leaving Berlin for Riga, where, ironically, he had hoped to find a conducive environment for his work, he considered making aliyah, only to reject the idea.[4]

"I move easily in time, but not in space," he wrote to a friend. "In my researches I can move swiftly from period to period, from the twelfth to the sixteenth century, for example; but to move several thousand kilometers from Riga to Jerusalem is not within my powers."[5] Because he was the most insistent defender of the Diaspora the Jewish tradition ever produced, Dubnow's execution came to symbolize the failure of the ideas he had advocated. "It would be unfair to say that he paid the price for his optimism," writes Ruth Wisse, Harvard professor of Yiddish, "since the Germans arranged the same end for all Jews, irrespective of the ideas they had held. But some of his fellow intellectuals had been warier of establishing a politically viable autonomy in Europe, warning that Jews must first be granted their natural rights as Jews, not merely citizens, as a precondition for their national recovery."[6] Unfair indeed, but Wisse's comment leaves the impression that Dubnow's stubbornness on the question of Zion was not just an intellectual error but also a personal disaster.

Dubnow spent his life advocating what he called "autonomism." In true Hegelian fashion, he defined it as the synthesis emerging out of two radically different, and flawed, alternatives. For most of their history in the Diaspora, Jews lived in their own subcommunities cut off from the larger world around them. There were certain advantages in "isolationism," as Dubnow labeled this proclivity, for such a way of life was "complete and consistent." The one thing the old order lacked, however, was what modernity brought in its wake: civic and political rights. Because of his liberalism, Dubnow viewed enlightenment as an advance over isolation. But he also worried that enlightenment would end in "assimilationism," which to him was nothing less than a "doctrine of national suicide."[7] Autonomism combined the best features of both approaches. Like isolationism, it insisted that Jews should be in charge of their own affairs. Like assimilationism, it affirmed the priority of rights and rejected religion as the basis of Jewish identity in favor of community building.

Although there had existed many self-governing boards throughout Jewish history in the Diaspora, Dubnow's favorite example of autonomism was the Council of Four Lands, in which Jewish leaders exercised authority over Jewish life in Poland and Lithuania from the sixteenth to the eighteenth centuries. With a greater influence of lay leadership than was common in this form of organization, as well as a more extensive degree of autonomy due to the size of the local Jewish community, the council conducted a census, collected and distributed tax monies, passed laws, and even engaged in relations with foreign countries. Its activities fit with one of Dubnow's key notions: While the Diaspora is global by its very nature, Jews throughout history informally adopted one place or another that came to act as the center around which Jewish life revolved. In the years of the council's existence Lublin had served that function; at other times, so had Baghdad, Córdoba, and Berlin. How were Jews able to create thriving communities in such hostile environments? Jewish law, the wisdom of the rabbis, messianism—all these aspects of religious life played a role. But for Dubnow they were secondary to the fact that Jews, lacking a state of their own, had little choice but to develop a "will to live" that elevated them as a special people; history, not God, had chosen them.[8]

During his time in Odessa, which had itself become a great center of Jewish intellectual life, Dubnow, as one political scientist has put it, was the "polestar" around which a circle of young intellectuals, including Bialik and Jabotinsky, revolved.[9] Unlike them, Dubnow rejected any notion of negating the Diaspora. He did so partially on the grounds of political realism: In a perfect world, all Jews might be better off living in a Jewish state, but in the actually existing world, dispersion was a fact of life and Jews were therefore best off building upon the institutions and traditions they had created since their exile in Babylon. "'Hatred of the *galut*,' rooted in the hearts of many in order to honor 'love of Zion,' is dangerous," he stated, in words that summarized his life's work. "Love that springs from hatred generally is suspect, but especially so if the hatred is directed against a powerful historical phenomenon that is part of our very being and that, under the historical conditions in which we find ourselves, cannot be severed from the body of the nation without wounding its soul."[10]

More than realism marked Dubnow's approach to these matters: there was also the question of national pride. Dubnow never denied the persistence of anti-Semitism, but the ability of Jews to survive and even flourish while subject to such unrelenting hatred offered a reservoir of strength. "What was all of Jewish history in all its many periods," he wrote, as if he were addressing the question to his mentor the ever-gloomy Graetz, "if not the heroic struggle of a cultural nationality for its inner freedom—a struggle waged not by force of arms but by the spirit, a struggle for those lofty spiritual values which by their very nature cannot be achieved through discreditable means?"[11] Yehudah Mirsky, a researcher at the Van Leer Institute in Jerusalem, is in my view correct to argue that Dubnow's "exuberant love of Jewish history" is a welcome alternative to those who, in negating the Diaspora, alienated Jews from their own past.[12]

Although he never lived long enough to see Israel come into existence, Dubnow did witness what he called "the most important event in contemporary Jewish history."[13] This was not the Kishinev massacre, the event that sent so many Jewish writers into despair. Writing in 1903 in response to Kishinev, Dubnow instead turned his eyes across the Atlantic, where he saw the building of a new center, one that would rival all the great places of Jewish accomplishment in the past. Dubnow never came to the United States, although his daughter, Sophia, a poet and activist, did; she died in New York in 1986 at the age of 101. (For many years I attended a faculty seminar at Columbia University, one of whose members was Alexander Erlich, an expert on the Soviet economy, who was Sophia's son and Dubnow's grandson; his father, and Sophia's husband, was Henryk Erlich, a prominent member of the Jewish Labor Bund in greater Russia who had hung himself in a Soviet prison cell.) Yet even from a distance, Dubnow understood the importance the new world would assume in Jewish history. "When we see that within twenty-five years a 'Jewish America,' numbering two million, was created, mainly by Russian emigrants, that New York City alone has close to 700,000 Jews, and that the main stream of our emigrants flows increasingly to the great republic across the sea, then we have the right to believe that in the course of time America will become the major center of Judaism, alongside of Russia, and, under certain conditions, may even surpass it."[14] In contrast to those who could not take their eyes away from how many Jews were dying, Dubnow could only express his relief that so many more were finding a new place to live.

Dubnow was an important enough figure, and his life sufficiently long and varied, that legends grew up around him. One—that his dying words to his people were "Jews, write and record"—is most likely apocryphal.[15] The other—that his death proved the fallacy of his ideas—can no longer be taken seriously. Even if we leave out New York, where close to two million Jews now live in the freedom for which Dubnow so fervently hoped, it is helpful to remind ourselves that more Jews currently live in Chicago, Philadelphia, and Boston than did in Berlin, Odessa, Lublin, and Vilna in their heyday. Jews in the United States have not created self-governing institutions, at least outside the ultra-Orthodox, and the rates of assimilation among them are far higher than Dubnow would have wanted. At the same time, Dubnow's prediction that the Diaspora would always be an essential part of Jewish life has proven more accurate than the Zionist hope that a Jewish state would render the Diaspora irrelevant.

Because he was a critic of assimilation, Dubnow's thought contained strong traces of particularism: not only should Jews who convert to another religion no longer be considered part of the group, he insisted, but neither should Christians who convert to Judaism. Yet within the world of Judaism, his views proved to be unusually capacious. The secret to the success of the Diaspora, in his account, lay in the special historical conditions it faced that "converted Judaism into an all-embracing world view which encompasses religious, ethical, social, messianic, political and philosophical elements."[16] Dubnow included within the Jewish nation the Orthodox, the mystics, the messianists, the enlighteners, Reform Jews, and even those of Jewish birth without any religious identity whatsoever. His views are about as far from what I have called selectivism as it is possible to be. Diaspora implied difference, and with respect to the Jews, Dubnow loved them in all the forms they took.

The lessons of Jewish history, furthermore, possessed for Dubnow universal significance. The Hebrew Bible, he pointed out, is treated as sacred by people all over the world. But just as important are the lessons taught by the Diaspora. Who cannot be moved by the oppression faced by the Jews, Dubnow asked, and their determination to survive? "The inexpressible tragedy of Jewish historical life," he wrote in his essay on the philosophy of history, "is unfailing in its effects upon a susceptible heart. The wonderful exhibition of spirit triumphant, subduing the pangs of the flesh, must move every heart, and exercise influence upon the non-Jew no less than the Jew."[17] In such a way did Dubnow move beyond the particularism usually associated with nationalism. "At moments when Jews managed to transcend the limitations of their own culture and link their particularistic inclinations with universal ones," as the Stanford University historian Steven Zipperstein summarizes Dubnow's ideas, "the products reached spiritual heights: the Prophets emerged at a moment when Jews were able to see the interconnection between their preoccupations and those of humankind. But even manifestations of lesser universal importance were expressions of Jewry's desire to maintain its dignity, freedom, and integrity."[18]

It was precisely this quality of capaciousness that, in Dubnow's view, would be threatened by political Zionism's efforts to reduce all Jewish questions to those of statehood. Especially toward the end of his life, Dubnow came to approve of the Zionists' efforts in Palestine. But he also believed that a nation is not the same thing as a state: the former reflects the collective life of a people as shaped by its history and culture while the latter is artificial, legalistic, and formal. Over thousands of years the Jewish nation was forged out of the challenges of exile. Dubnow died believing that the drive for statehood, if not careful, could warp the spiritual nation. "Political Zionism," he had written in his early years, "is ... a web of fantasies: the dream of the creation of a Jewish state guaranteed by international law, the dream of colonizing a great part of the Jewish people, and the dream of finding the solution of the Jewish question in this manner."[19] In this he was not correct: the fantasy has most definitely become a reality. But his warning that statehood cut off from the ebb and flow of Jewish history would be in danger of losing the moral and ethical ideals that had constituted diasporic life at its best is, alas, proving prescient.

III

The circle of Jewish intellectuals that congregated in Odessa in the early years of the twentieth century included a man Dubnow characterized as "the greatest of the Zionist theorists" and "a distinguished author to whom I am closer in the field of national ideology than to any other writer of our time."[20] He was referring to Asher Ginsberg (1856–1927), who took the name Ahad Ha'am (Hebrew for "one of the people") and who must be included with Dubnow as a lover of the Jews who had serious qualms about political Zionism and the course it might take.

Ha'am's birthplace was Skvire, near Kiev, in what was then Russia. As his adopted name implies, Ha'am wrote in Hebrew, at the time a language used mostly for prayer. His love of Hebrew created a major disagreement with Dubnow who, in defending the Diaspora, also defended what he called "the powerful force of the folk language used by seven million Jews in Russia and Galicia, which for several generations now fulfills the function of a spoken language."[21] He meant, of course, Yiddish, and Dubnow's unwillingness to condemn it provoked Ha'am to intemperance. Writing to his friend from St. Petersburg in 1909, Ha'am lectured him that the Yiddish question had become "the acid test of Judaism." A victory for Yiddish would be "the most serious threat to Judaism as we understand it." "If the Jewish people really cannot survive unless Yiddish wins," he rather dramatically concluded, "then—absit omen*—I am prepared to forgo its survival."[22]

As this preference for what was then a classical language demonstrates, Ha'am was a thinker determined to hold fast to principle even if doing so set standards difficult to meet. "Jewish literature," he once wrote in this regard, "is the literature written in our own language; it does not include books written by Jews in other languages."[23] By this definition, anything written by a non-Jew on a Jewish subject—say, George Eliot's *Daniel Deronda*—would clearly be excluded. So, of course, would anything written by a Jew in German, Russian, Polish, French, or English. But Ha'am's strictures would even leave out the

*Translation: May no evil follow.

work of another well-known member of the Odessa circle, Shalom Aleichem (nè Rabinowitz, 1859–1916), the short-story writer who created Tevye the milkman of *Fiddler on the Roof* fame and thus brought to life the world of the Jews of the shtetl. Aleichem, after all, wrote in Yiddish, and as Ha'am bitingly wrote, "Jews are not going to sacrifice their lives century after century for the holiness" of a writer such as him.[24] For Ha'am, the only aspect of the Jewish tradition worth preserving was biblical Hebrew and the subsequent great works by Talmudic scholars such as Rashi (born Shlomo Yitzhaki, 1040–1105) or the poet and physician Yehuda Halevi (1075–1141).

As is often the case with disputes over language, Dubnow and Ha'am were really debating a larger point: the role of the Diaspora in Jewish life. Ha'am was incapable of romanticizing the Diaspora, because it was there, except for places such as Spain during its Golden Age, that the once-glorious Hebrew culture fell apart. One of his earliest essays, "Slavery in Freedom," written in 1891, expressed themes that a number of Zionists, including Chaim Weizmann, with whom Ha'am was close, would later echo. Writing about French Jews, who prided themselves on their Frenchness, Ha'am pointed out how transitory their accomplishments actually were and warned them that their so-called emancipation came at the cost of denying their peoplehood.[25] In another essay, Ha'am wrote that Diaspora Jews "fertilize other people's gardens while their own is neglected."[26] Never short of metaphors, in yet another he characterized them as "like the mendicant who goes from door to door, begging from others what he cannot give to others."[27] Christians, Ha'am insisted, will always be too convinced of the inferiority of the Jews to ever grant them equal rights in any meaningful sense of the term. Dubnow's notion that they could gain autonomy in foreign lands, and in that way achieve civic and political rights, was therefore laughable: "So when I read these terrific discussions about . . . 'national autonomy' in Russia, it seems to me that these people are discussing whether the cows of Pharaoh's dream should be eaten roasted or boiled."[28]

Given all this, one might assume that Ahad Ha'am belongs with the Diaspora negators, and not just because of his ideas; Ha'am had lived in London and, as he wrote Dubnow in 1907, "if I have to settle here, I think I shall always feel myself to be in a world which is not mine."[29] Certainly Bialik, the poet of Diaspora negation, viewed Ha'am as an ally: "For me," he declared, "Ahad Ha'am was the most important person in my life. . . . His work, which became the backbone of a whole period, was a ceaseless effort to direct the mind of the people to one central point: the sin or the punishment of *galut* is characterized by a disease of the spirit: namely, the weakening of the will which leads to ever diminishing confidence in our own strength."[30]

But Ha'am's views toward both Zion and exile were far too nuanced to put him in any one category. The key question for him was not where Jews should live but how. As much as conditions of exile had drawn Jews away from their glory days, Ha'am nonetheless recognized the fundamental truths of Dubnow's realism: the Diaspora was where Jews had lived for thousands of years, it was where many of them would continue to live no matter what Zionism accomplished, and for all its decadence, it was still the home of some of the great accomplishments in Jewish life. "Despite his conviction that life in the Diaspora was fundamentally unhealthy for Jewry," concludes the scholar David Weinberg, "Ahad Ha'am could not deny the element of continuity that allowed for the survival of Jewish ideals despite the separation of Jewry from the source of its creativity in the Land of Israel."[31]

For the same reason that he could never unambiguously negate the Diaspora, Ha'am was also unable to give his backing to Zionism's political objective of immediate statehood. Like so many Jews of his time, he was shaken by the events at Kishinev; along with Dubnow, he first heard the news when a group of refugees from the pogrom came to a lecture in Odessa being delivered by Jabotinsky.[32] But as devastating as those refugees' message proved to be, Ha'am did not respond by joining the Zionist movement: Herzl, whom he detested, was in his view an illiterate on Jewish matters and an opportunist on political ones. That Herzl could even contemplate building a Jewish state in Uganda left him aghast: For Ha'am, the whole point of Zionism was to bring Hebrew culture back to life—and Uganda had nothing to do with that. Reviving Hebrew culture was ancillary, if not hostile, to the political element in Zionism, Ha'am charged. It was not love of the Jewish tradition that spurred the political call to Zion, for one thing, but fear of anti-Semitism. And the hurry of it all, the quest for a "quick fix" that would settle the Jewish question once and for all, ignored the fact, obvious to Ha'am if not to Herzl, that the Jews had to be worthy of sovereignty before achieving it.[33] If the objective of political Zionism was to resolve what Ha'am called "material issues," that is, to help impoverished Jews of the Pale find better living and working conditions, then it made more sense for them to move to the United States than to the Holy Land.

In contrast to the political Zionists, Ha'am urged that Jews build a "spiritual center" in Palestine, a place of learning, memory, reflection, and language, but not, given his secularist inclinations, of religion. His was a long-term vision: Jews wherever they lived needed decades if not centuries to refamiliarize themselves with the greatness of their tradition, and only after that was achieved would they be truly worthy of a state of their own. In the meantime, and to help them achieve this goal, the creation of such a spiritual center "will strengthen the Jewish national consciousness in the Diaspora; it will restore our independence of mind and self-respect; it will give our Judaism a national content which will be genuine and natural, unlike the substitutes with which we now try to fill the void."[34] Diaspora and Zion were not two opposing poles but more like a circle with a center and a circumference, each of which required the other. Herzl, Ha'am believed, was more interested in Jews than in Judaism whereas for him it was the reverse.[35] This was not a position likely to lead to much political influence, and on that score, truth be told, Ha'am had little. Responding to the fears and despair of ordinary people, Herzl was, for all his dandyish intellectuality, in touch with popular sentiment. Ha'am, by contrast, elitist to the point of contempt for ordinary people and the struggles of their daily lives, worshiped neither Jewish ethnic solidarity nor an unseen God but the scholars and philosophers who formulated and then struggled to keep alive the Jewish tradition of ethics and law.

Far more than Dubnow, Ha'am ought to be characterized as a

particularist; his love of Hebrew and appreciation for Jewish accomplishment was accompanied by a triumphalism that in today's era of religious pluralism and concern for political correctness can sound downright embarrassing. On those rare occasions when he deemed to discuss other faiths, Ha'am took few pains to conceal his contempt. The British writer Claude Montefiore (1858–1938), a member of one of the grandest Jewish families in Europe, had published a two-volume work in 1927 that argued that while Judaism possessed a well-developed ethic of justice, Christianity contained a more satisfactory ethic of love. Ha'am responded with an essay replete with unsupportable propositions about how Judaism's faith in an abstract God, as opposed to personified figures such as Jesus or Mohammed, makes it ethically superior to its rival faiths, as if a thinker such as Immanuel Kant, who developed the most systematic (and abstract) moral philosophy of modern times, and who was steeped in a thoroughly Lutheran environment, had never lived.[36] If Dubnow was correct that Jewish history offered powerful lessons for non-Jews, Ha'am could hardly have cared less. There is a reason Tel Aviv contains a street named after Ha'am. For all his qualms about political Zionism, his Jewish nationalism was second to none.

At the same time, however, Ha'am's Cassandra-like warnings about the temptations of politics would inspire generations of thinkers who worried that the drive for statehood would corrupt the Jewish soul. "The salvation of Israel," he had warned in 1897 in response to the First Zionist Congress, "will be achieved by prophets not by diplomats."[37] This, the most famous sentence he ever wrote, helped elevate him into the role of prophet that he clearly intended to have. In 1904 Ha'am had published an essay about Moses, which, it did not take much to discern, was also about himself. "As for the Prophet," he wrote, "he dies, as he has lived, in his faith. All the evil that he has seen in the world has been powerless to make him despair of the future or to dim the splendour of his far-off ideal."[38] Simon Dubnow concerned himself overwhelmingly with the Jewish past. Ahad Ha'am could not take his eyes off the eventual Jewish future.

Prophets can sometimes find their messages received in unexpected

places. "My father was a great sympathizer of Ahad Ha'am," the lin-
guistic and Zionist critic Noam Chomsky told an interviewer in 2010.
"Every Friday night we would read Hebrew together, and often the
reading was Ahad Ha'am's essays."[39] (This was no mere happenstance;
William Chomsky, Noam's father, had taught at Philadelphia's Drop-
sie College for Hebrew and Cognate Studies, among other places, and
long before Chomsky's tenure there, Ha'am had considered the possibility of assuming its presidency.)[40] Chomsky especially recalled that
he and his father discussed Ha'am's essay on Moses, which suggests
that Chomsky's own tone and style, whether one finds it prophetic or
tendentious, had its roots in these childhood conversations. Political to his core, at least when he was not being a linguist, Chomsky
made a political point about Ha'am. "He was very sympathetic to the
Palestinians," Chomsky told his interviewer. "In fact he wrote some
very sharp essays, after a visit to Palestine, criticizing the way the new
settlers were treating the indigenous population."[41]

Is it possible that a Jewish nationalist not especially concerned with
the needs of other people could nonetheless have been sympathetic
to the Arabs? The answer is not quite as Chomsky recalls it. The 1891
essay that Chomsky mentions, "Truth from Eretz Yisrael," written on
a ship returning to Odessa from Jaffa, contains more than its share of
stereotyping: the Arabs are "indolent," "do not like to exert themselves
today for a distant future," and "know how to exploit the public and
to proceed furtively with all those with whom they deal, exactly as
in Europe."[42] Ha'am, the Jewish nationalist, never went as far as to
recognize that Arabs in Palestine might have national aspirations of
their own. "Once the cultural atmosphere of the land is shaped in the
Jewish spirit," he wrote on the eve of World War I, "it is possible that
the Arabs too can be absorbed. For haven't they been here since ancient times, and quite possibly some of them are members of our own
people?" This notion that at least some Arabs were once originally
Jews—after all, they were both Semitic peoples—may have helped
the early Zionist settlers rationalize their move to the Holy Land, but
it was as fanciful as it was neocolonial. That he bought into it does not
add to Ha'am's ethical sensibility.

And yet, as with all matters involving this complicated man and his ideas, Ha'am came closer than any Zionist thinker of his era to the recognition that some accommodation would have to be made to the Arabs and their needs. In part his sensibility was shaped by his deep immersion in diasporic Jewish thought, which made him fully aware that the Jewish writers he most admired, especially those in medieval Spain, were strongly influenced by the Arab culture and language surrounding them. (*The Guide for the Perplexed*, the most famous work of Maimonides [1135–1204], the greatest of the medieval Jewish philosophers, was originally written in Arabic.) The ethicist in him, moreover, appreciated what it might mean for a people to be treated badly by others they viewed as engaged in a hostile takeover of their land. "He feared that the attitude of many of the [Zionist] settlers toward Arabs was haughty," his biographer Zipperstein writes. "He mourned when he heard of incidents when Jews abused them."⁴³ Given the limits of his time and place, Ha'am, when it came to the Arabs, was farsighted, as prophets tend to be. In those 1891 reflections, he wrote that "[f]rom abroad we are accustomed to believing that the Arabs are all desert savages, like donkeys, who neither see nor understand what goes on around them. But this is a big mistake."⁴⁴ None of this led Ha'am to question his own particularist inclinations. But he paid sufficient attention to the Arab question to stand out among others who simply wished the problem away.

As his concern with the Arab question illustrates, Ha'am appealed to the conscience of his country, a second reason why there should be a street in Tel Aviv named after him. For anyone who spends more time wondering why a Jewish state ought to exist in the first place rather than asking how it can best protect itself by military force, Ha'am's insistence that the greatness of Judaism lies in its prophetic stance toward the world offers a starting point for the discussion. Israel, as it happens, currently contains a figure who has carried on that discussion. His name is Avraham Burg.

The son of Yoseph Burg (1909–1999), the leader of Israel's National Religious Party and one of the most prominent Israelis of his era, Avraham Burg had been speaker of the Knesset, the Israeli parliament, and chairman of the World Zionist Organization before becoming a social critic. His most incendiary book, *The Holocaust Is Over; We Must Rise from Its Ashes*, appeared in Hebrew in 2007 and was immediately greeted with a storm of invective.[45] "I was outraged by the book," Ari Shavit, a prominent Israeli journalist, wrote in *Ha'aretz*, by way of introducing an interview he had conducted with Burg.[46] Especially shocked by Burg's charge that an atmosphere not unlike that of Germany in the 1930s was emerging within the Jewish state, Shavit repeatedly demanded to know whether Burg still considered himself a Zionist. To Shavit, a Jew was either a Zionist and therefore a lover of Israel or an anti-Zionist and therefore an enemy of the Jewish state; Burg, to his great regret, had become the latter. Why do you despise us so much? Shavit wanted to know. Why have you turned your back on your people?

Shavit was not alone in concluding that Burg had gone over the edge. Although Burg's criticisms of the ultranationalist Israel right should have made him friends on the left, a number of Israel's most prominent liberals joined in criticizing him. "For the so-called head of the Zionist movement to say all this—to say, 'Get another passport for your kids,'" the distinguished Israeli philosopher Avishai Margalit told the *New Yorker*'s David Remnick, "It's like the Pope giving sex tips."[47] Others who expressed serious reservations about Burg's jeremiad included the feminist Shulamit Aloni, the peace advocate Yossi Beilin and, not surprisingly given his views on the negation of the Diaspora, the novelist A. B. Yehoshua. "They sensed in him a kind of undergraduate universalism," Remnick writes of these critics, "a table talk at once snobbish and half-baked." Burg is literally a long-distance runner, and politically speaking, he has been experiencing the loneliness that comes with it.

Yet all these thinkers who find Burg simplistic are making the same mistake Chomsky did in his appreciation of Ha'am: confusing politics with prophecy. In response to Shavit's persistent questioning about his Zionism, Burg answered this way: "Already at the first Zionist Congress, Herzl's Zionism was victorious over the Zionism of Ahad

Ha'am. I think that the 21st century should be the century of Ahad Ha'am."[48] Shavit never really heard, and was therefore unable to absorb, Burg's point that Zionism, from its very beginnings, had taken a variety of forms, making it all but impossible to divide the movement into those who love Israel and those who criticize it. "You are dichotomous, Ari, and I am inclusive," Burg told his interlocutor. "You slice off and I try to contain. Therefore I do not say that I am turning my back on being a sabra but that I am turning in a different direction. And this is true. Completely true." Burg may be living in the twenty-first century, but his mind is preoccupied with debates over the future Jewish state that preoccupied querulous Zionists in the last decades of the nineteenth. Perhaps that explains why Burg has been able to make explicit the universalism always implicit in Ha'am's particularism. "What I want to do is to expand the borders of Israel beyond land and location to include universalism and spiritual search," Burg told the American journalist J. J. Goldberg in a follow-up to the argument with Shavit. "We were raised on the Zionism of Ben-Gurion, that there is only one place for Jews and that's Israel. I say no, there have always been multiple centers of Jewish life."[49]

It is impossible to know what Ha'am would think of Burg were the former alive today. In my view, he would likely despise the latter's French passport, his comparisons of Israel to the Nazi era, and his insistence, closer to Dubnow than to Ha'am, that the story of the Jews contains a universalist imperative. But there can be little doubt that in style and tone, if not fully in substance, these two thinkers share much. Read either one and you know that you are dealing with a person who disdains practicality in favor of principle. It is not, in the end, Burg's views on this or that Israeli policy that matters but his effort to remind Israelis that there is more to statehood than security. A Jewish state, like any other state, must ultimately live up to an ideal—and must be warned, dramatically if need be, when that ideal has been corrupted. Israel in that sense is fortunate that the legacy of Ahad Ha'am lives on in some Israelis who still ponder what it means to aspire to the words of the Hebrew prophets.

IV

The one project in Palestine to which Ahad Ha'am gave his full support was the Hebrew University of Jerusalem. Created to embody a long-standing tradition of Jewish respect for scholarship, the goal of the Hebrew University was to be accepted among the world's great centers of higher education, one reason it received the strong support of Albert Einstein. At the same time, it was designed to reflect and nurture a Jewish and Hebrew sensibility, and for this latter purpose Ha'am's ideas provided a perfect fit. The new university, as Weizmann said in a speech to the Eleventh Zionist Congress in 1913, would become "a guardian of those values which are most precious to the future of the nation; it would cultivate the living Jewish national tongue; it would be a meeting place for all Jewish creative activity in literature, art, and science: In a word, it would be the 'cultural center.'"[50] As if to reflect its dual purpose, the Hebrew University established not only traditional academic departments but also one devoted to the study of Judaism; indeed the latter began months before the university officially opened in 1925.

All of this brings to mind the figure of Simon Rawidowicz, who as we saw in the previous chapter strongly expressed his opposition to the notion that only in the Holy Land could a Jewish university flourish. Rawidowicz is the third of the thinkers being discussed in this chapter whose love of Judaism encompassed the Diaspora as much as the Jewish state. Indeed, in part because he came from the generation that immediately followed Dubnow and Ha'am, Rawidowicz's thoughts are even more relevant to the competing claims of Diaspora and statehood than those of the two scholars with whom he otherwise shared so many concerns.

Born in 1896 Rawidowicz was raised in the intense Zionist atmosphere of the Pale at the end of the nineteenth century. His father, Chaim Isaac, had been active in Hovevei Zion (The Lovers of Zion), the same organization that had originally attracted Ha'am; had attended the Seventh Zionist Congress, the one that finally rejected the proposal to build a Jewish state in Uganda, in 1905; and had even-

tually settled in the Holy Land.[51] As a very young man, Simon Rawidowicz became an admirer of the Hebrew language; ironically, his
enthusiastic talks designed to convince others to follow his path, of
necessity delivered in Yiddish, undermined his efforts to consign the
latter language to oblivion. Like so many other European-born Jewish
intellectuals of his time, Rawidowicz lived in many places: Bialystok
in Poland, Berlin in Germany, London and Leeds in England, and
Chicago and suburban Boston in the United States. In all of them he
carried forward his life's work of writing about the Hebrew classics in
the same language in which those classics were written.

Rawidowicz is not especially well known, not even among scholars of Jewish studies. One of his expressions, the idea that Jews are
best characterized as "an ever-dying people," is well known, however,
even if it is not always attributed to him. (Sir Jonathan Sacks, the
former chief rabbi of England and a man of prodigious learning, mistakenly cites Dubnow as the author of the phrase.)[52] Appalled by the
persistent tone of defeatism associated with those who followed in
the wake of Graetz, Rawidowicz wrote an essay, conceived before the
Holocaust and published in Hebrew in 1948, in which he argued that
Jewish thinkers, religious or secular, Orthodox or liberal, Sephardic or
Ashkenazi, were given to reiterating, as if it were part of their liturgy,
that they were the last Jews, that the tradition for which they spoke
was coming to an end with them.[53] There were reasons aplenty for
such despair; Jews, after all, were a people "that has been disappearing
constantly for the last two thousand years, exterminated in dozens
of lands all over the globe, reduced to half or third of its population
by tyrants, ancient and modern." Yet the cost of following what the
American Jewish historian Salo Baron once called the "lachrymose"[54]
theory of Jewish history was high: "It has depressed the best and the
greatest, darkened the light of their lives, poisoned the well of their
creativeness." Jews, Rawidowicz argued, need above all else a sense of
realism, an appreciation of not only the challenges they have faced
but also the resources they have mobilized to face them. Only then
will they appreciate, as he put it, that "a people dying for thousands of
years means a living people."

The place in which Jews had survived was of course the Diaspora, and Rawidowicz's essay can be read as a stinging criticism of Diaspora negation. But to this way of thinking Rawidowicz added a religious twist. The Zionist call for a Jewish state in the Holy Land, he noted, was designed to offer Diaspora Jews a safe haven not only from anti-Semitism but also from "the entire heavy yoke of religion, or of Judaism in its present legalistic and restrictive form."[55] For all his talk of a spiritual center, even Ahad Ha'am hoped, in Rawidowicz's words, that Zionism "would bring a new stream of life to the heart of the Jewish people and free the captive Jewish spirit from its subservience to chapter and verse, so that Jews would cease to be a petrified 'People of the Book.'" From such a perspective, Zionism and Reform Judaism, movements that strongly distrusted one another, shared the same objective of emancipating Jews from traditional Judaism; on the contrary, Rawidowicz countered, it was essential that "Hebrew literature and the Hebrew movement in the galut emancipate itself from Ahad Ha-amism." Rawidowicz has been characterized by the scholar Noam Pianko "as part of the last generation of Eastern European maskilim (followers of the Haskalah or Jewish Enlightenment)."[56] Although a product of an essentially secular movement, Rawidowicz was not a freethinker in the sense of Dubnow or Ha'am. According to his son Benjamin C. I. Ravid, Rawidowicz, while clearly rejecting the Orthodoxy of his upbringing, remained mildly if not strictly observant.[57] It is for this reason Rawidowicz insisted that one show respect for the great classics of Jewish philosophy and theology, as well as the rabbinic texts, Talmudic laws, and the endless reinterpretations of both, all of which constituted the core of traditional Judaism. One need not accept what the Jewish tradition taught to admire its determination to teach.

In addition, Rawidowicz rejected Ha'am's metaphor of a center and a circumference in favor of the notion of an ellipse, with two equal foci. There was an important reason: Ha'am's imagery flew in the face of Rawidowicz's core conviction that "the state of Israel is not the people of Israel, it is only a part of the people of Israel, only one segment—a great, creative, and free segment—but only one link of many. . . . All Jews have the same pedigree: they are children of Abraham, Isaac, and Jacob. The people of Israel is an organic unity, with one body and one soul; every limb of that body has absolutely the same worth as the other."[58] Because Jews who live in the Diaspora and those who live within the borders of the Jewish state belong to the same nation, political Zionism, denigrating the former consigns them to second-class citizenship. Rawidowicz, who could be as sarcastic as any of the political Zionists with whom he disagreed, therefore condemned the "little Herzls" who "say that the Jewish problem is now really solved, the state of Israel on the one hand and complete assimilation and conversion [in the Diaspora] on the other—and so the Messiah will arrive and the redeemer come to Zion."[59]

In 1953 and 1954 Rawidowicz published his thoughts on this question in both an English and a Hebrew version. Call the new society Medinat Yisrael (the state of Israel) or Eretz Yisrael (land of Israel) if you must, he wrote, but because God had chosen to call all his people Israel regardless of where they lived, using the same word only for those who had made aliyah constitutes "a great menace" to Jews both inside and outside the Jewish state.[60] Rawidowicz felt so passionately about the matter that he sent a copy of his essay to Ben-Gurion, then between terms as Israel's prime minister. The two men had known each other in London, and such was the respect the politician showed for the thinker that a correspondence between them ensued. I appreciate, that you, Simon Rawidowicz, are able to lead an entirely Jewish life outside the state of Israel, Ben-Gurion wrote to him, but even you cannot lead a "complete" one. (As we have seen, A. B. Yehoshua would repeat the same argument many years later.) "Only in the State of Israel is a full Jewish life possible," Ben-Gurion went on. "Only here will a Jewish culture worthy of that name flourish."[61]

Who was right? The answer, of course, depends on which elements of Jewish teachings add up to a full Jewish life. Ben-Gurion had little doubt where he stood on that question. Without both a strong sense of Israeli patriotism and a military capable of defending the new state from its avowed enemies, there would be no possibility of any kind of Jewish life, let alone a complete one. "A whole Jew and a whole man, without any split or division between the citizen and the society,"

Ben-Gurion wrote to Rawidowicz, "is not possible on foreign soil." Jewish unity was political unity, the kind of bond established through common membership in a single state. Security came first, and security could only be achieved by statehood.

Rawidowicz could not disagree more. Skeptical toward violence and a passionate opponent of "cruel Zionism"—the kind that worshiped power and defended any means to achieve the end of statehood—Rawidowicz despised "the pseudo-Nietzcheans," as he called them, who in condemning Diaspora Jews for their alleged weakness made strength—brute strength, military strength—into a virtue.[62] Even before the state of Israel had come into existence, Rawidowicz had detected in political Zionism a contempt for compassion, the very quality Diaspora Jews, dependent upon each other for support in countries in which they were a minority, had required for survival. After that state came into being, he, like Martin Buber, saw great danger in the Israeli adoration of Samson, the biblical hero who destroyed the Philistines by pulling down the pillars of the Temple of Dagon but killed himself along with them. I am not a pacifist, Rawidowicz informed his readers, but he did warn "against an exaggerated faith in force and in the decisiveness of force. . . . One can strike one's enemy again and again, with all the ten plagues, and not reach the end thereby; even when successful, force is no more than a means of winning time to prepare for an atmosphere of coexistence with friend and foe."[63]

Rawidowicz had become friends with Dubnow when the two of them had lived in Berlin in the 1920s, and it was the older man who suggested to the younger one that he collect his topical essays and publish them in a single volume. Rawidowicz took the advice, but by the time he became seriously involved with the project many years later, roughly at the same time he entered into his correspondence with Ben-Gurion, it had evolved into an entirely new book. Rawidowicz never lived to see his book in print; he was working on the index when he died. But then again, neither did many others. Running to more than nine hundred pages and published in Paris in 1957 in stilted Hebrew, *Babylon and Jerusalem* attracted little attention. There does exist a paraphrase in English of the book's major themes, included in a collection of Rawidowicz's writings edited by his son, but it is fair to say that *Babylon and Jerusalem* has not entered the canon of Jewish classics. Based on what has been translated, the book is nonetheless important. Rawidowicz's magnum opus can best be understood as a historical and theoretical effort to demonstrate the importance of the idea, so central to nearly everything he wrote, that the Diaspora and the state of Israel are best viewed as "two that are one," to cite the title of one of his articles. Judaism's history, Rawidowicz maintained, could best be understood through the metaphor of two houses. The first, corresponding to the period of the First Temple of Jerusalem, offered Jews the advantages of their own home, but it also made them like any other people whose existence was defined territorially; political power, law, faith—all were experienced through direct observation and felt in unmediated fashion. But once the Jews went into the exile, they were taught "a new and great secret, a secret of secrets" that "provided a new reason for existence."[64] Here in their second house, in the absence of political sovereignty, Jews found themselves relying on powers of imagination, memory, and interpretation to solidify their communal ties. If Jews are a chosen people, what makes them special is the fact of their two houses, one that gave them a sense of normality and the other that expanded their minds.

When he brought his analysis up to date by discussing the twin events of the Holocaust and the birth of the state of Israel, Rawidowicz insisted that what had been true throughout all Jewish history remained true even in much darker times: the Hitler years, far from teaching the end of the Jewish people, taught instead the remarkable survival of the Diaspora. "In short, what the wretched years that followed 1933 could not achieve, the happier circumstances of 1948 are not to achieve either. As it was before 1948, so shall it be afterwards: *Jerusalem-and-Babylon.*"[65] Rawidowicz considered himself a Zionist "no less than those who discharge their obligations by 'negating the Diaspora' or reciting 'kaddish' for Diaspora Jewry," as he put it.[66] As such, he was thrilled to see Jews able once again to live in their first house, and he urged Jews everywhere to commit to its economic and political strengthening. But for him statehood should never be made a condition for Jewish survival. Apocalypticism did not serve the Jews well: Jerusalem may be the end destination, but Babylon is the means to get there. Without Jerusalem there is no security, but without Babylon there is no dynamism. "Babylon represents not complacency and satisfaction with the status quo but an inner struggle against the status quo. In Babylon there is no room for incompetence, ineptitude, or slovenliness. Babylon represents only unlimited, unconditional, single-minded commitment."[67]

The most prophetic chapter of *Babylon and Jerusalem* was not published with the rest of the book. Rawidowicz had made a vow to himself that he would never discuss either Israeli foreign policy or the Arab question. But so convinced was he of the benefits of Babylon that he could not help worry about how Jerusalem would treat the Arabs who lived there. Convinced that if he published his thoughts on the matter all his other work on Jewish history and philosophy would be ignored, and not wishing to undermine a country whose existence he supported and that was home to much of his family, he wrote a chapter on the Arab question but did not include it in the eventual published version of the book. In 2008 the UCLA historian David Myers translated and published the chapter, allowing readers to hear a voice more prophetic than that of Ahad Ha'am, if for no other reason than the one voice was speaking when the Arabs were forced from their land in 1948 while the other was not.

"Nothing stands before me—before Israel and the entire world—except this simple fact," Rawidowicz had written in his self-censored chapter. "Hundreds of thousands of Arabs, man, woman, and child, left this country, and the State of Israel will not permit them to return to their homes and settle on the land, the land of their fathers, and of their father's fathers."[68] The refugee problem was the price paid for Jersualem, and the price was high. "So the Jew was given sovereignty in a small patch of land—and he acts like every Gentile under the sun? Your enemy lashed out, so kill him. He killed one or more from your camp, go and seek him out and kill him—and the family and the family of his family. Because this is the 'only language' understandable to your enemy." At no time did Jersualem need Babylon more than in the first years of Jewish statehood. "No Jewish minority in the Diaspora would ever dream of discriminating in this fashion," he insisted. "And if it did dream of this, it would not have the chance to implement it." This passionate protest against Arab displacement grew, at least in part, out of political rather than philosophical concerns: If Jews proved themselves cruel to the Arabs, would this not, Rawidowicz reasoned, give a green light for the rest of the world to be cruel to the Jews? To the degree that his dissent contained a moral and ethical component, moreover, it was closer to particularism than to a universalistic concern with human rights. "The question of these Arabs is not an Arab question," Rawidowicz pointed out. "It is a *Jewish question*, a question that 1948 placed upon the Jewish people."

As was also true of Dubnow and Ha'am, Rawidowicz's particularism nonetheless stretched to univeralist considerations. Having lived long enough to witness World War II, Rawidowicz found himself fascinated by Franklin Delano Roosevelt's declaration that the world was fighting for four freedoms: of speech, of religion, from want, and from fear. Because the Jews for so long "dwelt alone," always at the mercy of the non-Jewish majorities surrounding them, their particular history, in his view, taught the need for an additional freedom, indeed a foundational one that made all the others possible. Rawidowicz called this *libertas differendi*, the right to be different. "The oneness of man," he wrote in 1945, "will be fulfilled when the world is not dominated by any doctrine that forces smaller groups to adopt themselves to stronger ones, and causes assimilation and imitation by force between group and group by compelling the weaker and small groups to surrender their own group character and tradition, actions that have led to many catastrophies in recent history." Later on we would call this multiculturalism, and it is impossible to know what Rawidowicz, had he lived even longer, would have made of it. Still, the right to be different, as Rawidowicz understood it, blended the particular and the universal, teaching that "mankind is one and indivisible" while also demonstrating that "man is different, and every group is entitled to be as different as it is able to be."[69]

Although he must be counted as a defender of the Diaspora,

Rawidowicz worried that if Jersualem was failing the test of state-hood, Babylon was failing the demands of statelessness. As early as the 1950s, he saw emerging a pattern in which Diaspora Jews, espe-cially those in the United States, would cheer the state of Israel on rather than serve as its conscience. His only option was to write as if an Old Testament prophet had suddenly appeared in Waltham, Massachusetts, where his last place of work, Brandeis University, was located. Rawidowicz asked the most uncomfortable of questions and in the most biblical of ways: "Can we dare face ourselves and say: We are righteous and did not sin. There is no thorn in the crown of our kingdom, the kingdom of 1948, no stain in the vestments of our glory; our garment is pure through and through." As these passages suggest, few thinkers have ever enumerated the costs of Israeli statehood as thoroughly as Rawidowicz. "The period between 1948 and now [1951] places in question the very morality of Judaism itself," he cried out in his last years.[70] Jews, history's victims, had become the victimizers. Only time would tell whether Pharaoh's robe would fit them.

Among scholars who are familiar with the work of Simon Rawido-wicz, there is a tendency to dismiss him as "an obscure and lonely thinker whose ethical thought was ... both lacking in solid founda-tions and rather unrealistic," in the words of Allan Arkush of the State University of New York at Binghamton.[71] Certainly in comparison to Ben-Gurion, his correspondent from the 1950s, Rawidowicz, when it comes to having an impact on the world, pales in significance—even if his ideas are beginning to attract attention from those who find in his writings a dissenting and at times moving approach to the ques-tion of Zion. No full-length biography of him has yet been published.

Still, the recent history of Jewish studies in Israel suggests that perhaps his time is coming. In 2011 Israel's Council of Higher Edu-cation authorized a committee, chaired by the philosopher Daniel Dahlstrom of Boston University, to examine the status of Jewish studies both at the Hebrew University and at other institutions of higher education in the country. The committee painted a grim pic-ture, suggesting that cutbacks in the humanities and a preference for investing in more lucrative fields such as science and engineering were responsible for a shrinkage too dramatic to ignore. "Maimonides and the Kabbalah have an immense universal influence and it is very surprising that exactly at the same time the entire cultural world draws an interest in Jewish thought," said one committee member, Moshe Idel, from the Hebrew University, "in Israel the whole subject is submerging. Every culture that forsakes its past will end up being impervious to its future generations, and risks severing the cultural bond."[72] Given his views about the Diaspora, I believe Rawidowicz would not have been surprised to learn that the study of Judaism is more alive there than in the Jewish state. Nor, given his suspiciousness toward the military, would he be shocked to hear that Israel's success in science and technology is not being matched in the humanities. This is what happens, one can imagine him saying, when Israel the state confuses itself with Israel the people: it no longer feels it needs a conscience, and it is in danger of losing the one that the classic works of the Hebrew and Jewish traditions can provide.

As obscure as he may be now, Rawidowicz was once a thinker of considerable renown. At a reception at the White House during the 1960s, Abram Sachar, then the president of Brandeis University, was introduced to the presidents of both Israel and the United States, Zalman Shazar and Lyndon Baines Johnson. "Brandeis—that's where Rawidowicz is," explained Shazar as he turned to LBJ, holding up the receiving line to sing the man's praises.[73] There was a time when Rawidowicz, the defender of the Diaspora, was better known in Israel than in the United States. It can only be considered a shame that his views these days are so little known in both places.

V

Only one of these three thinkers, Ha'am, made the *yishuv* his home, and then only toward the end of his life. And only one of them, Rawidowicz, lived long enough to see the Jewish state come into existence. Yet the ideas of all three men nonetheless suggest two conclusions about the relationship between the state of Israel and the Diaspora today—one important, the other vital.

The important one is to emphasize just how mistaken it is to view Zionism as an open-and-shut proposition in which one is either a Zionist and loves the Jewish people or one is not and hates them. The notion that men such as Dubnow, Ha'am, and Rawidowicz were somehow incomplete Jews because they lived all or most of their lives outside Israel rings hollow, given their deep immersion in Jewish history and Hebrew language and culture. The more venomous charge that Jewish critics of Israel, and especially those who worry about its treatment of the Palestinians, are self-hating seems even more out of bounds: call these thinkers anything you want, including overly idealistic or haughty and contemptuous, but the term *self-hating Jew* can never be applied to any of them. Arguments about the future of Zionism require something more than invective and accusations of bad faith; greater familiarity with the ideas of these men can provide that missing ingredient.

More important, however, is the determined effort of all these thinkers to move beyond the tendency of so many Jews to view the world as implacably set against them. One of them, Ha'am, never lived to see the Holocaust, while another, Dubnow, was killed by it and a third, Rawidowicz, viewed it from abroad. Yet despite their different life trajectories, the issues with which they wrestled offer an alternative to the ways in which the events of the 1930s and 1940s have colored so much of contemporary Jewry's understanding of history and fate. If one is convinced that anti-Semitism is as powerful as ever and can only be deterred by military force, and if one accepts that the only way Israel can remain a Jewish state is by driving the Arabs away or treating them as second-class citizens, then Dubnow, Ha'am, and Rawidowicz have little to offer. All these men were prophets, and prophets never quite grasp matters of realpolitik.

For this very idealism, however, it would be a serious mistake to dismiss the ideas of these thinkers. Whatever form criticism of Israel takes in the future—that there will be criticism cannot be doubted— it is important to remember that the Zionist movement from the start was filled with argument, idealism, invective, and changes of mind. When the day comes that Simon Dubnow, Ahad Ha'am, and Simon

Rawidowicz are given greater recognition, we will know that Israel has reached that more mature point in its history when it has become possible to accept that that those who are critical of the way it goes about its business may have its best interest at heart. The proof of the Diaspora's necessity is not only that Zionism was born there but also that Zionism's most loving critics understood its importance.

CHAPTER 3

The Secularization
of Particularism

I

In 2012 Nechemya Weberman, a Satmar Hasidic rabbi from the Williamsburg section of Brooklyn, was found guilty of sexually abusing a twelve-year-old schoolgirl for whom he had been serving as a spiritual mentor.[1] His sentence—103 years in prison—was unusual. So was the case. Hasidic Jews are insular and distrustful of outsiders, which led many in Brooklyn to rally to Weberman's defense, some going so far as to accuse the girl of wanton conduct and her family of disloyalty. In trying to protect one of their own, furthermore, various Satmar members offered to bribe the judge and posted photos of the victim on the Internet. A long-existing code of silence prevented many others from appearing at the trial, finally forcing Brooklyn's district attorney to rely on the word of only one of them, the victim herself. The trial, in short, brought to light the inner workings of a religious community that generally avoids it, and the resulting exposure was not a pretty sight.

Legal trials often raise issues, not only of the guilt or innocence of the parties involved but also of matters relevant to society as a whole. So it was here. The self-protective nature of the Hasidic community in Brooklyn offers an extreme but nonetheless revealing illustration of what Jews call particularism. "For the particularist," as Svante

Lungren, a Finnish scholar of Jewish Studies who has written the definitive book on the question, puts it, "Jewishness, Jewish culture and religion are what matters. What the Jews can bring to the world is not important."[2] Out of their understanding of particularism, Brooklyn's ultra-Orthodox Jews insisted that whatever had happened between Weberman and the girl was their business to judge.

Particularism's appeal in the wake of both the Holocaust and the birth of Israel, as I argued in my introduction, was all but inevitable. Moreover, as the postwar years went by, it seemed if anything to gain strength. Jewish organizations in the Diaspora became increasingly preoccupied with the defense of Israel abroad and threats from anti-Semitism at home. Worries about assimilation and intermarriage led rabbis to warn Jews to focus more on themselves and their survival. Neoconservatism, a reaction against secular humanism, took root and began to spread, at least among intellectuals. The combination appeared too powerful to resist: influenced by particularism, Jews would become like everyone else, protective of their identity as Jews. This did not make the great bulk of American Jews anything like the Satmars. But the impulse to be wary of outsiders sprang from similar roots.

To the surprise of many, including those who joined its bandwagon, particularism in recent years has begun to show its age. Many reasons can be advanced to account for its loosening hold on Diaspora Jews. In this chapter, I will emphasize one that in my view has not received sufficient attention. The tendency of Jews to look inward in the years after World War II, unlike the particularism of Jews throughout much of their history and indeed unlike the particularism on display during the Weberman trial, was thoroughly secular. This severance from its religious roots broadened particularism's appeal: one did not need to attend synagogue, be active in Jewish communal life, or even be married to another Jew to become protective of one's Jewishness. At the same time, secular particularism offered no compelling reason, especially to younger and more idealistic generations, why Jews should remain Jewish. It helps Jews to know that like all other ethnic groups they can defend their own. It hurts them to realize that in being like everyone else there is nothing special about them.

II

Particularism emerged out of the idea, adhered to by so many of its greatest classical thinkers, that Judaism was superior to all other faiths. An example can be found in the writings of Yehuda Halevi, the spiritual and romantic poet of the Spanish Golden Age. Known to this day for his love lyrics and the beauty of his Hebrew, Halevi responded to the burdens of exile, let alone the fear of assimilation, by insisting upon Judaism's unique virtues. In his *Kuzari*, a philosophical dialogue between a pagan king and a Jew, Halevi wrote that Moses was fortunate enough to have seen the light of God, whereas the prophets of Christianity and Islam "have poor eyesight, and they cannot see the sun or find its place" and so wander to either the North or the South Pole, where it is completely dark, searching for a genuine spirituality that will always elude them.[3] A physician as well as a poet, Halevi was given to a biologically based view of Jewish superiority; just as humans were better than animals, Jews received from their maker a divine soul that non-Jews did not. Such a view can sound terribly ethnocentric, and Hillel Halkin is correct to conclude that despite the appeal of his poetry, Halevi's genetically based way of thinking constituted "an anticipation of modern racist ideologies."[4] At the same time Halkin is also correct that no writer before him, and not many after him, made yearning for Jerusalem, which has always been part of Judaism, as emotionally powerful as Halevi was able to do.

An emphasis on biology was not apparent in the work of Maimonides, although he too nonetheless held to ideas of Jewish superiority, if in matters of law rather than genetic fitness. A great philosopher of his or any other time, Maimonides enriched Judaism by bringing the tools of reason associated with Aristotelian philosophy to biblical interpretation and the demands of piety. It is not his profound and complex philosophy that is relevant to my concerns here, however, but his belief in the ethical superiority of monotheism, especially its Mosaic form. For Maimonides there was only one true God, and he was the one to whom Jews prayed when they recited the Shema: "Hear, O Israel, the Lord is our God, the Lord is one." This helps explain why he frequently used terms such as *heathen* and *pagan* to characterize other faiths and even calmly discussed whether killing by the sword or stoning was the proper punishment for non-Jews under Jewish law.[5] It also suggests why Maimonides concluded that although gentiles were capable of righteousness, it would be conditional on obeying the so-called Noahide Laws, which Jews considered obligatory on all human beings, as well as accepting that such laws were divinely inspired, that is, that they reflected the teachings of the Hebrew God.[6] (The seven Noahide Laws banned idolatry, blasphemy, murder, theft, sexual license, and the consumption of live animals and required the establishment of a legal system.) Because he accepted the proposition that conversion to Judaism was possible, something a biological emphasis such as Halevi's did not permit, Maimonides cannot be characterized as an ardent chauvinist. On the contrary: the fact that Jews were the followers of the one true God imposed on them the special obligation of adhering to the moral law; as Lundgren states, Maimonides "considered the Torah to be superior to all other laws, and . . . expected a morally better behaviour from the Jews than from other peoples."[7]

Are the ideas of Halevi and Maimonides at all relevant to life in the contemporary world? Michael Broyde, an Emory University law professor and rabbi, believes they are, especially in the case of Maimonides. Broyde, as it happens, publicly commented on the Weberman trial in an interview with the *Village Voice*, and his views were not what one might have expected.[8] The Torah, he pointed out, does contain an injunction against Jews cooperating with gentile authorities. But this has everything to do with the experience of earlier eras when Jews lacked political rights and were treated in unjust ways. In modern times, and especially in situations where accusations involve violent crimes such as murder (or, presumably, sexual abuse), Jews *are* under an obligation to give testimony in civil trials or even to inform on each other. Broyde is no casual observer of these matters; he is America's leading Orthodox authority on the family and the rules that ought to govern it. (So high is his standing among Jewish scholars that his name was prominently mentioned as a candidate to replace Sir Jonathan Sacks as chief rabbi of England, a position that was eventually filled by Ephraim Mirvis, former chief rabbi of Ireland.)⁹ Broyde knows Halakhah, as the tradition of Jewish law is called, better than the Satmar rabbis who invoked it in defense of Weberman.

An entirely different and far less attractive picture of Broyde's understanding of particularism emerges, however, when he discusses the obligation of Jews to pass judgment on the crimes committed by non-Jews. The most highly publicized contemporary cases of sexual abuse within a religious context in our time involve Catholic priests taking advantage of young boys. Although Broyde did not address this problem directly, there can be little doubt about his response: what happens among Catholics is of no particular concern to Jews. Even if non-Jews are obligated to obey the Noahide Laws, "classical Jewish law," he says, "does not compel a Jew to persuade or entice a people generally to observe the [secular] law."¹⁰ As a matter of politics or pragmatism, Jews may choose not to remain silent while non-Jews engage in criminal behavior. But nothing in their tradition requires them to act as watchdogs for the morality of society in general. There is, to be sure, the long-standing teaching that Jews are under an obligation to repair the world. But Broyde believes that *tikkun olam*, as that obligation is called in Hebrew, is as voluntary as it is utilitarian: "One can," he writes, "choose, in particular circumstances, not to fix the world now if the consequences of fixing are deleterious to one's long-term interest." The notion that Jews ought to be a light unto all nations only means that they ought to please their own God in the hope that gentiles will learn from them.

For all their emphasis on Judaism's superiority, both Halevi and Maimonides engaged with the gentile world around them, one reason their work can be admired by people of all faiths today. Broyde's indifference to non-Jews, by contrast, reflected in his lack of concern for the cruelties inflicted on sexually abused Catholics, grates on modern sensibilities. This much, however, can be said about the form of particularism he embodies: Orthodoxy is based on a long tradition of thought, commentary, and argument, which, though it does little to make Orthodoxy appealing, at least to me, does give it a history and a methodology. Whatever one thinks of his reasoning, Broyde does offer reasons: reading what he has to say on the Weberman case is like overhearing a thousand-year history of debate and interpretation. Halakhah, Broyde teaches us, is not something just made up on the spot. The learning that goes into it is impressive and the conclusions can be unexpected.

The same cannot be said for the secular particularism that emerged among Jewish thinkers and activists in the years after World War II. Like the rabbis of old, they argued that Jews should be concerned primarily with their own. In contrast to a Halevi or a Maimonides, however, let alone a Broyde, their views were not rooted in biblical teachings, rabbinic texts, or the commands of a supreme being. Lacking grounding in religious authority, their particularism became purely political, at best an excuse for avoiding self-reflection and at worst a rationalization for exclusion and militancy. It also became subject to the caprices of the moment; once the conditions that brought it into being changed, its appeal began to dissipate. Speaking for nothing but power, devoid of the narrative strength that religion at its best can furnish, appealing to no better world, it can hardly be surprising that the postwar triumph of secular particularism also signaled its eventual decline.

III

In June 1938 representatives from four major Jewish organizations—the American Jewish Committee, the American Jewish Congress, B'nai B'rith, and the Jewish Labor Committee—met to present a united front against the increasingly visible Jew hatred of the Nazi regime. The group they formed, the General Jewish Council, lasted for only one year. But in that time it articulated a general consensus among American Jewish leaders that Hitler's actions constituted an attack on all people irrespective of their faith. Something must be done to save the Jews, the GJC urged, "not primarily because they are Jews but because they are human beings and as such represent a fraction of the dignity and the potentialities of humanity itself." It is important, the GJC continued, to "always remember that by saving the innocent Christian and Jewish objects of persecution we shall fortify and safeguard the very elements of modern civilization—democracy, liberty, and justice."[11] It is an unarguable fact of contemporary political life that the Nazi regime, which took upon itself the task of exterminating the Jews, firmly lodged itself on the political right. No wonder that in the wake of the Nazi defeat the initial reaction of so many Jews found succor in a universalist outlook generally identified with the left.

As the Nazi killings went on, and as the extent of them became increasingly apparent, this capacious concern with all humanity increasingly came to be viewed as a luxury Jews could no longer afford. This first step in the direction of such particularism can be illustrated by the views of Maurice N. Eisendrath (1902–1973), executive director and president of Reform Judaism's Union of American Hebrew Congregations. Responding to the approach of the American Jewish Committee, which took the lead in arguing on behalf of humankind in general, Eisendrath called for a more focused alternative. "In seeking to establish the inalienable rights common to all men," he informed his colleagues at the second session of the American Jewish Congress in 1944, "we cannot ignore the Jew, qua Jew, nor dissolve an entire people out of existence by ignoring its presence, in our anxiety to secure for all men an International Bill of Rights."[12] Eisendrath had considerable foresight: as the historian Peter Novick has demonstrated, it took a couple of decades before the Holocaust became central to American Jewish consciousness. When it did, Holocaust awareness strongly reinforced the message Eisendrath had already drawn from it. "Those whose outlook is basically optimistic and universalist—as Americans, including American Jews, were in the fifties—are not going to be inclined to center the Holocaust in their consciousness," Novick pointed out.[13] Those who subsequently made the Holocaust part and parcel of their outlook on the world, in turn, would be both pessimistic and particularist. How could Jews not be particularist, people of this persuasion believed, when Hitler's single-minded obsession with them was so pronounced?

A similar movement in the direction of particularism took place in domestic affairs. It had been a staple of Jewish activism during the 1930s that anti-Semitism was a by-product of prejudice, and that prejudice existed not only against Jews but also against any other minority group struggling for acceptance in a society dominated by people unlike themselves. It followed that Jews ought to join together with other minorities to fight for inclusive principles of social justice. Consider a report called *Full Equality in a Free Society*, which was issued by the American Jewish Congress in 1946. Its author, Alexander Pekelis (1902–1946), wrote that "there is nothing new in the realization that the ideals, the tradition, and the fate of the Jews are indissolubly bound to those of the forces of liberalism and progress, and are opposed to those of social, political or economic reaction."[14] (Pekelis was born in Odessa one year before the first Kishinev pogrom, taught law in Florence and Rome, moved to Lisbon, lectured at the New School for Social Research, wrote a path-breaking law-review essay on welfare rights, and died in an airplane accident in Ireland at the age of forty-four, just after his report was issued.) He was by no means alone in expressing such views; Benjamin Epstein (1912–1983), who assumed the position of national director of the Anti-Defamation League in 1947, retained a similar outlook on the world: "We approach life in America with the premise that the progressive development of a democratic society will bring with it for the Jews, as for other groups, the freest and fullest development as individuals and as a community," he announced one year after taking office.[15] When critics said that the primary focus of his organization should be on Jews and Jews alone, he rebuked them. "We are concerned with human rights, inter-group harmony, with fighting bigotry; with promoting equal economic, social, and educational opportunities for all. These are pertinent contemporary applications of ancient Jewish ethical precepts."

This understanding of Jews as one minority group among many also began to lose steam in the decades after World War II. As they experienced postwar economic success and gradual social acceptance, Jews, while retaining much of their political liberalism, stopped thinking of themselves as a disadvantaged minority group along the lines of African Americans or Puerto Ricans. When affirmative action began to be used as a way to address problems of racial inequality, they worried that goals would turn into quotas, the very same kind, they feared, that had once kept them out of leading American universities. As black nationalism made inroads into civil rights rhetoric, especially during the meeting of the National Conference for a New Politics (NCNP) in Chicago in 1967, they realized that the days when Martin Luther King Jr. marched alongside prominent rabbis such as Abraham Joshua Heschel and Joachim Prinz were coming to an end. Tensions between Jews and African Americans in particular erupted in May 1968 when a newly empowered school board in Brooklyn's Ocean Hill–Brownsville district, under the rubric of community control of the schools, fired a number of teachers, most of them Jewish.

Israel's victory in the Six-Day War of 1967, which took place just three months before the NCNP meeting in Chicago and eleven months before Ocean Hill–Brownsville, continued this movement away from universalism: the seemingly miraculous triumph over Israel's Arab foes did more to transform Diaspora Jews into Zionists than any other event since Israel's founding. At the same time, the war also spurred black nationalists to identify themselves with the Arab victims of Israel's military actions. As far as universalism was concerned, the result was a double whammy. "For both African-Americans and Jews," Stanford historian Clayborne Carson explains, "the 1967 Arab-Israeli war signaled a shift from the universalistic values that had once prevailed in the civil rights movement toward an emphasis on political action based on more narrowly conceived group identities and interests."[16] (Whether expressions of black power convinced Jews to turn more particularist, or whether an inward turn among Jews influenced the move toward Afrocentrism, is difficult to say; in all likelihood, both happened together.) When World War I had broken out, socialists in Europe, committed to the proposition that workers of the world should unite, rushed to defend their own countries. When wars in the Middle East took place, Jews and African Americans went their own ways in similar fashion.

An intensive campaign to save Soviet Jewry was also stimulated by Israel's victory. The Soviet dictator Joseph Stalin had been a pronounced anti-Semite, and the conditions facing Soviet Jews after his death remained intolerable. Jews throughout the Diaspora, feeling a greater sense of self-confidence due to Israel's 1967 success, took the lead in rallying on their behalf. The campaign to help Soviet Jewry, as the historian Marc Dollinger points out, "borrowed a page from the African-American civil rights strategy book, imitating the style, technique, and rhetoric of earlier liberal protests."[17] At the same time, it lacked the broad base that had characterized the early days of the civil rights movement. Although the language of rights was used during the campaign, this was an effort by one ethnic group to come to the defense of its own. Neither left wing nor right wing, the campaign to free Soviet Jews was a civil rights movement of the strong. It combined all the aspects of outsider protest with all the success of insider influence.

None of these developments, as important as all of them were, served as the key factor that brought about the victory of particularism in post–World War II American Judaism. The same cannot be said of the events in Illinois that took place a decade later. In 1976 Frank Collin, head of the National Socialist Party of America (NSPA), began planning to hold a demonstration in Skokie, a northern suburb of Chicago. (Collin was half Jewish. His father, Max Cohn, had been imprisoned by the Nazis at Dachau.) Skokie contained a large number of Jews, a significant portion of them Holocaust survivors. The prospect of brown-shirted men wearing swastikas on their sleeves parading in front of the village hall was not one many residents welcomed, and a variety of legal means, ranging from court-ordered injunctions to ordinances passed unanimously by the Skokie village council, were relied upon to prevent the rally from taking place. "We never thought in our wildest dreams that it could happen like that again, that they would have a right to confront us . . . to say those obscene words without being punished," said one of the most passionate of the survivors, Erna Gans. "This realization brought back a terror . . . here we are again, in the same position."[18]

Given the special role that the Holocaust had assumed in American Jewish life by the mid-1970s, the events in Skokie presented a difficult dilemma to the leaders of the three major liberal Jewish organizations:

the American Jewish Committee, the American Jewish Congress, and the Anti-Defamation League (ADL). All three, as the attorney Stuart Svonkin has shown, were committed to the idea that in US domestic affairs there was no necessary conflict between universalist ideals and particularist needs.[19] These imperatives could be reconciled, they insisted, because liberal democratic values, such as equality before the law, religious freedom, and laws prohibiting discrimination, were held to be Jewish values as well. By supporting freedom and equality for all Americans, these organizations did what they also considered best for the Jews.

The proposed Skokie demonstration made it impossible to balance universalism and particularism in such a fashion. Among the most important of liberal democratic values are freedom of speech and assembly, both protected by the US Constitution. Unfortunately for the Skokie survivors, the general consensus among constitutional lawyers, and the conclusion of nearly all state and federal judges who heard the cases growing out of these events, was that the NSPA, as noxious as its views were, did have a First Amendment right to hold its rally. The American Civil Liberties Union, one of the most principled organizations in the United States, was in no doubt on the matter. Although not a Jewish organization per se, its national executive director at the time of the Skokie march was Aryeh Neier, three of whose grandparents had been killed by the Nazis and whose remaining family was among the last to escape Germany. Because the ACLU defended the rights of Nazis to have their demonstration, nearly all the critical letters he received, Neier later wrote, asked the same question: "How can you, a Jew, defend freedom for Nazis?" As a committed civil libertarian, his response also never varied: "How can I, a Jew, refuse to defend freedom, even for Nazis?"[20] This was Jewish universalism in its purest form. Majorities have power. Minorities have rights. As a minority, Jews would be foolish not to seek to protect the rights of as many as they can, even if that meant including their enemies.

Any claim that the defense of free speech in this case would benefit the Jews, however, was all but impossible for the more explicitly Jewish organizations to advocate, especially after Skokie's survivors relived their nightmares, spoke of their fears, and pleaded with their leaders for protection. The position of the ADL was especially precarious. At first, the ADL tried to dodge its dilemma: its initial response was to hold to its so-called quarantine policy. "In essence, to quarantine is to ignore and avoid a demonstration in the hope that it will pass away, without causing disturbance and without attracting widespread publicity," as political scientist Donald Downs describes it.[21] Quarantine had often worked well in the past: demonstrations are meant to call attention to the demonstrators, and nothing does this better than efforts to prevent them from demonstrating. In this case, however, the ADL was being threatened by more militant groups to its right such as the soon-to-be-violent Jewish Defense League. It also fully understood that not coming unambiguously to the side of the Holocaust survivors would constitute a public relations disaster. It was not long before its quarantine policy was abandoned.

When the ACLU went to court seeking to overturn the ordinances that were designed to prevent the demonstrations from going forward, the ADL, led by its Chicago affiliate, took the other side. Searching for an appropriate legal rationale, the organization's lead attorney, Jerome Torshen, proposed the term *menticide* to capture the psychic harm the demonstration would inflict upon Skokie's survivors.[22] (It was also Torshen who called an ACLU attorney, David Goldberger, a "neo-Nazi lawyer.") As Torshen's overheated rhetoric makes clear, emotions were as much on display in the Skokie affair as legal technicalities. From a legal point of view, the ACLU's position was unassailable. From an emotional point of view, the ADL's was more so. In Skokie, Holocaust suffering presented an unanswerable argument: put abstract principles about civil liberties on one side and the horrors of the Final Solution on the other, and the former have no chance. Even Frank Collin, in his own perverse way, understood this. The so-called rally, which proved a dismal and insignificant affair, was eventually held in Chicago's Marquette Park (where Collin had wanted it to take place all along). In the final analysis, Collin's main objective was not demonstrating the value of free speech; it was garnering publicity for his organization, which he certainly managed to obtain.

Skokie was "yesterday's news," Peter Novick wrote in 1999, something unlikely to leave much of an impression.[23] On the contrary, Skokie brought the postwar retreat from universalism to a fever pitch. Before Skokie, many survivors viewed their treatment at the hands of the Nazis with shame; after Skokie, their defiance was unmistakable. Unlike the usual pattern in which organizations take the lead and ordinary Jews, save for a financial contribution or two, play a passive role, Skokie featured a genuine outpouring of popular sentiment from below to which established organizations had no choice but to respond. Skokie in the years before the ruckus over the demonstration had been a well-off and leafy suburb, symbolizing the welcome of Jews into what had once been Christian enclaves; Skokie's own country club had once been closed to Jews. After the Nazis threatened to come there, anti-Semitism and the struggle against it once again became central to Jewish consciousness. Nineteen seventy-six, the same year in which Collin began thinking about his demonstration, witnessed the airing of the film *Network*, written by Paddy Chayefsky, the son of Lithuanian-born Jews, in which a frustrated character, Howard Beale, declares that he is mad as hell and not going to take it anymore. Skokie was a declaration by American Jews that they too were fed up: no longer were they going to play the victim role assigned to them by so much of their history.

For all the attention it received, however, Skokie's impact was ethnic and cultural rather than political and ideological. The survivors who spoke up were not offering a view of how the world ought to work so much as they were crying out in pain. Because it lacked ideological coherence, the particularism that emerged during the Skokie events can best be described as soft. In coming out so strongly against freedom of speech and assembly for the Nazis, Jews were not changing political parties or rethinking their history and traditions; they were simply putting the world on notice that, like every other racial and ethnic group learning how best to express its identity during the 1970s, they would, to paraphrase a popular expression of the time, be looking out for number one.

IV

Much ink has been spilled dealing with the legacy left by the social movements of the 1960s and the 1970s. The bulk of that legacy— greater equality for women, the election of an African American president, the acceptance of gay marriage—leans to the left. The political awakening of American Judaism during the same decades carried with it one important shift to the right. This has little to do with the voting behavior of ordinary Jews, including those in Skokie, which remains disproportionately liberal. (In the 2012 presidential election, Niles Township, of which the village of Skokie is a part, voted 65.19 percent for Obama-Biden and 33.64 percent for Romney-Ryan.)[24] I am referring instead to that group of intellectuals determined to harden the particularism on display during the Skokie events into an ideological outlook on the world. The name given to their efforts is *neoconservatism*.

In theory, neoconservatism is universalist: its criticisms of modern society identify trends and single out villains without respect to religion, and its proposed remedies are designed to apply to all. Yet while some writers associated with this way of thinking are not Jewish—among those, Catholics tend to predominate—it is simply a fact that an overwhelming majority of them are. To point this out is not to say, as some critics of these thinkers charge, that neoconservatives are so preoccupied with Israel that they put that country's interests first.[25] Quite the opposite, in fact, is the case. Neoconservatives are undoubtedly strong supporters of Israel. But it was conditions in the Diaspora that initially shaped the development of neoconservative thinking, and support for Israel followed only after that.

This was certainly the case of the man generally held most responsible for the success of neoconservatism, the late Irving Kristol (1920–2009). "Never in the history of the Diaspora has there been anything comparable to the American experience," he wrote in 1994, and he meant his statement to be gushingly positive; if negating the Diaspora is a crucial feature of Zionism, Kristol was no Zionist, at least not in the sense that so many of the Zionist pioneers were.[26] Unlike other defenders of the Diaspora discussed in the previous chapter, however, who believed that minority status would ensure that Jews always retained a certain sympathy for the underdog, Kristol held that the Diaspora offered Jews a safe place to live, and in return the least they could do was to be unstinting in their American patriotism and warmly sympathetic to capitalist values. By clinging so fiercely to forms of universalism that viewed patriotism as suspect and capitalism as unfair, American Jews, Kristol lamented, instead ran the risk of destroying all the opportunities their new home had offered them.

Kristol developed a theory meant to account for what be believed to be such a disastrous mistake. When the Enlightenment came to Europe in the eighteenth and nineteenth centuries, Jews, he wrote, bet on the wrong horse. Convinced that commitments to reason, science, and progress would make it easier for them to assimilate into European society, and that their major enemies were defenders of unearned privilege, they not only rejected conservatism but also preferred the more radical liberalism of the French Revolution to the more moderate reformism of England and Scotland. For Kristol, there are two kinds of Judaism: the "rabbinic," best represented by Orthodoxy, which is committed to custom and tradition, and the "prophetic," which is "less interested in God's word or Jewish law than in realizing, here on earth, a universalist version of the teaching of the Prophets."[27] The masses of Jews who arrived in the United States from Eastern Europe at the end of the nineteenth century and the start of the twentieth, to his regret, brought prophetic universalism with them—and then held tenaciously to its outlook on the world even as the children of other immigrant groups began to move to the right. The consequence of this misplaced idealism was both serious and unfortunate: Jews became major contributors to the triumph of secular humanism, which for Kristol constituted the dominant, and truly dangerous, belief system of our time.

Kristol was convinced that the incoherence of secular humanism was becoming increasingly apparent; neoconservatism's major task was to expose its flaws. In spite of liberalism's lingering appeal to Jews, he detected signs that things might be changing. "Ever since the Holocaust and the emergence of the state of Israel," as he put the matter, "American Jews have been reaching toward a more explicit and meaningful Jewish identity and have been moving away from the universalist secular humanism that has been so prominent a feature of their prewar thinking."[28] If there is one individual who best articulated the case for Jews to become more particularist in the aftermath of the great events of the 1930s and 1940s, it was Irving Kristol.

One key question nevertheless remained: What form should this emerging Jewish particularism take? The obvious answer for Kristol was Orthodoxy, the one tradition in Judaism always resistant to modernity and for that reason the one most committed to the time-tested teachings of the rabbis. Of Judaism's two ways of life, Kristol had argued, "the rabbinic is the stronger pole, always."[29] Only rabbinic Judaism offered something real, because only it offered something deep. Kristol therefore insisted that as Jews rethought the universalist assumptions of the Enlightenment, they would come to appreciate the branch of Judaism with the deepest roots in particularism. It all seemed to make sense, for the ultra-Orthodox, especially when compared to other ways of being Jewish including modern Orthodox, withdraw from gentile society as best they can to devote themselves to God; seek as much autonomy in running their own affairs as possible; and, as we saw with respect to the Weberman case, take little interest in the morality of society as a whole. Neither secular nor humanist, Orthodoxy for Kristol would, if one may borrow a Christian phrase, be the saving grace of the Jews. Yet from the very start there arose complications, rendering the task of reconciling secular political views with an otherworldly religious tradition far more difficult than Kristol realized.

To begin with, Kristol, following Leo Strauss, whose thinking was so important to him, was pro-religion rather than actually religious; as he told a group of theologians in 1979, he was "nonpracticing—or non-observant as we say."[30] Can one keep God at arm's length and still be, as Kristol went on to say of himself, "in principle, very sympathetic to the spirit of orthodoxy"? Doing so would require a greater familiarity with Orthodox theology than Kristol possessed. "One searches through his essays in vain," writes Rabbi Meir Soloveichik, who comes

from America's most distinguished family of Orthodox Jewish thinkers, "for any engagement with the tradition that is the foundation of
Orthodox Judaism. . . . This intellectual whose worldview was deeply
informed by a reverence for the classics of Western civilization had little to say, indeed little apparent interest in, the Talmud itself, the study
of which essentially dominated Jewish intellectual life for two thousand years."[31] (Soloveichik's name was also floated, along with that of
Broyde, as a contender for the position of chief rabbi of England.)[32]
Like Kristol, Soloveichik is a political conservative; he delivered the
opening invocation at the 2012 Republican National Convention. Yet
the rabbi, while generally admiring the political theorist, cannot help
but point out, as if mildly annoyed that Kristol never underwent it,
just how demanding Orthodox study really is.

Beyond this unfamiliarity with classical rabbinic texts, Kristol also
had little or no use for Orthodoxy's spiritual otherworldliness. Unlike those for whom God is ever present, Kristol's understanding of
the nature of faith owed more to the pragmatist tradition in philosophy and modern sociology than to the rabbis and poets of Golden
Age Spain or the Vilna Gaon, the eighteenth-century Talmudist and
scholar. We need to honor the traditions that came before us, Kristol
insisted, and "it is the function of religion to instill such respect and
reverence."[33] True of all religion, this reassuring functionalism is especially evident in the case of conservative religion. What Orthodoxy
offers and prophecy does not, from his perspective, is not awe, mystery, or transcendence but the decidedly this-worldly task of instilling
"a somewhat stoical temper toward the evils of the world."[34] Religion
is a good thing because it allows us to ignore issues of social justice in
favor of learning to live with unfairness—it all sounds like Broyde's
insistence that Jews are under no obligation to repair the world. But it
is not: Kristol's understanding of the role of faith expresses near-total
opposition to Broyde's argument that Jews have no business offering moral lessons to society as a whole. Kristol's lifelong purpose was
to find roots in the Jewish tradition, or in any other religious tradition, that could make society and all its members, whether Jewish or
not, morally healthy, at least as he understood it. Kristol *did* want to

repair the world, but in a way that would make the world conservative rather than liberal. His engagement with this-worldly matters cannot be questioned. His commitment to an Orthodox spirit, as he calls it, very much can be.

Broyde's Orthodoxy, furthermore, drew upon thinkers such as Halevi and Maimonides who believed that Jewish law was superior to that of any other faith. For all his insistence that diasporic Jews ought to cultivate a more meaningful Jewish identity, Kristol, by contrast, advanced no hint of Jewish superiority. Once religion is assigned a sociological role in preserving the political order, all religions are equal—equally flawed if they take a liberal form and equally helpful if they do not. The details—including such messy questions as whether there exists a covenant between God and his chosen people, whether salvation can be found outside the church, whether faith or deeds matter most, whether Jesus is the son of God, or whether a new prophet named Mohammed improved on the faiths that had come before him—are not matters on which Kristol dwells. When he spoke to theologians, Kristol spoke about politics: he did not proselytize, and he did not expect to be proselytized. All this is to Kristol's credit: religious triumphalism, especially when civilizations clash, is not especially admirable. Still, Kristol's statement that he found Christianity "more intellectually complex" than Judaism is one that no Jew committed to the Orthodox tradition would be inclined to make.[35]

Far from superiority, Kristol, in one important respect, argued that Jews would always be inferior to the gentiles with whom they lived. The most significant religious development in the United States over the past four or five decades has been the rise of the religious right, a movement once associated with anti-Semitism, anti-intellectualism, and anticosmopolitanism. Yet despite the nativist populism that is so far removed from Judaism's respect for scholarship, Kristol, rather than viewing the Christian right as lacking in theological depth compared to Torah study, urged Jews to welcome its presence in American life. "If America is to become more Christian," he wrote with equanimity, "Jews will have to adapt" by showing "a greater sensitivity to Christian feelings than has been evident in certain Jewish organizations in recent years."[36] Halevi, who was so convinced of Jewish superiority that he set off for a journey to the Holy Land, which was evidently fruitless, would have blanched at the idea that Jews who live among Christians should be so understanding of their hosts' insecurities.

To the argument that the Christian right had not fully managed to shed its anti-Semitic origins, moreover, Kristol had a ready answer. Surprisingly enough, and again to Kristol's credit, it contradicted the widespread assumption that anti-Semitism is so much a feature of Christian societies that Jews have no choice but to create subcommunities of their own. "While there might be a revival of such discrimination," Kristol wrote of anti-Semitism in the United States, "it is unlikely. In our increasingly multicultural society, it is hard to see why hostility to Jews should be a ruling passion for large numbers of Americans, especially since Jews are now so firmly established in the mainstream of American life." Kristol was far too much the political strategist to remind his new allies in the Christian right of the errors of their anti-Semitic ways. He was also far too clear-eyed to subscribe to any notion that the fate of American Jews would in any way resemble those who were slaughtered in Europe.

Only after exploring all these varied aspects of diasporic life did Kristol finally turn to the question of Israel. When he did, Kristol, who as we have seen rarely discussed the Talmud and other classic rabbinic teachings, not only refused to negate the Diaspora, he also ignored Zionist thinkers of any political and cultural point of view: Herzl, Bialik, and Ha'am are as difficult to locate in his essays as Halevi and Maimonides. As with his approach to religion, Kristol was more pro-Zion than he was a Zionist; the two major volumes that brought together his leading essays contain only one chapter on Israel, and it deals with the Yom Kippur War. As we have seen, far from engaging in any form of Diaspora negation, the one proposition to which nearly all the otherwise contentious Zionist thinkers were committed, Kristol was thrilled that the Jews had found a home in exile. His overriding fear was that because of what he called their "political stupidity," Jews would spoil that home by taking up the cause of everyone but themselves.[37] Israel, he hoped, would show them another way.

Founded by socialists and left wing in its ideology, Israel could not offer Kristol, at least in its early years, much of an alternative to the temptations of secular humanism. But as Israel moved further to the right politically,[38] Kristol's approach to Zionism, like his taste for Orthodoxy, assumed a functionalist stance: Israel's task was not to provide a safe home for Jews threatened by anti-Semitism, since he acknowledged that they no longer really were, but to demonstrate to Jews in the Diaspora why their historic affinity with liberalism had to be abandoned. Kristol did share one thing in common with the Zionist thinkers who did so much to bring the Jewish state into existence: he was as unmoved by religion as they were. For that reason, his sympathy for Orthodoxy had everything to do with politics and almost nothing to do with faith; it was, after all, on religious grounds that so many Orthodox Jews, fearful of interfering with God's monopoly on salvation, very much unlike Kristol rejected the promise of Israel no matter how much political power it might accumulate. As the so-called godfather of neoconservatism, Kristol played an instrumental role in luring Jews away from their sympathy for prophetic universalism. But no one should conclude that his reasons for doing so had much to do with theology or even faith. Kristol was a political person through and through, and the particularism he taught was as secular as it was possible to be.

V

Odd as it may sound, Irving Kristol, the founder of neoconservatism, was never a full-throated neoconservative. He was to be sure a particularist who wanted the Jews to act more like Jews, but unlike more recent neoconservatives, whom we shall meet in a moment, he nonetheless stopped short of defending all things Jewish. For Kristol, Israel was important but not everything; for those who followed in his wake, Israel is everything and any critic of the Jewish state must be an enemy of the Jewish people. Kristol tended to judge people and movements by a single standard: if they were liberal, he found them problematic but if they were conservative, he admired them. Today's neoconservatives live in a world of double standards, absolving Israel of mistakes while bending over backward to find fault with its critics. Jewish neoconservatism since Kristol has become far more apologetic and defensive, as if, despite the wonders of the Diaspora that Kristol so much admired, Jews around the world remain so vulnerable to the venom of anti-Semitism that they must be constantly on guard. Revolutions have a way of turning their backs on their founders. Neoconservatism today is not the same as it was when Irving Kristol was in his prime.

Many examples could be offered of this more single-mindedly political form of Jewish particularism. Let me begin with two writers, both of whom are specialists in literature rather than politics and both of whom, with respect to their literary achievements, are individuals of unquestioned brilliance. One is Harvard's Ruth Wisse, whom I cited in a previous chapter lamenting the fate of Simon Dubnow in Riga. The second is the novelist and critic Cynthia Ozick.

Born in Romania in 1936 and raised in Montreal, Wisse is the Martin Peretz Professor of Yiddish Literature at Harvard. Over the course of her career she has translated and given critical attention to a number of Yiddish poets and writers such as Shalom Aleichem and I.L. Peretz—the great-great uncle of Martin—and, collaborating with figures such as Irving Howe, the socialist and New York intellectual par excellence, published classic anthologies of Yiddish literature: if Yiddish survives as a literary language, it is fair to say it will be in large part because of her efforts. Wisse, however, has a political as well as a literary side. Shocked by the 1975 United Nations General Assembly Resolution 3379 condemning Zionism as a form of racism, she began to write more topical essays, most of them appearing in *Commentary*. In one of them, from 1998, she characterized Palestinian Arabs as "people who breed and bleed and advertise their misery," a formulation that led to a rupture in her friendship with Howe, after *Dissent*, which he edited, criticized it as racist.[39] Although the two eventually reconciled on a personal level, Howe never became a neoconservative. Wisse unquestionably did.

Wisse has written two books on politics, *If I Am Not for Myself:*

The Liberal Betrayal of the Jews (1992) and *Jews and Power* (2007). The latter develops two major themes: Jews ought to have more power, and no matter how much they have obtained, they never have enough. From these assertions she develops an account of the situation facing world Jewry that combines the long-established view that Jews are an ever-dying people with the contemporary observation that a Jewish state can spare them their otherwise inevitable fate.

Unlike Kristol, Wisse insists that powerlessness is the defining condition of Diaspora Jewry. It is true, she acknowledges, that Jews in both Christian and Muslim lands survived for centuries under extremely hostile conditions. It is even the case that in certain times and places, individual Jews thrived; forced to develop their talents in highly competitive environments, they found themselves in a fairly good position as the transition to modernity began to take place. But for Wisse these accomplishments, however impressive, are insufficient. Certainly survival itself offers little to brag about and may in fact be a problem. "This pride in sheer survival," she writes, "demonstrates how the toleration of political weakness could cross the moral line into veneration of political weakness. Jews who endured exile as a temporary measure were in danger of mistaking it for a requirement of Jewish life, or worse for a Jewish ideal."[40]

Furthermore, emancipation, the source of hope for so many in eighteenth- and nineteenth-century Europe, did not help; if anything, "the new political situation in Europe proved more threatening to the Jews than the old," because "the replacement of a single autocratic ruler by an elected assembly potentially reduced rather than increased their political influence." Moreover, no sooner had the Jews convinced themselves that at long last they could take their place as full citizens of the societies in which they lived than anti-Semitism, "the ideology of the twentieth century that came closest to fully achieving its goal," showed them otherwise. Taken as a whole, Diaspora means humiliation, disloyalty, and softness. *Jews and Power* has no chapter, or even commentary, on the fact that both England and France have elected Jewish heads of state or that Jews have achieved positions of influence in the United States. When Heinrich Graetz wrote his tale of Jewish woe, Jews had in reality very little political power. Now they do, but Wisse nonetheless finds the theme of Jewish powerlessness too powerful to resist.

Having dispensed with the Diaspora, Wisse proceeds directly to a discussion of Israel. Continuing with her theme of Jewish weakness, she deplores that as a state, Israel is small, unappreciated, and constantly threatened by its enemies. (That Israel is the major military power in its region is not something upon which she dwells.) Statehood, however, has produced one major and, in Wisse's view, positive outcome. Fully conversant with the Jewish tradition—far more so than Kristol—Wisse summarizes the premodern understanding of the Jewish condition in these terms: "The power of God, emphatically including his eventual action in history, was the guarantee that justice would eventually triumph." However important such a religious way of thinking may have been back then, it is, in her view, too passive to be applicable today, because "lacking such faith in God's intervention, modern Jews could not claim to be moral unless they themselves intended to supply the missing dimension of power."[41] It would be difficult to find a more succinct expression of what I am calling the secularization of particularism. In a direct reversal of the ideas of Ahad Ha'am, Wisse is arguing that ethics and justice have nothing to do with the prophets but can be achieved only by diplomats, politicians, and, never even contemplated by Ha'am, generals. What makes Jews different is that nothing makes them different. Because power, not justice, is the appropriate language of states, Jews, like every other people, are best off when they have less of the former and more of the latter. The most important consequence of statehood is that it makes universalism superfluous.

By shifting the Jewish concern for morality from a by-product of minority status to a feature of statehood, Wisse not only defends Israel against its enemies but also gives Israel the benefit of moral doubt for whatever it chooses to do. Those who surround Israel and wish it harm, by this sleight of hand, are by their very nature immoral, including the Arabs, once major supporters of the Nazis, in Wisse's view, and now leaders in the emergence of a vicious new round of anti-Semitism. Given such attitudes, it cannot be surprising that Wisse, in the comment that so upset Howe, resorted to stereotyping when she spoke about the Arabs. United only by their determination to rid the world of the Jewish state, Palestinian Arabs, she insists, are a twisted people, unable to live in peace and unwilling to accept their situation. "The national consciousness of Palestinian Arabs is so politically focused on what belongs to the Jews," she writes in *Jews and Power*, "that they cannot concentrate on what is theirs to enjoy."[42] In Wisse's understanding of the world, statehood is something the Jews require—and something the Palestinians must learn to live without. If there are indeed blessings associated with exile, those blessings belong to the enemies of the Jews. Wisse need not make the case that Jews are superior given her certainty that Arabs are inferior.

Cynthia Ozick, born in New York in 1928, is an internationally recognized novelist and short-story writer, cited as "the grande dame of Jewish literature" when in 2011 she received the Jewish Book Council's Lifetime Achievement Award.[43] Largely self-taught in the Jewish tradition—at one point she consumed Graetz's massive *History of the Jews* in order to enrich her fiction writing[44]—Ozick, among her many works, writes powerfully about Jewish women, especially in the "The Shawl," a haunting 1980 *New Yorker* short story about a baby killed during the Holocaust, and her 1997 novel *The Puttermesser* * *Papers.*[45] Whether she ranks at the same level as contemporaries such as Philip Roth, Saul Bellow, and Joseph Heller, I leave for others to decide. But no one can deny that she is one of the major literary voices of our time.

Like Wisse, Ozick has refused to confine herself to literary matters. She too has especially strong views on the Middle East, and perhaps because she writes fiction, she has spelled out in dramatic, even lurid, detail the implications of where her unvarnished version of particularism leads: since Jews are a special nation, the Palestinians, who claim the same land, must be an illegitimate one. "By replacing history with fantasy," she wrote in the *Wall Street Journal* in 2003, "the Palestinians have invented a society unlike any other, where hatred trumps bread.

Puttermesser is German for "butter knife."

They have reared children unlike any other children, removed from ordinary norms and behaviors."[46] Nations are about culture, and what, Ozick asks, is the culture of the Palestinians? "On the international scene: airplane hijackings and the murder of American diplomats in the 1970s, Olympic slaughterings and shipboard murders in the 1980s. And toward the Jews of the Holy Land, beginning in the 1920s and continuing until this morning, terror, terror, terror, terror." It goes without saying that Ozick would view anyone who spoke of Jewish culture in such broad terms as an anti-Semite. But because she is speaking about non-Jews, indeed a people she considers the enemy of the Jews, she feels free to generalize at will.

In her fiction, Ozick demonstrates a deep and moving capacity for empathy. In the character of Ruth Puttermesser, for example, she invented a figure whose life never quite works out the way she had hoped, yet is nonetheless rendered fully human through humor and insight. (Puttermesser is raped and murdered, or as Ozick puts it, "murdered before she was raped," and eventually finds herself in a paradise that turns out to be little different from hell.)[47] No such taste for wonderment characterizes Ozick's writings on the Middle East. Deadly serious, didactic, chilling, this inventive creator of characters whose absurdity makes them all too real is incapable of seeing real people in those actual human beings whose existence her state of choice finds so troubling. Ruth Wisse's former collaborator Irving Howe wrote a classic book, *Politics and the Novel*, devoted to figures such as Conrad and Stendhal, who found ways to bring to the events of their time the techniques of master storytelling.[48] Ozick is not a political novelist in that sense; her fiction and her political commentary not only fail to reinforce each other, they also work at cross-purposes.

VI

Both Wisse and Ozick are citizens of the republic of letters, cultivated writers and thinkers who belong to a humanistic tradition but who are so supportive of the Jewish state that, at least when it comes to Palestinians, their humanism is rendered difficult to detect. In this sense they are distinct from another group of particularistic Jewish writers who, like them, defend Israel and attack Arabs, but who do so not out of any humanistic convictions but from a deeply Manichean sensibility that views the world as hopelessly divided between good and evil—with Israel and its Jewish supporters, needless to say, embodying the former. As Jewish intellectuals move further and further to the right, there comes a point at which the modifier *neo* no longer applies. That point, it would seem, has already been reached. One can see it at work in the ideas of flamboyant Muslim bashers such as Pamela Geller, a blogger quick to find an Islamic link to every act of terrorism taking place in the world; Melanie Phillips, an especially acerbic journalist who described the leaders of the left-leaning British Independent Jewish Voices as "Jews for Genocide"; the pro-war Middle East commentator Daniel Pipes; and the Marxist intellectual turned right-wing political activist David Horowitz.[49] Of all of them, Horowitz, the most prolific as well as the most unyielding, offers the best example of such posthumanistic particularism.

Upon receiving the Ben Hecht Award for Outstanding Journalism from the Zionist Association of America in 2012, Horowitz characterized himself as a secularist whose views are uninformed by a theological commitment to bringing God's light to the world. Given particularism's secularization in the years after World War II, this should not be surprising. Horowitz, however, went much further. Realizing correctly that Herzl, the dreamer of Zionism, was in fact something of a universalist, he also rejected him and the idealism for which he stood. Herzl's approach, Horowitz told his audience, "proved to be a fairy tale, as delusional in its way as the dreams of socialism, communism and progressivism, whose believers hoped would provide solutions to the conflicts and sufferings that blight our human state."[50] A proud Diaspora Jew, Horowitz defends Israel in much the same way zealous cold warriors defended the United States: the world is bitterly divided between us and them, they are out to kill us, and we must do everything in our power to resist them. Accepting the charge made against him that he is a "muscular Jew," Horowitz believes that force rules the world and Israel needs all the force it can obtain: "I want a Jewish nation-state possessing in its arsenal the most advanced modern weapons available, a state that can be counted on to defend Jews from their global enemies, and particularly their enemies in the Muslim world who are legion and who have sworn our destruction, and who are openly planning to complete the job that Hitler started. I want a Jewish state, armed to the teeth, because Islamic Nazis, who are the storm troopers of a second Holocaust, are already mobilized, and because—as we discovered during the first Holocaust—there are not enough non-Jews in the world who are willing and prepared to defend us." We have heard such ideas before: they were best expressed by Ze'ev Jabotinsky, although he did so before nuclear weapons appeared on the scene.

If Wisse and Ozick reject the prophetic universalism of the Jewish Enlightenment, Horowitz goes further back and turns against the classical forms of religious particularism that long preceded it. Maimonides, the reader may recall, insisted on Jewish superiority but also believed that precisely because Jews were better than others, they should act according to a higher moral standard. Lacking a religious sensibility, Horowitz accepts the superiority while leaving behind the morality: not only are Jews unbound by the laws of the Torah, they need not obey any laws at all that might weaken their militancy. Horowitz teaches us that as unattractive as the religious side of particularism can be, the militant side is even uglier. With him there is no tradition of debate and interpretation; it is all arrogance and assertion. I never thought I would long for the parochialism on display in Halevi and Maimonides. Reading Horowitz inclines me in that direction.

The views of David Horowitz move as far as possible from the capacious understanding of humanity that earlier generations of Jews brought with them to their new home in America. It took just seventy-five years for the 1938 universalism of the General Jewish Council to be transformed into the unadorned worship of state power that characterizes Horowitz's outlook on the world; far from the notion that Jews ought to be saved because they were human and not just because they were Jewish, we are now being told that the only human beings worth being saved, at least with respect to the two parties at war in the Middle East, are those who are Jewish. Even less time has passed since the assertions of early postwar universalists such as Alexander Pekelis and Benjamin Epstein that Jews and liberalism were made for each other; in Horowitz's account, Jews ought to inherit the mantle of a conservatism committed to the proposition that "there is no solution to the dilemmas of the human condition."[51] With Horowitz, secular particularism reaches the point where anything that Jews need to do to protect their own is justified, not because of any ideals for which Jews have long stood but because we live in a world in which all ideals are illusions.

VII

Although Jews have moved back and forth throughout their history between particularism and universalism, the form particularism took when they lacked political power is worlds apart from the form it takes since Israel came into existence as a Jewish state. Yesterday's particularism never played the role of justifying injustice, because in earlier times Jews lacked the political power to impose injustice. Classical religious particularism, it is important to recall, is a diasporic phenomenon; it emerged out of the exilic condition in which the Jews found themselves. "Any Jew," Halevi wrote in the *Kuzari*, "could immediately become a friend of his oppressor by simply uttering a word. . . . However, if we would endure this exile in the proper fashion, we would be the pride of the generation that will arise with the coming of the Messiah, and we would hasten his salvation for which we yearn."[52] Lacking statehood and its accompanying access to power, Jews overcame their political weakness by insisting on their religious strength. Their God was almighty even as his people were not; indeed, jealous God that he was, he may have preferred things that way. Assertions of Jewish superiority in religion amounted to confession of Jewish inferiority in politics.

In our time, by contrast, Jews are not only politically stronger than ever before in their history, they are also not as religiously cohesive: increasing numbers of them have turned their back on religion or found themselves embroiled in endless quarrels among Judaism's often contentious branches. Under conditions such as these, secular particularism lacks both the poetry of a Halevi and the philosophical rigor of a Maimonides. Its preference for political argument over rabbinic sources raises the question of what specifically is Jewish about it. Its chauvinism reduces it to all other forms of nationalism in the contemporary world. An exercise in apologetics, it appeals to those who believe that intellectual inquiry is more about defending entrenched positions than being open to new evidence. Its bitterness offers no hope and its descent into racist stereotyping relies on ways of thinking so often deployed against the Jews. It calls upon Jews to take pride in their heritage while stripping that heritage of everything that ought to make a Jew proud. It even finds itself unsympathetic to Zionism whenever the idea of a Jewish state is defended on idealistic grounds. Unlike thinkers such as Dubnow and Ha'am, whose particularism grew into universalism, today we are confronted with writers whose universalism has shrunk into particularism. When the secularization of particularism reaches its final destination, it appeals only to bitter-enders, who are determined to view the world through the eyes of the Jews only, dismissing as hostile everyone who sees the world differently and entering more and more deeply into the self-righteous conviction that this very isolation proves the validity of one's worldview.

All these contemporary thinkers offer examples of the pseudo-Nietzscheans who advocate what Simon Rawidowicz had called "cruel Zionism." Shorn of all nuance, this harsh version of particularism does not reflect, as ultra-Orthodoxy all too often does, indifference to the gentile world. On the contrary, it knows that the non-Jewish world, shocked by what the Jewish state has been up to, is prepared to judge the actions of the Jews as it does the actions of everyone else. That is not something these writers are prepared to accept; far from repairing the world, Jews should thumb their noses at it.

CHAPTER 4

A Tale of Two Rabbis

I

Is their dispersion a sign of God's displeasure with the Jews? The Hebrew Bible certainly leaves that impression. Obey God and all good things will come to you; dishonor him, and, as it is said in the book of Deuteronomy, "the LORD shall scatter thee among all people, from the one end of the earth even unto the other; and there thou shalt serve other gods, which neither thou nor thy fathers have known, even wood and stone (28:64)." Not all the Jews of yesteryear accepted the notion of Diaspora as punishment; that idea was more common among Christians seeking to blame the Jews for the death of Jesus. Yet even when they viewed their homelessness as a test of faith they might eventually pass, the Jews could not help wonder what sins they had committed to have made God so angry. As the rabbis who contributed to the Talmud and the Midrash sought to interpret the meaning of the Bible, the number of such possible sins multiplied. "Exile comes to the world on account of idol-worship, sexual crimes, and bloodshed," said one commentator, while another blamed the punishment for those times when the Jews "denied the one God of the universe, the Decalogue, circumcision, . . . and the five books of the Torah."[1]

So long as the Jews continued to view the Diaspora as punishment for their sins, they would never be in a position to offer themselves as a model for others: who would want to learn from a faith with which God was so displeased? There was from the start, however, another way of thinking about the issue within Judaism, one that became increasingly important in modern times: far from being punished, the Jews may well have been spread around the world to bring the light of reason to as many as possible. It was out of this more positive conception of diasporic obligation that Jewish universalism grew. We have just seen how particularism can come in a variety of forms. The same is true of universalism. If universalism is once again becoming attractive to Jews in the Diaspora, it is helpful to ask which type of universalism is the most appropriate under contemporary conditions.

II

Modern universalism's roots lie in the ideas of Moses Mendelssohn, the brilliant and largely self-taught German Jewish philosopher who arrived in Berlin (from the provincial town of Dessau) in 1743 at the age of fourteen. In his writings, Mendelssohn, the founder of the Haskalah, or Jewish Enlightenment, argued that Judaism was a religion of reason and in so doing paved the way for separation of church, religious toleration, and the idea that the rights of Jews were best protected when the rights of all were most honored. The thinkers who followed in his wake were diverse and contentious, but what united all of them was a conspicuous broadening of perspective. As Amos Elon, the most erudite of those who have told this story, points out, their "ideal of self-improvement and refinement allowed these spirited young men and women—all born of devout Jewish families—to accomplish in two or three decades a journey that their peers elsewhere, especially in Eastern Europe, would take much longer to complete: from a hermetically closed system centered on divine sacraments to an emancipated agonistic culture centered on man."[2]

As Elon's account makes clear, this was not a great epoch in the history of the Jewish religion; some of the best-known figures of the

Haskalah sought to drop what was distinctive about Jewish religious practice, converted to Christianity (and back again), or, like the poet Heinrich Heine, the most sardonic of them all, concluded that "all religions are the same; some skin their clients from the top down; others from the bottom up." But it certainly was a great moment in the lives of individual Jews. No arena of creative endeavor, from philosophy to politics to science, was without the presence of people whose grandparents, whether residents of smaller German cities and towns or immigrants from the vastness of the Pale of Settlement, had been excluded from all aspects of European public life. Indeed so powerful was the trend toward enlightenment that it would soon spread to the Pale itself, embodied in such figures as the Pole Joseph Perl (1773–1839), a critic of the Hasidim, or ultra-Orthodox, who founded the first modern school teaching secular subjects to Jewish children, and Antoni Eisenbaum (1791–1852), creator of the Warsaw Rabbinic School, which trained a new and more worldly Jewish elite.[3]

Being enlightened could mean abandoning religion, but it did not have to: Reform Judaism, especially in Germany, interpreted the idea of enlightenment to mean that Jews were charged by their God with the special task of bringing messages of peace and social justice to those with whom they lived. In contrast to the inward-looking spirituality of the Orthodox, its rabbis, such as the Bavarian-born David Einhorn (1809–1879), sought direct engagement with this world.[4] German Reform rabbis taught that the essence of Judaism lay in a code of ethics rooted in monotheism that was applicable to all; in this, one can see traces of Jewish superiority. But they also insisted that the rigid rules and codes of conduct emphasized by the Orthodox were developed in response to specific historical conditions and thus lacked eternal significance, and they also asserted with considerable vehemence, as historian Michael Meyer puts it, "that the events which had evoked mourning for nearly 2,000 years were in fact providential, not a punishment for sin but a necessary condition for universal priestly activity."[5] Typical of the way these men thought were the words of Mendel Hess (1817–1871), chief rabbi of the Grand Duchy of Weimar, who wrote that "as previously through its teaching [and] now through its example, Israel must be exemplary for all peoples, must reach the highest rung on the ladder of moral perfection."[6] It was not Judaism's mission to proselytize; one cannot find much evangelicalism in either Jewish particularism or universalism. Instead, Germanic Reform rabbis believed that chosenness implied an obligation to bridge the gaps between all the world's leading faiths.

Irving Kristol reminds us, if disapprovingly, that Reform Judaism, when it moved to the United States, brought with it this tradition of prophetic universalism. The most immediate reason was the arrival on American shores of rabbis such as Einhorn himself, who in 1855 became the leader of Baltimore's Congregation Har Sinai, where he almost immediately began attacking slavery from the pulpit, forcing him, with considerable haste, to flee the border state to which he had just moved. America's German-born nineteenth-century Reform rabbis synthesized their major ideas into one document, the Pittsburgh Platform of 1885, and even though Einhorn was no longer alive, his ideas pervaded it. (One of Einhorn's sons-in-law, Kaufmann Kohler [1843–1926], convened the Pittsburgh meeting.) "We recognize in Judaism a progressive religion, ever striving to be in accord with the postulates of reason," the platform declared. "We are convinced of the utmost necessity of preserving the historical identity with our great past.... We acknowledge that the spirit of broad humanity of our age is our ally in the fulfillment of our mission, and therefore we extend the hand of fellowship to all who cooperate with us in the establishment of the reign of truth and righteousness among men."[7] Traditional obedience to law, such as eating kosher food or creating separate synagogue spaces for women, was deemed unimportant. Maintaining an ethical stance toward the world was considered vital. Nothing could have been more repellent to the German-born Reform Jews of the nineteenth century than the Orthodox teaching that Jews were under no compelling obligation to improve the moral standing of the non-Jews with whom they lived.

Although this shift to a more universalist way of thinking assigned a positive role to the Diaspora, it still left unanswered the question of Zion. For those who endorsed the Pittsburgh Platform, nationalism of any sort was offensive to reason and justice; Zionism for them was a step backward, because identifying with any one particular group, even one's own, was little more than a romantic and emotional reaction against modern movements bent on establishing the brotherhood of all people. "We consider ourselves no longer a nation, but a religious community," the platform stated, "and therefore expect neither a return to Palestine, nor a sacrificial worship under the sons of Aaron, nor the restoration of any of the laws concerning the Jewish state." The United States was now the home of these Jews, and it was there that they would engage in the work of repairing the world.

At the time it was written and even more as the years went by, the Pittsburgh Platform's hostility to Zionism would prove extremely controversial; indeed, one can trace both the rise of Conservative Judaism and the success of the Jewish Theological Seminary in New York to the opposition the Pittsburgh Platform stimulated.[8] (Before the JTS established itself in 1886, the intellectual center of American Judaism had been Reform Judaism's Hebrew Union College in Cincinnati.) American-born Reform Jews also found Pittsburgh too radical, and its ideas were subsequently repudiated in another meeting of Reform rabbis that took place in Columbus, Ohio, in 1937. Although those who endorsed the Pittsburgh Platform committed themselves to principles of social justice and the importance of maintaining an ethical stance toward the world, Reform rabbis' reformulation of what universalism required with respect to a Jewish state was strikingly different from what had been taught by the German Reform tradition: "In the rehabilitation of Palestine, the land hallowed by memories and hopes, we behold the promise of renewed life for many of our brethren," those who gathered in Columbus declared. "We affirm the obligation of all Jewry to aid in its upbuilding as a Jewish homeland by endeavoring to make it not only a haven of refuge for the oppressed but also a center of Jewish culture and spiritual life."[9] In the United States, in short, prophetic universalism found itself divided on the question of a Jewish state: One side was critical of everything for which Zionism stood while the other believed in the possibility that a Jewish state, as the Columbus consensus expressed the matter, could further the mission "to cooperate with all men in the establishment of the kingdom of God, of universal brotherhood, justice, truth and peace on earth."

For any revival of prophetic Judaism to have lasting significance, it will have to address the question of which kind of universalism it will be: one that views Zionism as a mistake or one that strives to improve upon it. To draw out implications of each position, I will focus on the life and work of two American rabbis, one of whom followed the lead established in Pittsburgh, the other more comfortable with the direction taken in Columbus. The former was Elmer Berger. The latter was Stephen Samuel Wise. The differences between them have been argued out every time universalist Jews disagree about the nature and meaning of the Jewish state, none more so than at the present moment.

III

The rabbis who gathered in Pittsburgh were followers of what has come to be called Classical Reform Judaism. Much like nineteenth- and early twentieth-century Orthodox Jewry, with which it had little else in common, Classical Reform viewed Zionism as a secular political movement at odds with the commands of faith, if, in its view, faith was embodied in the words of prophets such as Amos and Micah rather than in obedience to Halakhah. Primarily German American, and therefore not especially fond of the multitude of Yiddish-speaking Eastern European Jews who began arriving in the United States toward the end of the nineteenth century, advocates of Classical Reform were assimilationists who considered themselves American by nationality and Jews by religion. For that reason their approach to their faith took on many features of Protestant religious practice: men did not wear head coverings, women sat next to them in the synagogue, prayer books were written in English, organ music was introduced, and services were even held on Sundays.[10] Classical Reform rabbis tended to look favorably on political activism, engaging themselves in campaigns for the minimum wage or the regulation of working hours. To call Classical Reform a Jewish version of the Social Gospel movement, the Protestant effort to link Christian teachings with social reform, is an exaggeration, but only a minimal one.

San Francisco, home of an especially prominent and wealthy German Jewish community, became exemplary of Classical Reform during the first three decades of the twentieth century. (Among the most prominent Jewish families in San Francisco were names such as Magnin, Haas, Gump, Zellerbach, and Strauss, as in Levi Strauss.) As such, it offers a good example of just how far Classical Reform rabbis could go in their opposition to Zionism. One of the leading San Francisco Jews was Irving Reichert (1895–1986), the rabbi of that city's Temple Emanu-El, whose left-wing and pacifist views were so pronounced that when Japanese Americans were sent to internment camps during World War II, a move supported by nearly all America's leading rabbis, Reichert spoke out in dissent.[11] Reichert was so strongly committed to assimilationism—he believed that the true Zion could be found in the hills surrounding the Bay Area—that he once told a friend, had he not been born a Jew, he could just as easily have been a Unitarian. He was also a strenuous advocate for the Diaspora: "If my reading of Jewish history is correct," he said in a 1936 sermon, "Israel took upon itself the yoke of the Law not in Palestine, but in the wilderness at Mount Sinai, and by far the greatest part of its deathless and distinguished contribution to world culture was produced not in Palestine but in Babylon and the lands of the Dispersion." Given such views, Reichert had no qualms about offending the Zionists in his congregation. "There is too dangerous a parallel between the insistence of some Zionist spokesmen upon nationality and race and blood, and similar pronouncements by Fascist leaders in European dictatorships," he added in that sermon.[12] For Jews, these were fighting words and Reichert was determined to fight.

The organization created to take on that fight was the American Council for Judaism, which emerged out of Classical Reform to become the most prominent anti-Zionist movement within American Jewry. Founded in 1942, the ACJ attracted a number of well-known Reform rabbis, Reichert included, but the clear leader among them was Elmer Berger (1908–1996), who left the pulpit of Temple Beth El in Flint, Michigan, to become its executive director.[13] "I do not believe," Berger wrote in a 1942 pamphlet called *Why I Am a Non-Zionist*, "that any exclusively Jewish salvation program, in and of itself, can be permanently beneficial to Jewish life for the Jew is inseparably a part of civilization."[14] That is a position to which he adhered until the end of his life; the ACJ under Berger's leadership first fought against its formation and then, after it came into existence, denounced the policies of the Jewish state. It did so by lobbying US State Department officials on Middle Eastern issues, sponsoring articles for popular magazines, seeking alliances with clergy and intellectuals of other faiths, and trying its best to respond to the criticism it received from Zionists.

Berger and the ACJ's leaders certainly received considerable amounts of such criticism. In May 1963, for example, William Fulbright, chairman of the Senate Foreign Relations Committee, spoke to the ACJ annual conference. Fulbright is now remembered as a man after whom America's leading cultural exchange program is named, as an eloquent opponent of the Vietnam War, and as one of the many Arkansas mentors to a young Bill Clinton. But Fulbright was not only a Southern segregationist—he would vote against the Civil Rights Act one year after his ACJ speech—he was never known as a friend of either the Jews or Israel. His appearance before the ACJ sparked a furious reaction from Philip Bernstein (1901–1985) of Temple B'rith Kodesh in Rochester, New York, who was president of the Central Conference of American Rabbis and chairman of the American Israel Political Action Committee (AIPAC). "I must say this is a handful of sick Jews," he said of Berger and the ACJ. "They are self-hating Jewish anti-Semites. They have been repudiated by every Jewish religious body, lay and rabbinical."[15]

Berger took sides in the political controversies in which he engaged, and the side he took, following from his firm opposition to Zionism, was the Arab one. An example was his decision to work together with pro-Arab officials in the Eisenhower administration, some of whom, such as diplomat Loy Henderson (1892–1986), had been known for their indifference to the plight of the Jews during the 1930s. Berger also supported the efforts of American Friends of the Middle East, a front group for Arabist positions that was funded publicly by Saudi Arabia and privately by the Central Intelligence Agency.[16] While many American Jews became more supportive of Israel after the 1967 Six-Day War, Berger became, if that was possible, less so, corresponding with the Palestine Liberation Organization during its most militant phase, appearing on stage with the radical activist Stokely Carmichael, and traveling to the Middle East, where he was "lavishly treated by his Arab hosts," as Jack Ross, his sympathetic biographer, writes.[17] Politically speaking, all this makes a certain amount of sense; if you strongly oppose a state, you are naturally drawn into an alliance with others who do so as well. There is, furthermore, a case to be made for Palestinian nationalism just as there is one to be made for the Jewish variety. The problem here is not the taking of sides per se but the way political struggle and universalism rarely go together; by lining up so predictably with Israel's enemies, Berger, while claiming to act in the name of universalism, simply chose a different nationalism to be particularist about. With Berger, the universalism of Classical Reform had devolved into a way of thinking in which the enemy of my enemy must be my friend.

A similar unfolding of events took place in the realm of domestic politics. From the days of Einhorn in Germany through the years of Reichert in San Francisco, Classical Reform located itself on the left end of the political spectrum. The advent of the Cold War, however, reshaped the contours of left and right in American politics. Nineteen forty-eight, the year in which Israel came into being, was also the year in which the American presidential election featured both a Democratic candidate, Harry Truman, and a Progressive Party candidate, Henry Wallace. Many of those who supported the latter were either fellow travelers or members of the Communist Party, USA. Truman backers, by contrast, adopted a position now described as "Cold War liberalism," which combined strong support for domestic reform measures with an aggressive approach to national security issues. Although the Soviet Union had initially granted diplomatic recognition to Israel, it quickly shifted to a search for allies in the Arab world, leading many Truman-oriented liberals to conclude that a strong Israel would be a key Cold War ally against the Russians. That Israel in its early years was widely considered to be engaged in a socialist or at least a social democratic experiment solidified their position. The upshot of all this was to put the Democratic Party, and most of the leading liberal lights in the United States, firmly behind the Zionist project.

This link between liberalism and Zionism left Berger in an awkward position. Again feeling the need for allies wherever he could find them, and despairing that few of them were on the left, he flirted with a number of fringe groups on the American right. A segment of that fringe was Jewish, including the libertarians Frank Chodorov (1887–1966) and Murray Rothbard (1926–1995), as well as one of the more flamboyant figures ever to pop up on the conservative scene: Morrie Ryskind (1895–1985), who had been a Hollywood writer for the Marx Brothers and a Pulitzer Prize–winning collaborator with George Gershwin and George F. Kaufman on *Of Thee I Sing*, not the kind of background one associates with a man who became a funder of William F. Buckley's *National Review* and even joined the John Birch Society for a brief period. (Ryskind, however, was not sui generis; Ralph de Toledano [1916–2007], born in Morocco to Sephardic Jewish, if American, parents, not only was a founder of the *National Review* but also a violinist and jazz critic.) These days we tend to think of right-wing Jews as neoconservative; in the early 1940s a number of them were isolationists, despite isolationism's wariness of taking on the fight against Hitler. That Berger saw in them potential political allies led to the assumption that he may have provided the model for Lionel Bengelsdorf, the rabbi featured in Philip Roth's *The Plot Against America*, who supported the best known of the American isolationists, Charles Lindbergh.

In no way were Berger's allies on the extreme right confined to the few Jews who could be found there. As the Cold War set in, Berger began to consort with Freda Utley, who had worked with Senator Joseph McCarthy to compile his list of suspected communists in the

US government and who had frequently named alleged subversives before congressional committees. Utley's views were so extreme—the historian Deborah Lipstadt considers her a Holocaust denier because of her insistence that the crimes committed by the United States were equal to those of Nazi Germany—that Buckley would drop her from *National Review*.[18] Politics can certainly make for strange bedfellows, but it is difficult to deny that Berger managed to find friends who would make the next generation's neoconservatives, even the most harshly particularist among them, seem moderate by comparison.

Neither Berger nor the ACJ ever became all that successful: Already before the group's founding, Reform Judaism had begun to develop a greater appreciation of liturgy and tradition than that expressed in the Pittsburgh Platform. A rapid increase in the number of Eastern European Jews, who lacked the social standing of their German co-religionists, moreover, had rendered American Judaism less overtly assimilationist in outlook. Finally, after the group came into existence, news of the Holocaust made Zionists out of most of those who had once been skeptical, and the 1967 war rallied most American Jews to Israel's side. For all these reasons, by the 1970s the ACJ had lost whatever little clout it may once have had. The organization still exists, but it is now a shell of what it once was: its annual budget in 2010 was $55,000 and its mailing list in the low thousands.[19]

Two major lessons can be learned from what, under Berger's leadership, the ACJ tried to accomplish. The first is that taking one side does not require demonizing the other. Critical Zionists such as Ahad Ha'am and Simon Rawidowicz took the side of the Jews while understanding the plight of the Arabs. Berger and his allies, by contrast, took the side of the Arabs but rarely showed any understanding of why the Jews might deserve a state of their own. In so doing, they opened themselves up to the charge that anti-Zionism, which may have had a certain credibility before the Holocaust, was not only cruelly indifferent to the massive suffering experienced by European Jews in the 1930s and 1940s but was also lacking in influential allies willing to support the creation of international norms of human rights in the aftermath of World War II. Universalism demands that all nations be treated by the same standard. By assuming the Arab cause was just while the Jewish cause was not, Berger and his allies failed that test.

The second lesson is that if engagement in politics means at some point sides have to be taken, one must be careful about which side to take. The problem with Berger was not, as Philip Bernstein and other mainstream Jews charged, that he was anti-Semitic: lifelong rabbis rarely are. The problem was that Berger made political alliances with anti-Semites. There has to be a point, even in the most fraught political controversies, where one says, there, I will not go. For an allegedly progressive Jewish leader to ally himself with libertarians who hoped to return society to the untrammeled laws of the market was to abandon any claims to a prophetic tradition of social reform. For him to work with reactionaries who were so blinded by their anticommunism that they had a soft spot for nativism and racism, if not overt Nazism, was worse. A man whose political views emerged out of Classical Reform, Elmer Berger wound up in a position that was antagonistic to the very outlook on the world that had shaped his early days as an activist.

IV

Stephen Wise (1874–1949) was a Reform rabbi committed to universalism whose views on the Jewish state stood in diametrical opposition to those of Berger. Born in Hungary to Sabine and Aaron Weisz, he arrived in the United States at the age of one month.[20] (The family changed the name to Wise on the grounds that Weisz, pronounced in Europe with a *v*, would sound like "vice," not a name a member of the clergy, as Aaron Weisz was, should have.) Wise rapidly followed his father's footsteps into the rabbinate, serving at Beth Israel in Portland, Oregon, before being lured back to New York, a more appropriate home for this very ambitious man, in 1906. He was a brilliant speaker and tireless organizer, and his rise to prominence was only a matter of time.

At the start of his career, Wise appeared to be in the tradition of Classical Reform; hearing him make the case for his Free Synagogue, a place that would be "pewless and dueless,"[21] Emil Hirsch (1851–1923), who was then the rabbi of Temple Sinai in Chicago, a living embodiment of Classical Reform, and the other son-in-law of David Einhorn, could barely contain his enthusiasm.[22] Wise's approach overlapped with Classical Reform's universalism in two ways. One was Wise's commitment to working together with other faiths; in 1910, for example, he joined Protestant preachers in nonsectarian services that proved to be wildly popular—and drew the wrath of more insular Jewish leaders.[23] In addition, Wise became a well-known advocate for social reform, defending union organizing, urging better working conditions, and arguing on behalf of equality for women and African Americans. "Wise's belief in the need to improve the socioeconomic conditions of the toiling and disenfranchised classes," writes the historian Mark A. Raider, "resonated with Reform Judaism's mission ethos."[24] Had times never changed, Wise might well have evolved into a figure such as Irving Reichert.

But times did change, and the most significant shift with respect to the future of American Jewry was the arrival of those fleeing from Eastern European persecution. When Wise left Portland for New York, which was just one year after the second Kishinev pogrom, New York's Jewish community was divided by geography and theology: the well-off "Our Crowd" of German Jews tended to live in Manhattan, and especially on the Upper East Side, while the newly arriving Jews from the Pale settled on the Lower East Side or in the outer boroughs. Whatever the latter lacked in income and education, they more than made up in Jewish pride: Zionism, in their view, was a program developed in their part of the Old World that spoke to the fears of nonacceptance they felt in coming to the new one. They, and especially their children, found in the liberalism of Reform Judaism much that attracted them, but in the process of joining Reform temples, they also reintroduced more traditional forms of religious practice that Classical Reform rabbis had scorned; even San Francisco's Temple Emanu-El found itself appealing to the religiosity of Eastern European Jews.[25] Between 1900 and 1920, Reform Judaism in

America began to take on a whole new shape, complete with Temple Sisterhoods; Hadassah, a women's Zionist organization; men's clubs; youth-oriented activities; and the transformation of synagogues into Jewish community centers. This environment, a far more explicitly Zionist one than that offered by Classical Reform, shaped and was shaped by Stephen Wise. There is no reason to doubt that Wise came by his enthusiasm for Zionism genuinely; that it also helped him reach out to the demographic future of American Jewry was a secondary consideration. But help him reach out it did.

For Wise, support for Israel was axiomatic for anyone committed to universalist principles of social reform. A hater of oppression in nearly all its guises, he favored Woodrow Wilson's internationalism for the same reason he approved a strong role for government in the domestic sphere: oppressed Jews threatened by reactionary regimes in Europe deserved as much protection as vulnerable workers threatened by arbitrary bosses in Chicago. While sharing the political agenda of Classical Reform, Wise, temperamentally speaking, simply could not abide the cautiousness of the German Jewish aristocrats, and this only fueled his Zionist militancy. Speaking of one of them, the banker Felix Warburg, he announced that he "would give one thousand Warburgs for one [Chaim] Bialik. Warburg gives out of his surplus, while Bialik gives out of his soul."[26]

During the early 1930s Wise's Zionism and the Reform agenda became ever more firmly linked, if for no other reason than these were the years that witnessed both the rise of Nazism and the political arrival of the New Deal. Wise traveled to Palestine in 1935 and there he saw something closely resembling the reclamation projects being built by the Works Progress Administration and Civilian Conservation Corps. "I do not know such a miracle as our young fellow-Jews have wrought," he told his secretary about the efforts being undertaken by *yishuv* pioneers to reclaim the land. "I am more Zionist than I ever was. I have moved from 100 to 200 percent."[27] The same trip also helped him overcome some of the skepticism he had once felt about the Histadrut, the Labor Zionist movement in the *yishuv*. "Labor is one of the great forces here for the implementation of Zionism," he realized. "It must not be broken." It seemed to Wise a truth so obvious that it needed no elaboration: all those who believed in the universalist ideals of truth, justice, and peace would be liberals at home and Zionists abroad.

Matters did not work out the way Wise had hoped. For better or worse, Wise was a progressive, and "the Progressive mind . . . was preeminently a Protestant mind," historian Richard Hofstadter wrote decades ago.[28] Wise not only made friends with prominent Protestant pastors; he also borrowed from their mental outlook on the world. Hofstadter did not think much of that outlook, finding it rigid, moralistic, and often at odds with the needs of the very urban immigrants to whom Wise, for one, appealed. While overstated, Hofstadter's critique remains a powerful one. As Woodrow Wilson's entire career demonstrated, progressivism's high-mindedness was its own worst enemy. True, it was universalist in the sense that it insisted both on the individual's right to a better life and on the rights of nations, including small ones, to self-determination. But it also was a doctrine unprepared for the complexities of real-world politics. Its method of operation was to proclaim a goal, weigh the most efficient ways to reach it, and, without much nuance, begin marching in that direction. Wise's universalism, shaped by Protestant ideals of moral reform as much as the prophets of the Hebrew Bible, shared all too many of the flaws of progressivism in general.

Just as the limits of Wilson's progressivism were put on display when, like a character in a Henry James novel, he traveled to Versailles to be outmaneuvered by wily Europeans, Wise revealed his limits when, in 1933, he went to Prague to attend the Thirteenth Zionist Congress. There, in his usual militant fashion, he took the podium to denounce the British, warn against Chaim Weizmann's persistent diplomatic efforts to negotiate with them, and reject compromises that would delay the arrival of statehood. All that may have made sense to an American social reformer, but it fell on deaf ears among the European veterans of Zionist political debate. Wise, for example, was a severe critic of Jabotinsky, but this speech put him on the Revisionist's side. He also never seemed to appreciate that Weizmann's approach, frustrating as it may have been at the time, understood that in the long run Israel would need friends, Britain among them. In contrast to Europe where Zionism tended to be ideological, faction ridden, and simultaneously ruthless and utopian, American Zionism in the 1930s, so strongly influenced by progressivism, tended to be plain spoken, pragmatic, and hopeful. The two Zionisms found it difficult to understand each other, not only because they had different programs and personalities but also because they viewed the world in different ways.

Back in the United States Wise's progressive version of universalism also ran into considerable political trouble. In contrast to its near-cousin populism, which put its faith in ordinary people, progressivism tended to rely on leaders claiming to stand above the fray in order to promote the common good. This trust in leadership proved to be a serious problem for Wise. For Berger involvement in politics meant choosing sides. For Wise it meant choosing people. At a time like the present when a number of prominent conservative religious leaders have become publicly identified with the Republican Party, and in so doing have lost any aura of holiness generally associated with religious figures, it is instructive to ask whether Wise paid a price for his unyielding defense of the president who had assumed the mantle of progressivism after Wilson's death: Franklin Delano Roosevelt.

As historian Elizabeth Bryant demonstrates in her doctoral dissertation, Wise worked tirelessly to bring public attention to the plight of the Jews in Europe.[29] There can also be little doubt that he was willing to use his friendship with FDR to lobby on their behalf. But Wise also possessed a larger-than-life ego, loved his access to the Oval Office, was in poor health and near the end of his life, and knew that he could push FDR, who was ever sensitive to the isolationist sentiment of the American people, only so far. This did not endear him to Zionists even more militant than he, such as his main rival in the Reform tradition, Cleveland's Abba Hillel Silver (1893–1963), who compared Wise's protective approach to FDR to the methods used by the court Jews of eighteenth- and nineteenth-century Europe.[30] Historians have engaged in a debate over whether Wise did enough for the European

Jews; Bryant, for one, thinks he did all he could. Others, however, disagree, and the consensus among them is best expressed by Mark Raider who judged Wise "cautious and ineffective" in his actions with respect to the Holocaust.[31] If these later historians are correct, Wise shared something with Berger: the latter gave up prophecy for partisanship, while the former gave up prophecy for influence. In both cases, the result was the same: a biblical injunction to confront power with truth was sacrificed for the sake of Zionist positions, one for, the other against.

Another comparison between these two figures is worth emphasizing. Berger may have taken the wrong side, but he understood that a side had to be taken, whereas Wise's straight-and-narrow progressivism seemed incapable of realizing that there was a side to take. "We cannot say 'our land' as long as we only hold six percent," Wise said during his 1935 trip to the Holy Land. "Upon our return to America, our cry will be 'Land! Land! Land!'"[32] Arabs, needless to say, lived on the land Wise craved. European thinkers such as Jabotinsky, who had no concern for Arab well-being, at least knew they were there, if only as an obstacle to be removed. For Wise, on the other hand, Arabs and their real and future displacement were simply not part of the conversation, surely an odd position for a man attuned to suffering in so many places. Wise was aware of the Arab riots of 1929 that erupted after serious disputes over access to holy sites exploded into violence; he used them as an opportunity to speak against British policy, which, in becoming increasingly evenhanded between Arabs and Jews in the Middle East, was angrily taken by Zionists as a rejection of British support for their efforts. One therefore has to wonder how he could so thoroughly ignore a conflict that had already begun and that would eventually become the biggest challenge facing the new state.

Wise lived just long enough to see Israel come into existence. Had he lived longer, he may well have begun to express some reservations about the form it took; Silver, for all his militancy, quickly found himself isolated from David Ben-Gurion in large part because the new prime minister's Diaspora negation had little room for those who believed, Silver among them, that Jews might also have a home in America.[33] But it is not Wise's personal views that are of concern here as much as the lessons that can be gleaned from a vision of universalism that, rather than taking a critical stance toward all forms of nationalism, viewed one kind of nationalism as embodying universal values applicable to all. The danger in this way of thinking is its myopia, and Wise, much like Woodrow Wilson, fell victim to it. Like many other progressives, Wise was so convinced that history was on his side, and so certain that his side was the right one, that he was simply unprepared for the complexities involved when high-flown rhetoric expressed in the language of universal values winds up ignoring the claims of nations with insufficient power to speak for themselves. Wise's conviction that the Israel he saw coming into being would be egalitarian and democratic cut short the need for any further thinking about it.

Progressivism is a distinctly American phenomenon. Israel, however, is not an American state. Nor is it the European one envisioned by some at its birth. It is, for better or worse, a Middle Eastern state existing in a part of the world shaped by a political culture that has little in common with Protestant traditions of political and moral reform. Getting Middle Eastern politics right requires a taste for complexity and an appreciation for the tragic. For all their other mistakes, most of the European Zionists understood this. For all his good intentions, Stephen Wise never did.

V

By and large immune to significant criticism from the Diaspora since the 1967 war, Israel in recent years has begun to hear considerably more of it. (Concerns from within about Israel's direction are long-standing.) Such criticism is unlikely to come from particularists, who view Israel as the embodiment of the particular values they seek to protect. Nearly all this recent questioning of Israel's actions, therefore, emanates from a universalist perspective. For that reason, the question of whether universalists should oppose Israel or try to reform it still lingers. Is it even more true now than it was a half century ago that any effort to create a Jewish state in the Middle East is bound to corrupt universalistic ideals because it will inevitably appeal to the baser emotions of nationalism? Or can Israel, which after all grew out of the horrors revealed by the Nazi Holocaust and remains a democracy, once again come to stand as a state opposing hatred and combating oppression? Elmer Berger and Stephen Wise may be gone from the scene, but the questions with which they wrestled remain very much with us.

That the American Council for Judaism no longer offers a significant place for the expression of anti-Zionism does not mean such views receive little attention at this moment. On the contrary, the ACJ has been rendered superfluous by the many other individuals and organizations, especially among those who find Israel's actions in the Gaza Strip and the West Bank morally repulsive, and who have moved from critics of Israel to opponents of its existence as a Jewish state. Two venues for the articulation of such views have gained special prominence in our time. One includes political activists who lead protests, call for disinvestment, or urge boycotts. The other involves academic criticism, primarily coming from the left end of the political spectrum, that results in a rejection of Zionism and the form of statehood associated with it.

Just as Classical Reform had its Pittsburgh Platform, contemporary anti-Zionist activists have a central place to express their views: a website that brings attention to their campaigns and publishes justifications for them. It is called Mondoweiss.net, and it was founded by a journalist named Philip Weiss. Weiss's Zionist criticism is rooted in the ideas once associated with Classical Reform. "Zionism as an ideological movement," he wrote in a 2012 blog entry, "has called on very good currents in Jewish life for the last century, from liberation to intellectual dreaminess to socialism to manual labor to a new Jewish relationship to land. But in the end Zionism has worked itself out to be militant ethnocracy. Full stop."[34] Ethnocracy being the quintessential form of particularism, Weiss views himself as a universalist. "There is a family of man and woman, not ethnicities," he wrote in the same blog post. "This is the great challenge of modern democracy, and Zionism is fundamentally opposed to it." For all his objections to

Israel, Weiss wants his anti-Zionism to be viewed as an expression of his Jewish identity. "Herzl said, 'Anti-Semites made me Jewish again,'" he told the American journalist Michelle Goldberg. "I would say that neo-conservatives made me Jewish again."[35]

Academic anti-Zionism has been no less forthcoming, both in the United States and in Europe, and a substantial part of it contains expressions of Jewish identity similar to the one offered by Weiss. Perhaps the most important example is the work of Judith Butler, professor of rhetoric at the University of California, Berkeley. Like Weiss, Butler, although a critic of the Enlightenment and its legacy, finds herself engaged with Judaism's universalist tradition. The thinkers most relevant to her are not theologically oriented rabbis such as David Einhorn but the secular philosophers who followed in their wake. One of the most important of them was Hermann Cohen (1842–1918), the leading neo-Kantian of his time, who advocated a religion of reason rooted in monotheistic ethics and for whom messianism represented "the dominion of the good on earth."[36] Cohen made one major mistake that has severely damaged his contemporary reputation: he was an opponent of Zionism on the grounds that Jews would always be welcome in Europe, especially in Germany. Nonetheless, there is no doubt about his brilliance, and he became an inspiration for many crucial Jewish voices of the twentieth century, including Franz Rosenzweig, Martin Buber, Emmanuel Levinas, and Hannah Arendt, all of whom figure in Butler's work.

For Butler, the question of whether Israel has become a violent, oppressive, and inegalitarian society is settled—it has—and so the remaining issue is whether resources can be found within the Jewish tradition for exposing its flaws. The reality of Diaspora offers just such a resource. "I'm trying to understand," she writes (in prose that gives a sense of her style), "how the exilic—or more emphatically, the *diasporic*—is built into the idea of the Jewish (not analytically, but historically, that is, over time); in this sense, to 'be' a Jew is to be departing from oneself, cast out in the world of the non-Jew; bound to make one's way ethically and politically precisely there within a world of irreversible heterogeneity."[37] If Jewish history is one of dispossession,

Israel's has been one of occupation. In her view, therefore, Jewishness and Zionism, far from supporting each other, work at cross-purposes: the former requires understanding the world of the non-Jew while the latter simply ignores it. Those ethical values cultivated by Jews in the Diaspora not only permit one to question the assumptions of Zionism, they demand it.

Given their views, both Weiss and Butler have faced the same charges of Jewish self-hatred as anti-Zionists of the 1940s such as Berger. "Mondoweiss often gives the appearance of an anti-Semitic enterprise," one critic has written, while another has declared it "a hate site, . . . a virulent pusher of anti-Semitic tropes."[38] When in 2012 the City of Frankfurt announced that Butler was to receive the Theodor Adorno prize, named after the philosopher associated with the Frankfurt School of Critical Theory, Gerald Steinberg, a Hebrew University political scientist, charged in the *Jerusalem Post* that her views represented the "modern embodiment of anti-Semitism."[39] A blogger for the newspaper pointed out, furthermore, as if it constituted proof of the charges against her, that Butler, seeking a place to respond to her critics, had turned to the Mondoweiss website.[40]

As with similar-sounding accusations against the American Council for Judaism, the problem with the views of Weiss and Butler lies not in the murky psychology of presumed Jewish self-hatred but in the real world of political choice. Berger and the ACJ lost their universalist sensibilities when they became partisans in the war over the Middle East. One might have hoped that a younger generation would have learned a lesson from that. It does not appear to have done so. Weiss, for example, is a great admirer of Berger; he posted an item praising Ross's biography of him as a "glorious intellectual achievement."[41] Perhaps this admiration is what has now led Weiss into the same traps into which Berger fell more than a half century ago. If neoconservatives for Weiss are the enemy, and if what makes conservatives "neo" is their support for a strong state, especially in the area of national security, then to oppose their Zionism is to oppose their statism. This, I believe, explains why Weiss seeks allies among libertarians. One of his favorites among them, much like those close to Berger, is Jewish: Sheldon Richman, grandson of an anti-Zionist Orthodox rabbi and the former editor of the *Freeman*, one of the longest-lasting libertarian publications. Richman considers himself a left libertarian who supports free markets but not corporate monopolies and who warns against state involvement in personal life and fears growing militarization.[42] Yet for all this, his ideas, if implemented, would, like those of earlier generations of libertarians, undermine many of the gains achieved by ordinary people who have relied on governmental programs to obtain a certain degree of economic security. By endorsing them, Weiss is taking leave of his universalism.

Nor do the parallels between Weiss and Berger stop there. Like Berger's flirtation with extreme right figures such as Freda Utley, Weiss has something of a soft spot for those who embody reactionary ugliness in its purest form. The clearest case is offered by Weiss's assessment of the ideas of the explicitly anti-Semitic writer Kevin MacDonald, a California psychology professor described by the Southern Poverty Law Center as "the neo-Nazi's favorite academic."[43] MacDonald once reached out to Weiss, but because he believed that MacDonald was strongly committed to fixed racial categories, and therefore was far removed from universalist ideals, Weiss rejected his "embrace." But Weiss also added that MacDonald "understands how important Jewish history is to this moment" and "is concerned about Palestinian human rights and the Israel lobby's astonishing ability to remove Palestinian suffering from the American discourse," all of which make his ideas "bracing and bold."[44] No one can doubt that Weiss, more than any other figure in contemporary American public life, has brought public attention to the anti-Zionist cause. Nor can one doubt that in doing so, he has shown something of a blind spot toward unsavory figures.

In a similar manner, academic critics of Israel often move from the universalist outlook out of which their ideas grow into a narrow defense of national privilege, even if unintentionally. Butler's ideas, especially as expressed in her book *Parting Ways: Jewishness and the Critique of Zionism*, illustrate the problem. As befits her appreciation for German philosophy, Butler is especially attracted to the writings of Hannah Arendt, who like so many universalists of her time was a skeptic of nationalism. In a 1943 essay that sought to apply the insights learned from European history to what was then called the Near East, Arendt had written that "the attempt to solve national conflicts by first creating nation states, and then guaranteeing minority rights within state structures, has suffered such a spectacular defeat in recent times that one would expect no one would even presume to think of following that path again."[45] It followed that neither a Jewish state promising to protect Arab rights nor an Arab one claiming to respect Jewish ones would work. Instead Arendt offered the prospect of a "federation." If we could imagine Palestine as a place within the British Commonwealth, both Arabs and Jews, she argued, would be in a position to express their national sensibilities without dominating each other. Federation, halfway between state sovereignty and statelessness, was for her an attempt to recognize the power of particularism while upholding principles of universalism.

The prospects for federation ended when the British gave up their role in the Middle East. Federation nonetheless serves as an interesting thought-experiment for Butler. Although sympathetic to the goals federation seeks to achieve, she ultimately finds Arendt's solution "naïve," too tied, in her view, to the Eurocentrism that colored both her writing and Hermann Cohen's.[46] We need another approach, she argues, and she finds it here: just as the Jews were historically a diasporic people, the Palestinians have now inherited the same status. Because the Jews were allowed to return to their ancient home, equality between these two peoples requires that the Palestinians also be allowed to come back to the lands from which they were expelled by force in 1948. Doing so will not result in the destruction of the Jewish people, Butler insists, but only in "the dismantling of the structure of Jewish sovereignty and demographic advantage." Vague on the details, she believes that in what she calls "complex and antagonistic modes of living together," Jews would make the case for Arab acceptance of them based on their own history of exile. Presumably, then, Palestinian Arabs would recall their more recent history of exile and understand why they should live together with Jews.

It is difficult to imagine such a proposal ever getting off the ground. In reality, Butler's thought-experiment amounts to a one-state solution in which Jews would always be at the mercy of the Arab majority dominating them. Although sympathetic to the Palestinians and their plight, Butler is not an apologist for them the way Berger proved to be. But like him she urges steps that if followed would bring the entire Zionist experiment to an end. Butler is no anti-Semite. At the same time, she clearly is an anti-Zionist. In this she is little different from earlier advocates of the same position whose universalist roots withered under the force of nationalistic appeals. There may have been a time when universalism stood against the notion of statehood in itself. In our time, when so many oppressed peoples view statehood as necessary for their survival, the goals of universalism may be better filled by recognizing that because states are here to stay, the best course is finding political solutions that can allow them to live in peace. Short of that, one winds up critical of particularism on one side while understanding and appreciating it on the other.

VI

Stephen Wise also has his intellectual descendants. Two writers, neither of them rabbis, have taken it upon themselves to articulate the contemporary case for a Zionism rooted in a Wise-like commitment to universalist ideals of social justice. Gershom Gorenberg, an American-born, Jerusalem-based writer, published *The Unmaking of Israel* in 2011. It was quickly followed by *The Crisis of Zionism*, a cri de coeur from Peter Beinart, a senior political writer for the *Daily Beast* and an associate professor of journalism and political science at the City University of New York.

Explaining his decision to make aliyah, Gorenberg writes that "I thought there was a chance of realizing liberal Zionism, of creating a society in which Jews are the majority, in which Jewish arguments are the arguments of the general society—but also a society with full rights for non-Jews, a democracy in the fullest sense."[47] He realizes the hour is getting late and his dream may never be fulfilled. But it is not that difficult, he argues, to understand what steps would need to be taken if it were to be realized: the settlements must end, the influence of ultra-Orthodox Jews will have to be reduced by more firmly separating synagogue and state, and the legal system—Israel does not have a constitution, in large part because Orthodox Jews oppose the writing of one—should be reformed so that all ethnic groups are treated equally. His goal, in short, is to avoid the creation of what Philip Weiss believes Israel has already become: an ethnocracy.

Unlike Weiss and Butler, Gorenberg desperately wants Israel to survive as a Jewish state; his book is filled with love for a public life spoken in the Hebrew language. Anti-Zionists insist that the crisis of Israeli society began in 1948 when the new state came into existence by displacing Palestinians from their homes. For Gorenberg, by contrast, the crucial year is 1967, when Israel evolved into what he calls "an accidental empire," a term anti-Zionists would never accept, but to Gorenberg means a state with an ambition to expand, even into areas in which it did not belong and in which continued occupation would threaten its Jewish character.[48] The idea of Israel is not wrong. The current politics of Israel very much are.

An American whose family has roots in the Jewish community of Cape Town, South Africa, Beinart writes explicitly in the shadow of the liberal Zionists of the 1930s and 1940s. For him these figures— he cites not only Wise, Brandeis, and Silver but also Henrietta Szold, the founder of Hadassah—are to be admired precisely because their Zionism was an offshoot of their universalism. "In the half-century between World War I and the Six Day War," he states, "American Jewish organizations repeatedly linked the struggle for Jewish acceptance to the broader struggle for a more just and tolerant America, even when that meant allying with the more despised and brutalized groups in American life."[49] Not only that, Beinart continues, their commitment to liberal democratic values led them to the conclusion that America's leading Zionist organizations should be run in a democratic spirit. Were they alive today, Beinart believes, they would view America's major Jewish organizations, funded by wealthy contributors and taking positions far to the right of most American Jews, as a nightmare come true. True, they did not pay much attention, Szold excepted, to the Arabs. But right up to the 1967 war, when so many American Jews rushed to Israel's defense, liberal Zionists believed that one could be a nationalist and a strong supporter of individual rights at the same time. As one 1964 statement of the American Jewish Committee put it, "As Americans, we have not hesitated to withhold . . . support or to disagree publicly when Israel's actions appear to depart from the principle [of human rights]."

The crucial question facing both Gorenberg and Beinart is whether contemporary political conditions permit any kind of reconciliation between support for Jewish nationalism and the maintenance of a universalist sensibility. For both writers, there is only one possible way out of this dilemma. Because they are Zionists, they insist that Israel has every right to maintain its sovereignty as an independent state. But because they are also universalists, they believe that Israel should be a relatively small state, certainly significantly smaller than it is now. Gorenberg does not discuss Arendt, but his solution of two smaller states comes closer to her ideal of a federation than Butler's conception of mutual cohabitation. It is true that a smaller Israel would be surrounded by Arab states unlikely to feel especially warm toward it. But by relinquishing heavily Arab-populated lands, such a state has a much better chance of maintaining its Jewish and democratic character. Beinart agrees. So opposed is he to Israeli occupation and settlement that while he rejects any call for a boycott of Israeli goods, he does advocate a boycott of Israeli companies located in the West Bank. Israel, in his view, needs a lesson in modesty, a position not very different from Gorenberg's.

Liberal Zionists may have the right idea, but the reforms they advocate seem hopelessly utopian in the current political atmosphere. Israel's leadership is not interested in hearing about prophetic universalism. Any attempt to roll back let alone end the settlements is likely to produce violent resistance from those Jews, whether ultra-Orthodox or entirely secular, who would be affected. There is little or no chance that established Jewish organizations in the Diaspora will change their funding strategies or general political outlook, at least in the short run. Like the progressivism of the 1930s and 1940s that energized Wise, there is and will likely always be an element of naïveté in liberal Zionism. Progressivism appeals to the intellect while nationalism speaks to the heart. For those who still live under the spell of the destruction wrought by the Holocaust and the protection offered by Israel, the heart will continue to rule the head in all things Jewish for some time.

Still, there does exist evidence that liberal Zionists have learned more from the mistakes made by their predecessors than anti-Zionists. One course correction especially stands out. Like Wise, who placed so much hope in Franklin Delano Roosevelt, Beinart at first saw considerable potential in the man he calls "the Jewish president," Barack Obama.[50] He points out that although American Jewish opinion turned in a more particularist direction after 1967, the tradition of prophetic universalism lived on with such rabbis as Arnold Jacob Wolf (1924–2008). An organizer of Breira (Hebrew for "the alternative"), which led the way in endorsing the idea of a Palestinian state in the West Bank and Gaza, Wolf was Chicago based; his congregation was KAM Isaiah Israel in that city's liberal Hyde Park neighborhood, the same place in which Obama lived. Obama was introduced to Wolf and his circle, and they in turn helped shape the future president's views about the Middle East. Once he was elected, Beinart writes, prophetic universalists had a friend in the White House for the first time in decades.

Beinart, however, quickly learned otherwise. Whatever Obama's personal views may be—and it is not difficult to see that he does not fully trust Israeli prime minister Benjamin Netanyahu—the realities of domestic politics make it far too risky for any American president to express public disapproval of Israel's actions. In an odd way, this is probably a good thing for Beinart's analysis, since it prevents him from repeating Wise's mistake of placing too much trust in one elected official. Although Beinart is a political journalist, he realizes that politics can take the cause of liberal Zionism just so far. This explains why, as his argument progresses, he turns his attention away from politics in the direction of education; Beinart is a strong advocate of Jewish schools so that young Jews can learn about universalism by learning more about Judaism.

Beinart may well be correct that for those concerned with Israel's actions, an immersion in the Jewish tradition, rather than politics, may be the more effective path to take for now. As we shall see in my concluding chapter, growing numbers of Jews throughout the Diaspora, and even in Israel, are finding in the Jewish tradition good reasons to take a universalist stance toward the world. It is quite possible that this emphasis on education today could produce new political movements tomorrow. In theory it ought not matter where criticism comes from: if such criticism resonates, it hardly matters whether it originates from Jews, Christians, or Muslims. In the reality of actual politics, however, criticism of Israel's current policies is more likely to have an impact if it comes from those, religious or secular, steeped in Jewish values. Far from self-hatred, criticism of Israel rooted in universalistic Jewish values could become a major form of self-expression.

VII

Unlike the Reform Judaism that emerged in nineteenth-century Germany before spreading to the United States, today's universalists operate in a world in which a Jewish state is no longer a distant dream. The challenge facing universalism in our time is therefore greater now than it was then. Before the state of Israel came into existence, prophecy required only imagining a blessed future. Now that such a state exists, prophetic universalism, while appealing to future hopes, also has to consider the consequences of its ideals for present political arrangements: messianism now has to be accompanied by realism. Neither the anti-Zionists nor the liberal Zionists have successfully met this challenge. Nonetheless, the latter, I believe, are in a better position to do so than the former.

Anti-Zionists consider themselves critics of nationalism, especially when embodied in states and even more so when those states use their economic and military might to rule over others. Yet Israel casts its shadow over all Jews, even those who oppose it, and for this reason the ideological zeal, utopian longing, and sectarian proclivities of the early European Zionists reappear in the convictions of those who oppose the very idea of Zion. Like the early Zionists, today's anti-Zionists have a dream and hope to make it come true.

But there the difference ends. Herzl's vision that a Jewish state could come into being, highly impractical during his lifetime, was eventually realized. Dismantling the Jewish state would, I believe, prove to be an even more impossible objective than establishing it. No matter how many genocides have taken place since Hitler, the Nazi genocide, singular in its evil, makes it seem heartless in the extreme to argue against the proposition that those who experienced its brutality were justified in having a state capable of protecting future generations, even when that state acts in ways contrary to international law and opinion. Despite the Jewish state's birth on land that belonged to others, moreover, there are more than six million Jews now living there whose existence cannot be ignored. Universalists who argue on behalf of the dignity and rights of all people are correct to take the sufferings of the Palestinians into account. For the same reason, they are wrong to propose solutions that would deny the Jews a state of their own. A two-state solution may be enormously difficult to achieve. But it is the only solution currently under discussion that by recognizing the rights of both peoples is capable of fulfilling universalist ideals.

Liberal Zionists, who generally favor a two-state solution, face a different problem: while Israel has retained its Zionism, it is rapidly dispensing with its liberalism. Liberal Zionists are determined to bring to the Jewish state a message from the Diaspora at a time when Israel, except in its quest for financial and political support, is not all that interested in hearing what the Diaspora has to say. It never occurred to Stephen Wise that the Israel he saw as the best antidote for oppression would itself become a force for discrimination at home and militarism abroad. Now that it has, and no one of a liberal sensibility can deny that it has, the inevitable gap between liberalism and nationalism has become that much harder to bridge. Under such conditions, the best that liberal Zionists can do is to serve as Israel's conscience, reminding its citizens of historical realities and moral dilemmas they seem all too willing to forget. When Zionism came into being, those Jews who had already moved to Palestine were in desperate need of the financial and political help that could only come from abroad. Now that Israel is a powerful state, it is desperately in need of the moral help that also can come from abroad.

Many Israelis know the course that their country is presently pursuing destroys the values that brought the state into being. Because of a political system that gives disproportionate power to extremist parties, as well as a population that has seen too much war to put any hope in peace, they lack the means to lead their country in a new direction. They need allies where they can find them, and the Diaspora is one place that can offer them. Were Jews in the Diaspora to play a greater role in helping Israel come to its senses, the tradition of Jewish universalism that began long ago will have brought the light of reason to all nations, including the one created by the Jews themselves.

CHAPTER 5

The Lost Jews, the Last Jews

I

One question majorities rarely have to answer seems to preoccupy minorities endlessly: what to do about assimilation? To blend in with everyone else threatens to obliterate all those features that make a minority distinctive. To opt for separatism is to choose a certain degree of alienation, cutting oneself (and one's group) off from the dominant culture. Because Jews have lived in the Diaspora for so long, they have debated the question of assimilation more thoroughly than most. The creation of a Jewish state has not changed matters all that much. If anything, the existence of a Jewish majority in one place makes the question of how best to live as a minority everywhere else all the more compelling.

The passions aroused by assimilation are deep and divisive—and with good reason. For those who lean in a particularist direction, the attractions of gentile society constitute one more warning the ever-dying people must heed: if anti-Semitism does not obliterate them, assimilation will. The issue is just as important to universalists: Diaspora Jews cannot serve as the conscience of the world if because of assimilation no Diaspora Jews are left. What, then, is happening to those Jews who continue to live as a minority, especially in the largest of such places, the United States? Are they losing either their Judaism or their Jewishness? Or are Jews simply adapting to new conditions the way they have done in the past? Such questions need answers, not just to satisfy sociological curiosity but to address the question with which this book has been concerned: whether a concern only with themselves or with the needs of all is the best way to carry Jewish traditions into the future.

II

In his youth Theodor Herzl had been an advocate for intermarriage, as well as an enthusiast for a nationalist fraternity proud to affirm Germanic virtues.[1] (He even shocked Vienna's chief rabbi, or so the story goes, who once found him at home lighting Christmas candles for his children.)[2] Herzl's subsequent shift from assimilationism to Zionism was never fully completed; even after his change of heart, he loved to challenge anti-Semites to that most barbaric of Central European rituals, the duel. Still, once Herzl realized just how deep the virus of anti-Semitism had entrenched itself in Christian societies, especially after the Dreyfus affair, he was moved to write the book that changed Judaism forever.

Many of the Zionists who followed Herzl, by contrast, dropped all such ambivalence: gentile societies, they were convinced, either would not willingly allow the Jews to assimilate or would poison the minds of those who nonetheless did. Simon Dubnow and Jacob Klatzkin represented opposite poles within Zionism, the former an enthusiast for the Diaspora who only reluctantly and late in life supported the idea of a Jewish state, the latter a confirmed Zionist who believed that assimilation "was not a matter of great regret, for the Judaism of the diaspora was not worthy of survival," in the words of Walter Laqueur.[3] But both agreed that in the absence of a counterweight, whether it be autonomy in Dubnow's case or statehood in Klatzkin's, nothing would stand in the way of Diaspora Jews losing everything that was Jewish about them.

The arrival of the Holocaust in the one country in which assimilation had been so prominent—I speak, of course, of Germany—did more than furnish seemingly irrefutable evidence for the case against assimilation; it also offered the ultimate metaphor for antiassimilationist warnings in succeeding years. "If we fail to act now, if we fail to share with our young Jews the beauty and meaningfulness of Jewish life and Jewish heritage," proclaimed the Orthodox American rabbi Ephraim Buchwald in 1992, "there will be few Jews left in the next generation who will even know that there ever was a Holocaust of European Jews. The 'silent Holocaust' will have done its job. Hitler will have emerged victorious."[4] No less a figure than the former Israeli minister of justice, Yaakov Neeman, expressed his agreement with such a position in 2011; speaking at a panel in Jerusalem, he told the audience that "the problem is not conversion, it's assimilation."[5] "Let's face the truth," he urged. "What Hitler—may his name and memory be forgotten—didn't manage to do is happening in the Diaspora with its horrific assimilation."

Those killed by the Nazis were the lost Jews. Any person who assimilates becomes "the last Jew in a line stretching perhaps three thousand years, turning their energy to other causes, deciding not to reproduce someone like themselves, taking as role models those who had been their persecutors," wrote the late Barry Rubin, an American-born Israeli scholar.[6] Assimilation is the fate for which particularism is the remedy: lost or last, Jews face the constant prospect of disappearance. Defenders of the faith must therefore do everything in their power to hold out against those who marry gentiles, raise their children in two faiths rather than one, lose their sense of ethnic attachment, or otherwise fall victim to the pressures toward homogenization so characteristic of modern society.

Despite all these warnings, no consensus among Jews has ever existed on the question of assimilation. In contrast to the particularists, universalists believe that assimilated Jews, as Herzl himself wrote in an 1882 book review, are in a position to "exert themselves diligently for the sincere well-being of humanity."[7] From such a perspective, assimilation is an opportunity rather than a threat. In a commencement address delivered at Boston's Hebrew Teachers College in 1996, for example, Gerson Cohen, soon to become chancellor of the Jewish Theological Seminary and one of the first Conservative rabbis to sup-port the ordination of women, spoke about what he called "the bless-ings of assimilation." Cohen noted that Jews have always assimilated throughout their history, adopting the names, language, clothing, and customs of the societies in which they lived. Moreover, they were right to do so, since "the great ages of Jewish continuity were born out of a response to the challenge of assimilation, and there is no reason our age should not respond to this challenge with equal vigor." Of course there were dangers if assimilation went too far. But as a minority, Co-hen pointed out, Jews must adapt in order to preserve their traditions. "So it has always been, and so it will continue to be."[8]

Both sides in this debate are making a bet on the future. Who, then, has the better argument? That question, I believe, can best be answered with a lot less Hitler and a lot more data. Given the disproportionate number of sociologists among them, Jews are given to studying them-selves. The data they collect cannot offer a definitive resolution to the debate over assimilation, especially because surveys of the American Jewish population are accompanied by arguments over who should be counted as a Jew that reflect disagreements over the very subject being studied. Still, social scientists and historians have uncovered good reasons for concluding that Diaspora Jews are not only surviv-ing in the United States but they are doing so in ways that make a revival of prophetic universalism more plausible. That may not be good news for those who insist that Jews ought to marry only other Jews, teach their children obedience to Jewish law, and, if necessary, be prepared to move to Israel should matters turn sour. But it strikes me as good news for everyone else, including, if they would only listen to their overseas cousins, those who have made Israel their home.

III

In less emotional quarters than the one occupied by Buchwald and Neeman, the question is not whether a new holocaust is taking place. It is whether there will be such a thing as "Jewish continuity."

A discussion of continuity, by one name or another, has preoccupied Jews since they first appeared in the world, but it became especially urgent in the United States with the publication of the National Jewish Population Survey of 1990. The survey offered no evidence for Rabbi Buchwald's conclusion that two-thirds of American Jewry had already been lost. But to those worried about the robustness of Jewish life in the United States, the findings nonetheless came as a considerable shock. The Jewish population between 1970 and 1990 had grown at a slower pace than the overall American population.[9] In comparison to earlier periods, Jews had aged. Their rates of observance did not seem especially impressive; among those with the strongest sense of Jewish identity, only 11 percent claimed to attend synagogue weekly. Above and beyond all such findings stood the one that mattered most: according to the 1990 survey, 9 percent of American Jews who had married before 1965 married non-Jews, a figure that rose to 25 percent among those married between 1965 and 1974, to 44 percent for those who tied the knot between 1975 and 1984, and then to 52 percent of those joined together since 1985. If the intermarriage rate were to continue at anything like the same pace, the question would be not what kind of future Diaspora Jews would face but whether there would be any future at all.

"In some Jewish circles," Jonathan Sarna, a Brandeis University historian, has commented, "the intermarriage rate is as widely followed and analyzed as the inflation rate."[10] His comparison could not be more apt. In the 1970s and 1980s, inflation in the United States reached crisis-level proportions, rising to a peak of 14.8 percent in March 1980. It has come down considerably since then; in 2012, the monthly average was a little over 2 percent. Despite this decline, the economist Paul Krugman frequently cautions against "deficit scolds," those so committed to austerity that they urge radical measures, such as deep cuts in government spending, even when there exists little actual evidence of increasing prices.[11]

The intermarriage rate among Jews, coincidentally, hit its peak at almost the same moment as the inflation rate, prompting "intermarriage scolds," as they might be called, to fret that the meaning of a

Jewish marriage, like the dollar, had been losing its value.[12] Intermarriage, it should be pointed out, is not confined to Jews; while Mormons and Hindus overwhelmingly marry within, the rate of intermarriage among Jews is roughly the same as among evangelicals and is lower than that of Buddhists and mainline Protestants.[13] Not only that, but racial intermarriage has also become far more common in the United States, the percentage having more than doubled between 1980 and 2010.[14] Nonetheless, Jews have a special reason for their concern for *endogamy*, the term used by demographers to characterize those who marry within the group: they are the only people that have experienced the horrors of the Final Solution followed so quickly by the relief offered through statehood. (Armenians were the victims of genocide at the hands of the Turks, have also witnessed high rates of intermarriage in the United States, and also now have an independent state, but one rarely hears talk of a "silent holocaust" with respect to their marriage patterns.)[15] Those concerned with both extermination and state building assign a high priority to demography, the one by pondering the reason for so many deaths, the other by asking how many Jews are left and where they are best off living. It can hardly be surprising that in the aftermath of the two, Jews became obsessed with counting.

For leading Jewish organizations and activists, the findings of the 1990 survey quickly became a call to action. A much-discussed response was the publication of *A Statement on the Jewish Future*, signed by a distinguished group of rabbis, academics, and community professionals and coordinated by the American Jewish Committee. The statement addressed the problem of Jewish continuity by emphasizing five values that make Jews Jewish: *Torah*, a commitment to Jewish learning; *Am Yisrael*, identification with Jewish peoplehood; *Klal Yisrael*, or "catholic Israel," the acceptance of plural forms of Jewish expression, such as Reform, Conservative, and Orthodox; *Brith*, the maintenance of boundaries that keep Judaism distinct from other faiths; and *Keruv*, outreach to those who can be enticed back into the fold. Adherence to all five were considered essential for Jewish continuity. "Judaism consists of a complex structure of rules and beliefs," said one signer, Jack Wertheimer of the Jewish Theological Seminary. "Tamper with one aspect and another will be affected. . . . There is an integrity to the structure of Judaism. As we dismantle one section of the structure, we weaken the rest."[16] As an example, Wertheimer wrote that "there is a connection between kashrut [kosher] observance and sexual liaisons." You are either a Jew in full or not much of a Jew at all.

A *Statement on the Jewish Future* was not offered as a consensus position designed to unify American Jews. On the contrary, its signatories recognized that some would be excluded, especially those who in their view were unwilling to make the personal sacrifices a rich Jewish life demanded. In the debate that followed, the statement's signers were described as advocating "inreach": rather than trying to win over those so estranged from their Judaism that they could effectively be considered lost, let alone any Christians they may have married along the way, an effort should be made to strengthen the ties of those already committed to some degree to Jewish life. Religious communities require borders, the signatories insisted, both between themselves and other faiths as well as between their own denominations. American Judaism is losing such borders. Reform and Conservative Jews, therefore, and not just the Orthodox, have to take serious steps to reestablish them. The last thing Judaism needs is a nonjudgmental religion that refuses to define its key practices and beliefs.

A document deliberately intended to exclude is bound to attract critics. Among the fiercest was Deborah Dash Moore, then at Vassar College and now a professor of history at the University of Michigan. Moore belongs to Reconstructionism, a movement begun by Rabbi Mordecai Kaplan (1881–1983) that views Judaism as a culture or civilization, questions the God-centeredness of traditional Judaism, and rejects the idea of the Jews as God's chosen people.[17] There was no place for Reconstructionism within the narrowly drawn borders of *A Statement on the Jewish Future*, and Moore took her exclusion from the ranks of presumably authentic Jewry personally. "Why should we trust these self-appointed gatekeepers with their penchant for drawing boundaries and setting-up barriers?" she wanted to know. A feminist as well as liberal, she pointed out that the signers never explicitly called for a return to traditional gender segregation, "but given the logic of its argument, why should we not expect this in some future document?"[18] (The statement had thirty signatories, six of them women, including Ruth Wisse, whose views on particularism were discussed in a previous chapter.) Reaching in rather than expanding out, Moore argued, represented a fearful and ultimately self-destructive reaction to the increasing diversity and egalitarianism of the United States. Yes, American Jewry is changing. But what else is new? "If American Jews really want to focus their energies upon the future and Jewish continuity, . . . let the openness of American society and the voluntary character of its religious life stimulate Jewish imaginations and energize Jewish wills. Solutions will emerge through competition and debate, through syncretism and innovation." Advocates of inreach, she concluded, are little different than their Christian counterparts intent on maintaining sectarian purity. The Diaspora is where religious creativity takes place, and it is a creative Diaspora that American Judaism requires.

Both sides in this argument, it turns out, were responding to a statistic that proved to be incorrect. In something of an embarrassing admission, the 52 percent intermarriage rate was withdrawn when it was discovered that people who were classified as non-Jews in the 1990 survey were included among those Jews who had intermarried. The real intermarriage rate for the five previous years turned out to be 43 percent, still high but not quite as catastrophic.[19] Any relief, however, was short lived. A subsequent survey taken in 2001 showed an uptick in the intermarriage rate (to 47 percent), and even though the survey left the impression that some notable forms of revitalization were taking place in American Jewish life, the trend had clearly been established: Jews were marrying non-Jews in numbers that would have shocked their grandparents.[20] That point was confirmed beyond debate in 2013 when the Pew Research Center in Washington, DC, published the most extensive portrait of American Jews since 2001: 58 percent of those American Jews who had married since 2005, it found, had married non-Jews.[21] Not only that, but 32 percent of younger people with direct Jewish ancestry described themselves as having no religion, compared to 7 percent of those born between 1914 and 1927. Most members of the former group, finally, were not raising their children in a Jewish home. For technical reasons involving sampling, response rates, and question wording, it has proven difficult to draw direct comparisons between all these surveys. Still, the one published in 2013 seems to give empirical support to those who believe that Jewish life can continue in the Diaspora only if Jews continue to marry each other.

That, however, would be a premature conclusion. Consider once more the analogy between inflation and intermarriage. Krugman, for one, does more than believe that worries about inflation are excessive; he reminds us that especially in recessionary times moderate inflation may prove to be a good thing by reducing the value of the debt accumulated when the economy was booming and in that way encouraging future economic growth.[22] Could a rising rate of Jewish intermarriage also prove to be positive development, offering an entirely unexpected source for the revival of diasporic Judaism? Judaism is not, and never has been, an evangelical faith, intent on bringing new adherents to its way of life. Still, intermarriage can be viewed as the Jewish equivalent of Christian evangelization; any Jew who marries a gentile raises the prospect of exposing new individuals to the faith. In contrast to the intermarriage scolds, French philosopher Alain Finkielkraut, who is both a political conservative and a self-identified Jew, looks upon intermarriage as a unique chance to assert one's attachments. "Marrying a non-Jew doesn't mean one is abandoning one's tradition," he has written. "On the contrary, it demonstrates a desire to disseminate the message throughout the world. Those who wish to remain Jews in a world they don't care about are reducing Judaism to something no better than a lobby."[23]

The positive potential of intermarriage lies in what has been called the "enlarged Jewish population," defined by Sergio DellaPergola, an Israeli demographer, as everyone born Jewish plus "all those persons of Jewish ancestry who now hold another monotheistic religion, and all non-Jews who belong with the nuclear families of Jews."[24] Each time the born-Jewish population is reduced through intermarriage,

the enlarged Jewish population expands: there were, by one estimate, 6,588,065 such people in the United States in 2011, compared
to 5,828,000 in 1992.[25] If it is true, as Sarna writes, that "opposition to
intermarriage, once normative in Jewish life, is fast becoming excep-
tional," then the real question is not why intermarriage has become so
common but why it took so long to happen.[26] In-marriage, I believe,
lasted as long as it did because of the lingering effects of the events
of the 1930s and 1940s, which encouraged Jews to think about self-
preservation. Once they no longer were convinced that the concentration camps lay just around the corner, and as they began to understand
that Israel was becoming the major military power in its region, the
marriage floodgates opened. No one can ever predict the future, but
the chances that 91 percent of all American Jews will marry other
Jews, which was true of those who married before 1965, are virtually
nonexistent.

Concerns about intermarriage are premised on the idea that people
who belong to a long-persecuted minority will find the blandishments
of the majority culture impossible to resist. Yet the actual record is far
more mixed. The best studies of mixed-marriage couples are those
that, relying on qualitative methods, examine the lives of real people
through intensive interviewing. What they have found is instructive.
Sylvia Barack Fishman's *Double or Nothing?*, as its title suggests, emphasizes the extent to which mixed-married couples try to bring up
their children in two traditions rather than convert one or the other
spouse. Such findings represent good news, in the sense that they in-
dicate the extent to which prejudice against Jews has declined. Jewish
culture, moreover, has shaped American culture and vice versa, making it easier to cross once-high boundaries between them. At the same
time, she writes, "divided religious identities are problematic from the
standpoint of historical definitions of Jewishness."[27] Although her approach is balanced, Fishman, who was a signer of *A Statement on the
Jewish Future*, would have to be included among the worriers. Jewish
continuity requires a thicker Jewish life than intermarriage generally
allows.

The historian Keren R. McGinity, a Jewish woman who married a non-Jewish man, focuses on other women who made the same choice. Her work also conveys a mixed message, if one that is more positive toward intermarriage than that of Fishman. After interviewing forty-three Jewish women in the Boston area who had married non-Jewish men, she wrote that "although most Gentile husbands were significantly involved with their wives living a Jewish life, and indeed fostered the women's Jewishness and participated in raising Jewish children, most Jewish women in my sample, ironically and despite the positive qualities they described about their intermarriages, expressed sadness about not being married to a fellow Jew."[28] The sadness of these women is surely noteworthy, but its cause, we need to remember, lies not in a decision to leave Judaism behind but in one to remain attached to it. This explains why the involvement with Jewish life for many of these women *increased* after their marriages; among younger women who have married more recently, intermarriage resulted in greater observance than found among their mothers who had married Jewish fathers. Jewishness, McGinity's findings inform us, is not something automatically passed along the bloodline but, reflecting the feminist movements of the 1960s and 1970s, is a matter of personal choice. Responding to the notion that assimilation threatens the future of Diaspora Jewry, one of her interviewees said, "I'm doing more for the continuity of Judaism in this house with [her Gentile husband] than most of my Jewish girlfriends combined."

In 1977 Harvard demographer Elihu Bergman predicted that by 2076, the year of the American tercentennial, there would be as few as 10,420 Jews in the United States.[29] Twenty years later, Alan Dershowitz, a law professor at the same university, broadened the geographic scope; by the last quarter of the twenty-first century, he wrote, "American Jewry—indeed, Diaspora Jewry—may vanish."[30] Such gloomy prognoses, according to sociologist Calvin Goldscheider, are almost certainly untrue.[31] Just as important for the purposes of this chapter, they define Judaism biologically, based, as it historically has been, on the criterion of matrilineal descent. Jews, of course, are free to hold to such a definition, in which case the only hope for survival lies in traditional Jewish couples having larger numbers of children. Both in the Diaspora and in Israel, this is a task that Orthodox Jews have taken on, usually with considerable success.

For everyone else, the fate of Diaspora Jewry ironically now lies in the hands of gentiles, either those who convert or those who refrain from doing so but encourage their Jewish spouses in their personal quest for more meaningful forms of religious identity. This is not a situation that Jews have faced throughout most of their history, and it is understandable that it is accompanied by considerable anxiety. Still, biologically based conceptions of identity may have made sense in Yehuda Halevi's time, when Jews were a minority threatened by autocratic rulers, but in a society as open and fluid as the United States, religion, like everything else, will be based upon personal choice. The debate over Jewish continuity is all but over: *A Statement on the Jewish Future* proved to be really about the past. Those advocating outreach can be declared the winners, not because they are smarter people or their arguments are more impressive but because facts on the ground, so to speak, have shifted reality in their direction.

Not only does intermarriage offer a path to Jewish survival but it stands a good chance of softening the harsher forms of secular particularism described in chapter 3. Intermarriage is universalism in miniature: by bringing Jews together with non-Jews in the most intimate of ways, intermarriage, both as Herzl once hoped and as the work of both Fishman and McGinity documents, really does expand horizons. It is true that what intermarried couples practice bears little relationship to the Judaism of Maimonides, let alone to the religious practices of the East European immigrants who first made it to American shores. But spouses raised in different traditions who face the question of what values they will convey to their children stand little or no chance of rooting their religious identities in biology or tradition. No doubt some of the intermarried, as well as some of their children, will turn against religion. For those who do not, adherence will be preconditioned on acceptance. Lecturing Jews on why those who marry Christians are no different from those who walked unthinkingly into the death camps is not an effective way to gain that acceptance. Judaism has changed numerous times throughout its long history. It is clearly going through another such change now, one forced upon it by the era in which we live when human beings have so many options. When people have choices, religions do not: either they adapt or they wither.

IV

Although written by Jews for Jews, *A Statement on the Jewish Future* closely resembles a jeremiad, the quintessential Puritan sermon lamenting the decline from a golden age. It may seem odd that a people as persecuted as the Jews could ever have had a golden age; if one is nonetheless going to use the term, the most applicable period would be the years when writers such as Halevi and Maimonides thrived in medieval Spain. It is therefore significant that Benjamin Epstein, the early postwar director of the Anti-Defamation League, used that very term to characterize American Jewish life in the two decades after World War II. It was during these years, Epstein wrote, in a manner similar to Irving Kristol, that American Jews "achieved a greater degree of economic and political security, and a broader social acceptance than has ever been known by any Jewish community since the Dispersion."[32] Such postwar success was more than a matter of economics and politics. These were the decades of an American religious revival, and Jews were swept up with everyone else; it was at this time, as Sarna pointed out, that "religion became the major vehicle for Jewish identity, while secular Judaism as an ideology largely collapsed."[33] Those who worry about the prospects for Jewish continuity, however pessimistic about the future, can look back half a century to a time when American Jewish life seemed so much more vibrant.

It is, of course, impossible to turn the clock back and return American Judaism to the way it experienced the world in the 1950s and 1960s. Yet even if we could, it is by no means clear that we should. Far from constituting a model that future generation of Jews should emulate, the two or three decades after World War II were, in the long course of Jewish history, the exception rather than the rule. The reason why can be explained by considering the ways in which American

Jews during that period carried out one of the most basic tasks facing any religion: organizing the relationship between space and time.

From the moment the Jews were expelled from the Holy Land, they developed an ambivalent attitude toward specifically defined places. In ancient times, Rabbi Sacks points out, "Jews were a nation in the normal sense, bound together because they lived in the same land, under the same government. Shared fate, under such circumstances, requires no special faith, no theology, no leap of the imagination."[34] But once exile became the condition of the Jews, they developed a religion that could "be practiced anywhere, centered on the synagogue as an institution and on collective Jewish responsibility as an idea." Judaism in that sense could not be more different than Catholicism, the first of the monotheistic faiths to link itself with political rulers and to organize itself into administrative units resembling the federal structure of states. Reflecting such spatial commitments, Catholics could assert their presence through monumental churches and majestic mausoleums. Denied such a physical presence due to their diasporic existence, Jews, by contrast, possessed the advantage of portability: not only did they move themselves to new places when oppression repelled or opportunity lured, they also took with them their prayer books, traditions, memories, and, for the orthodox, distinctive clothing.

A distinctive religious style followed from the reality of diasporic existence. "Not having a functioning territorial state of their own and not even being concentrated in a particular territory," wrote the late Israeli American political scientist Daniel Elazar in this regard, "the Jews emphasized the temporal and organized time in the service of Jewish survival and self-expression. *Halakhah* . . . emphasizes the organization of time, the rhythm of its passage and the obligations of Jews to sanctify those rhythms—in daily prayers and study, the weekly Sabbath, and through holy days, festivals, and celebrations at representative seasons."[35] Space can be destroyed, as, indeed, the Second Temple was. But time, short of a nuclear Armageddon, will always be there. It is no small advantage when religious life can be organized by people who live apart but worship together. Jews around the world celebrated their holiest days at the same time, and in that way, the distances between them were shortened.

The most striking feature of American Judaism in the postwar years lay in its reversal of these historic priorities: space was now given priority and time sacrificed as a result. Time, for one thing, was in short supply in a society in which one parent worked long hours while the other had seemingly endless child-rearing duties. No one emphasized the time pressures facing early postwar Jews as much as Marshall Sklare, the leading sociologist of American Jewry during that period. One of his main conclusions was that large numbers of Jews were perfectly willing to celebrate annual holidays such as Hanu-kah and Passover but drew the line at more time-intensive practices such as weekly Sabbath observance. "Infrequently performed rituals," he wrote, "harmonize more with the secular component in modern American life than daily or weekly rituals. . . . Secularization under-cuts the emphasis of Jewish sacramentalism on the sanctification of the routine and imperils the continuation of those rituals which do not celebrate an extraordinary occasion."[36] Religiosity may have thrived during the 1950s and 1960s, but according to the (Jewish) former Marxist turned conservative theologian Will Herberg, faith in those years was more a matter of belonging than belief.[37] If so, the message for Jews was clear: one can believe anywhere but one must belong somewhere.

Because of this overwhelming need to belong, American Jews of the 1950s and 1960s began to inhabit what Sklare called "the suburban frontier."[38] Sklare chose an especially appropriate title: the Jews who had moved to these burgeoning enclaves, like those gathered in the forts in Hollywood Westerns, were seeking protection against hostile outsiders. Reform and Conservative Judaism were at the forefront of this protective suburbanization. "Why do temples look the way they do?" the Reform rabbi Daniel Hillel Freelander asked in a 1994 article.[39] His answer was that as Reform Jews become more secure and prosperous, sanctuaries with cinder-block walls, cheap carpet-ing, and retractable walls were left behind in favor of larger, more physically imposing synagogues with less space for prayer but more for classes, offices, and kitchens. In a similar manner Conservative Judaism celebrated its success in the suburban environment by building monuments as impressive as European cathedrals: Eric Mendelsohn's Park Synagogue in Cleveland Heights, Ohio, or Frank Lloyd Wright's Beth Shalom in Elkins Park, Pennsylvania, offer two such examples. As places to pray, synagogues had always been a feature of Jewish life, and a number of impressive urban houses of worship, many Moorish inspired, predated the postwar period in places ranging from Brookline, Massachusetts, to Cincinnati. Still, synagogue centers complete with day care, recreational facilities, book groups—even a "shul with a pool"—were something new.[40] Although both were densely populated with people of the same faith, the Jewish suburb was not the European ghetto: the former was expansive space the Jews took over and made their own, not, like the latter, confined space that autocratic rulers assigned to them.

The sense of permanence these impressive synagogues conveyed was matched by the increasing density and organizational heft of official Jewish life in the early postwar period. Building upon earlier efforts such as B'nai B'rith and Hadassah, American Jews in the years after World War II created an institutional structure that resembled Catholicism in its breadth and depth, composed of "a sophisticated political system, with hundreds of local and national organizations operating through a complex network of linkages to raise and expend hundreds of millions of dollars to carry out the 'public' business of American Jewry: support for the state of Israel, assistance to Jews abroad, maintenance of social welfare, recreational, educational, and cultural programs for American Jews, insurance of Jewish security and involvement in American society," writes Jonathan Woocher.[41] Because they did not move to Israel, postwar American Jews did not belong to a Jewish state. But in their diasporic homeland they nonetheless built a "Jewish polity," as Woocher calls it, one that resembled statehood in its reach and density. No wonder that when *A Statement on the Jewish Future* appeared, its signatories, reflecting the spatial orientation that had become second nature to American Jews during the middle of the twentieth century, spoke quite naturally about borders. Borders are what states or polities have; they are not what Jews through their long history of exile could count on.

It is certainly understandable that Jews would seek some kind of permanence while memories of the Holocaust were so acute. But not only was this attachment to place at odds with the long history of exilic Judaism, it also ran counter to the mobility and movement so prominent in the American experience. As soon as the new Jewish suburbs and their associated synagogue centers became established, their lure began to diminish in favor of movement: to Israel for some, to the "golden cities" of Miami or Los Angeles for others, and, ultimately, to a return to downtown for the younger generations.[42] "At the beginning of the twenty-first century," writes Uzi Rebhun, professor of Israel-Diaspora relations at the Hebrew University of Jerusalem, "American Jews have reached a high level of both individual and institutional spatial dispersion, which largely weakens the significance of geography for determining group identification."[43] Such dispersion may destroy tight-knit communities, but it is far more in accord with the diasporic life that had long characterized Judaism.

As geographic ties loosen, it should come as no surprise that postspatial ways of thinking about the organization of Jewish life are once again becoming the norm. Two examples, one Orthodox and one Conservative, are interesting in this context, because despite their ideological differences they share a similar movement from rootedness in a particular local community to a broad spatial outlook.

Of all the forms Judaism has taken, the ultra-Orthodox were most given to viewing themselves in spatial terms: in Europe, where they originated, their movements took their names from the places in which they lived, such as Lubavitchers, who originated in the Russian town of Lyubavichi. Even after they uprooted themselves for the New World, moreover, the *haredim*, as the strictly Orthodox are called, continued to congregate geographically; the headquarters for the Lubavitch movement became not only Brooklyn but the specific part of that borough called Crown Heights, which lies along Eastern Parkway. In part because of the Sabbath requirement of living within walking distance of a synagogue and in part because of their desire to create subcommunities of their own, the ultra-Orthodox did their best to create patterns of close residential proximity wherever they found themselves.

None of this means, however, that Orthodoxy lacks resources for responding to a more geographically dispersed world. Today, for example, the Lubavitch movement is best known for sponsoring Chabad, the most successful effort to encourage lapsed Jews to give Orthodoxy a new look. While traditionalist in its religious teachings, Chabad is anything but old-fashioned in its methods: in the place of dour chastisement and self-protective insularity, it offers potential new adherents warm support, relying on an impressive website, extensive houses and summer camps, Torah classes, and campus-based outreach activities. Most striking, these activities are global in nature, represented by Chabad's efforts to build *shlichim*, Hebrew for "emissaries," in one thousand cities spread throughout seventy countries.[44] It was a profound tragedy when Gavriel and Rivka Holtzberg, who ran the emissary in Mumbai, India, were murdered by terrorists in 2008. It was a testimony to Chabad's ambitions that they had left Crown Heights for India in the first place.

Representing another side of the spectrum, the most widely discussed and increasingly emulated synagogue in the United States may well be B'nai Jeshurun, which is housed on the Upper West Side of Manhattan, a neighborhood that historically was even more densely Jewish than Crown Heights. Ties to its neighborhood, however, are not what make this synagogue famous; if anything, reflecting that so many Jews had been moving to the suburbs through much of the postwar period, B'nai Jeshurun was in a state of serious decline throughout the 1980s. That all changed when new rabbinical leadership arrived from Argentina whose outlook had been shaped by resistance to a reactionary government. Through their efforts at revitalization, the place is now known for its lively Friday night services, vibrant music, life-cycle advice, recruitment techniques borrowed from MoveOn.org, and a strong emphasis on social justice. (In December 2012 its rabbis wrote and then partially retracted an e-mail message calling the

United Nations' vote recognizing Palestine as a nonmember observer state "a great moment for us as citizens of the world.")[45] What is so striking about all this is the way in which B'nai Jeshurun's Argentinean rabbis repeated the experience of the German Reform rabbis of the nineteenth century by expressing sentiments similar to those found in the Pittsburgh Platform. Moving to a new country seemed to underscore the universalism so often identified with liberal Jewish traditions.

Those who attend B'nai Jeshurun are almost as geographically mobile as those who lead it. The Upper West Side is not the same place it was when the synagogue first established itself there in 1918. No longer dominated by Jewish families who never gave up their apartments because they were protected by rent control, the young Jews who come to B'nai Jeshurun in many cases have recently arrived in New York— one attraction that Friday night services offer is an opportunity to meet people—and are probably not going to be living there in the future. These are individuals more likely to be connected through social media such as Facebook than encounters at Zabar's, the neighborhood outlet for bagels and lox. They are exemplars of what Caryn Aviv and David Shneer of the University of Colorado identify as Jews who "are making home in a global, not diasporic, world."[46]

Strongly influenced by postmodernism, Aviv and Shneer suggest that the geography of Judaism can no longer be viewed as Israel standing in the center surrounded by Jewish communities everywhere else; indeed, they question whether the term *diaspora* makes any sense at all now that Jews have taken their place in a global melting pot. The melting pot they describe, however, is not fully global; as Jonathan Sarna has written, "More and more Jews live in fewer and fewer places," and the places in which they live are the wealthier, liberal democracies of the First World.[47] Yet the fact that Jews have become more concentrated than scattered does not change their portability. Contemporary Jews, Sarna continues, increasingly speak a common language (English), visit each other's countries with considerable frequency, and find themselves in constant communication through the Internet. When the world is globalized, Jews no longer need be:

they have the means to leave such places as Iran, Morocco, and Cuba for such places as Tel Aviv, New York, Jerusalem, Los Angeles, and Haifa, five cities that contain more than half of the world's current Jewish population. Aviv and Shneer make a good point but express it wrongly; the Diaspora isn't disappeared but, rather, all Jews increasingly live within it, including those who have made Israel their home. The late Christopher Hitchens, author and critic, expressed this point well when he wrote that "the important but delayed realization will have to come: Israeli Jews are *a part* of the diaspora, not a group that has escaped from it."[48] (Hitchens's Jewish mother had become so assimilated in the English city of Portsmouth that Hitchens discovered her background only late in life.)

The major question facing Jewish continuity today is whether such geographical mobility will result in a revival of the temporal aspects of Judaism that were once so prominent in the historical Diaspora. Days devoted to prayer and learning are hardly compatible with modern conditions; and only the ultra-Orthodox, and within them only the men, are likely to keep that sense of daily routine viable. But there nonetheless remain ways in which a focus on the temporal can be developed to accommodate the schedules that modern Jews live. An example can be found in the efforts by Rabbi Eric Yoffie, past president of the Union for Reform Judaism, to change the ways Jews worship. To overcome the problem of "two-day-a-year Jews," those who attend synagogue only on the high holidays, Yoffie wrote, "Eighteenth-century Minsk is not our worship ideal. Neither is Berlin of the 1850s, nor suburban America of the 1950s."[49] He instead called for a "worship revolution," one that remains faithful to what he called "age-old prayers and time-honored chants" while accommodating itself to the busy lives that contemporary Jewish families live. One method for achieving this goal, he proposed, would be to rearrange the weekly calendar. At many synagogues Friday night services are for the elderly and Saturday morning ones for bar and bat mitzvahs. Not only does this segregate the audience, he pointed out, it also creates a conflict between synagogue and soccer, the dominant activity of contemporary Saturday mornings. To meet these challenges Yoffie proposed that synagogues might try to make every worship service a family event or to provide family services once a week instead of every month. The most interesting aspect of Yoffie's proposed changes is their explicit recognition that the challenges American Judaism faces require redefining concepts of time to support contemporary spatial realities.

Now that the dust between inreach and outreach has settled, it is important to note that the most significant determinant of how diasporic Jews practice their faith is neither the intermarriage rate nor attitudes toward Israel. It is the way non-Jews structure *their* religious lives. England has a chief rabbi because the Church of England has the Archbishop of Canterbury. French Jews who tend toward universalism resemble French secularists who do so as well. Russian Jews lost their ties to Judaism because the Soviet Union was formally committed to atheism. And the fast-moving and unusually mobile quality of life in the United States makes it all but impossible for any religion to look back to a presumed golden age. All American religions face the problem of adapting their time-tested beliefs and practices to the realities of a society undergoing constant change. The question is never whether they can find ways to stay the same, for no faith can. The important issue is whether they can adjust, which is precisely what American Judaism is trying its best to do.

V

Judaism is an ethnicity as well as a religion; indeed, so important is the ethnic dimension in Judaism that it contains more than one. Although they spoke different native tongues or once belonged to different social classes, German and Eastern European Jews, for all the historic hostility the former showed the latter, shared the common ethnicity known as Ashkenazi. In contrast, the first Jews to arrive on American shores were Sephardic, or Spanish and Portuguese Jews, and even that category includes the Eastern Sephardim (Iberian Jews who fled to Turkey, Greece, and the Balkans) as well as Mizrahim (Jews from the Arab world), and the Maghrebim (Jews from North Africa).[50] It reflects the global nature of the Jewish people that they not only find themselves living everywhere but that they come from everywhere as well.

Prominent Sephardic Jews have been in the United States from the time of the Revolution (Haym Solomon) through the twentieth century (US Supreme Court justice Benjamin Cardozo and Nobel Prize–winner Salvador Luria) to the present (the late popular singer Eydie Gormé, born Edith Garmezano, and her cousin Neil Sedaka, whose last name is a variation of the Hebrew word for charity, *tzedakah*). But American Jewish life since the great wave that arrived from the Pale in the late nineteenth century has been overwhelmingly dominated by the Ashkenazim, and it is they who have most experienced the great transformation in recent American Jewish life. Because that transformation involved changes in the nature of ethnicity as well as in religion, I will focus primarily upon them.

Ethnicity is an alternative to assimilation. If a few people arrive in a new location, they will likely be unable to resist the pressures to become like their neighbors. But when a million or so people arrive at roughly the same time, and the great bulk of them find themselves in the same city, they can develop an in-group consciousness capable of maintaining their distinctiveness. Although the term *melting pot* was coined by a Jew, the British playwright Israel Zangwill (1864–1926), first-generation American Jews were not all that interested in melting; their preference was for something more like *cultural pluralism*, the term developed by another Diaspora Jew, the philosopher Horace Kallen (1882–1974), to advance the idea that groups could maintain their distinctive features while also becoming part of the larger society to which they belonged. When we look back on an era in which Jews overwhelmingly married other Jews, it was not their faith that tied them together so much as their consciousness of sharing the same ethnic roots.

Far more than religion, ethnicity is spatial by its very nature. For the first generation of immigrants who arrived in New York, which rapidly became the largest Jewish city in the New World, ethnicity's most glorious manifestations could be found on Second Avenue in Manhattan, where the Yiddish theater flourished, or in Brooklyn's

Brownsville, overwhelmed by poverty but still recalled fondly by many for its bakeries, its libraries and schools, the impressive number of writers and intellectuals whose childhoods were spent there, and even mobsters such as Dutch Schultz and Louis "Lepke" Buchalter.[51] The children of those immigrants often found themselves with the means to move upward, finding more spacious apartments in areas such as Brooklyn's Flatbush or the Bronx's Grand Course, modeled on the Parisian Champs-Élysées, but even there they retained their ethnic consciousness; as Deborah Dash Moore writes in her history of New York neighborhoods in the 1920s and 1930s, "The Concourse did not forget its Jewishness in the pursuit of middle-class security."[52] While rooted, ethnicity can also be portable, so long as large numbers of people move together.

Moore's use of the term "Jewishness" in this context is significant. In 1957 the sociologist Nathan Glazer, who grew up in a Yiddish-speaking home in the East Bronx, made an important distinction between Jewishness and Judaism. Religion, Glazer argued, was only one aspect of Jewishness, and it found itself competing, often not very successfully, with socialism, communism, Zionism, and fraternal associations such as B'nai B'rith, let alone a dense world of "Jewish hospitals, orphanages, old people's homes, settlement houses, [and] social agencies for the poor."[53] Among those second-generation New York Jews who were moving up the ladder, synagogues continued to be built and Jewish education was emphasized, "but while all these material advances could be pointed out," Glazer wrote, "it was nevertheless true that the overwhelming majority of the immigrants' children had deserted Judaism. They did not convert, but they were either indifferent or hostile to traditional religion."

Despite its importance to the first and second generation of American Jews, rabbis and other spiritual leaders have never been all that comfortable with this preference for Jewishness over Judaism. Their attitude persisted long after Jews moved out to the suburbs or farther afield to Miami and Los Angeles. On a visit to Los Angeles's Hillcrest Country Club in the 1970s, for example, Edgar Magnin (1890–1984), known as the rabbi to the stars, caustically declared that "I see these guys with their yarmulkes eating bacon on their salads. . . . They want to become more Jewish, whatever that means. It's not religious, it's an ethnic thing. What virtue is there in ethnic emphasis? . . . You know, it's insecurity, the whole thing is insecurity. Roots, roots, roots—baloney."[54] Magnin was a descendant of one of the wealthy San Francisco Jewish families that were strong supporters of Classical Reform. His comments were in line with those of earlier German Jews who insisted that Judaism was a religion and not, God forbid, an ethnicity, the latter being something they identified with Jews from the Pale.

Even in the absence of such class snobbery, a conviction that Judaism matters more than Jewishness continues to characterize those rabbis who find ethnicity vulgar compared to the glory of the psalms or dignity of the Yom Kippur fast. This is certainly the case of England's Rabbi Sacks. "There is nothing challenging in ethnicity," he has written. "It embodies no ideals, no aspirations, no purpose or vocation."[55] So-called Jewish culture, he continued, is not even Jewish. "It is a lingering trace of what Jews absorbed from the circumambient non-Jewish culture: Polish dress, Russian music, North African food, the Spanish-Jewish dialect known as Ladino and a lexicon of local and essentially alien superstitions." In his own contribution to the debate over continuity, Sacks wrote a book entitled *Will We Have Jewish Grandchildren?* In it he warned against taking the findings of the American 1990 National Jewish Population Survey too literally, because for Jews, who are always small in number, counting will inevitably be hazardous. Unlike those who signed *A Statement on the Jewish Future*, furthermore, he argued that it would be a serious mistake to concentrate only on already affiliated Jews. For him the crucial question was what is worth preserving about Judaism in the first place, and his answer was "to be a member of the people of the covenant, an heir to one of the world's most ancient, enduring, and awe-inspiring faiths."[56] It is not the people but the tradition that the present generation's grandchildren ought properly to inherit.

Sacks may prefer Judaism to Jewishness, but to those who believe that Jews can best survive by drawing boundaries between themselves and everyone else, any kind of Jewishness, vulgar or not, offers a potential life raft: if the point is to avoid the next generation of Jews becoming the last one, ethnic consciousness, so long as it serves delaying assimilation and all its dangers, may not be such a bad thing at all. By the time *A Statement on the Jewish Future* appeared, this transition was complete: to its signatories, in contrast to generations of rabbis, Jewishness had become as important as Judaism. Ethnicity was in decline, as one signer of the statement, Steven M. Cohen, pointed out, and so long as that was the case American Jews would be less likely to support Jewish organizations and their agendas, rally to the defense of Israel, and come to the aid of their fellow Jews around the world. Cohen argued that with ethnicity in danger, nothing less than "the very fabric of Jewish life and the very definition of being Jewish" was at stake.[57]

Cohen's occasional collaborator Jack Wertheimer, also a signer of the statement, made an even stronger argument for the dangers that accompany the weakening of ethnic ties in a 2006 essay in *Commentary*. Not that long ago, he pointed out, a concern with Jewishness was readily apparent in American life because "the horrors of the Holocaust and . . . the significance of emerging Jewish statehood unleashed strong feelings of ethnic identification."[58] Not only were those feelings disappearing in a post-Holocaust world, he worried, but "most of the once-traditional props of Jewish peoplehood in this country—large immigrant populations, neighborhoods, Yiddish-inflected folkways, a distinctive cuisine—have faded from the scene. American Jews are now regarded, and appear largely to regard themselves, as part of the undifferentiated mass of American whites, not as a distinctive group in the multicultural 'rainbow.'" Even postmodernism came in for its share of the blame: "In the name of eliminating 'boundaries' between and among people, whether national, ethnic, or religious, this quintessentially postmodern movement celebrates the trans-national, trans-cultural individual. It urges us to sample civilizational offerings wherever they may be found, and from these to assemble our own private identities." For Wertheimer, all this ethnic blending was worse than a melting pot. It more accurately resembled mush.

Wertheimer's fears are not groundless; we do live in a world of spatial diffusion that makes it difficult for neighborhood-based forms of ethnicity to survive. But far from decline, a lack of dense ethnic ties is viewed by others as offering opportunities for what has been called "symbolic ethnicity," "ethnic options," "ethnic identity," or "post-ethnic America," terms proposed by leading American sociologists and historians to characterize the fact that ethnicity is no longer, and perhaps no longer should be, viewed as a process of groups imprinting their values on the individuals who compose them but, like religion, as an identity chosen by individuals to accommodate themselves to the demands of modern life.[59] The scholar who has most extensively explored this way of thinking with respect to Jewish life is Indiana University's Shaul Magid. "Post-ethnic Judaism," as he calls it, is a product of widespread intermarriage and the religious syncretism, or the blending of elements from different faiths, that accompanies it, as well as a trend toward multiple identities of Americans of all religions and races. Magid believes that future generations of Jews, no matter how they are defined or define themselves, will no longer be under the twin spell of the Holocaust and the birth of Israel and will thus be free to express their Jewishness in ways that earlier generations would not recognize but which would still be authentic. "The Jew will survive," he wrote, "perhaps not the ethnic Jew . . . but a new Jew, a figure who not only participates in the larger society, but is integrally, and even biologically, a part of it."[60]

As one might expect, Cohen and Wertheimer regard Magid's new Jew as not very Jewish at all. What Magid says may be accurate as description, they responded together, even if said too exaggeratedly. But such trends are hardly to be welcomed because "those of us who wish to build a strong and authentic Jewish life dare not communicate to our children that everything is up for grabs, that their Jewish descent is non-binding, and that Jewish living is merely one option among a broad array of lifestyle choices."[61] For Wertheimer and Cohen ethnicity remains intimately tied to that densely Jewish world of the 1950s and 1960s. "Sixty-five years after the Holocaust demonstrated the interconnected fate of all Jews, 62 years after the State of Israel was established as a heroic achievement of the Jewish people, and but a few decades after the epic struggle to free Soviet Jewry, a magnificent expression of Jewish solidarity, is Jewish peoplehood suddenly finished, all because America has gone post-ethnic of late?" This is the kind of rhetorical question that seems to contain its own answer, and not one that makes those who pose it happy. The world has become flatter and, lacking dramatic moments that can rally a people together, ethnicity will be on its way out.

Such pessimism, however, may not be warranted: the presumed decline of a rich Jewish life since the two or three decades after World War II does not mean the end of any meaningful conception of Jewishness. In reality, Diaspora Jews are not rejecting ethnicity but redefining it in ways that make sense to them. Continuity worriers such as Cohen and Wertheimer focus only on the negative: as befits their taste for the jeremiad, and as representatives of a once-dominant establishment in decline, they speak in tones of exasperation and dismay. Magid, by contrast, understands that in a world in which Jews confront conditions not fully of their own making, they must retain a positive attitude toward the challenges confronting them. In so doing, he reminds us that ethnicity is not, like the law, handed down by God to his chosen people but is invented out of the conditions of exile in which Jews have found themselves throughout their history. Jews in Golden Age Spain spoke in Judeo-Spanish, a language that ever since has faced extinction, and yet Judaism managed to survive. Jews in contemporary America are becoming increasingly distant from Yiddishkeit, as the Jewishness of Ashkenazi Jews is frequently called, and their ethnic identities will likely survive as well.

VI

"The assimilationist hunger among Jews is epitomized for me," wrote Rabbi Marc Gellman in December 2000, "by a clothing manufacturer named Ralphie Lipshitz, who, with the aid of some blond gentile models, some flannel clothes, and, yes, a few duck decoys, became Ralph Lauren—a Jew who out-gentiled the gentiles."[62] Lauren, Gellman goes on, may not have been the worst. Israel Baline, the Russian-born songwriter who changed his name to Irving Berlin, "stoked the assimilationist legacy with his music," writing not only "Easter Parade" but also "White Christmas," "the most popular Christmas song ever," and in 1942 "when Auschwitz was belching smoke." Finding parallels between assimilation and extinction by the Nazis is an exercise that never seems to lose its appeal.

Gellman was nonetheless willing to forgive both these men because the selection of Senator Joseph Lieberman to run for vice president in the year he wrote his article "definitively ended the assimilationist myth that to succeed in America you have to hide your Jewishness." Leaving aside Jews who change their names who may not be hiding their identity—Irving Berlin is not a name one would associate with gentiles—Gellman's comment is worth citing because it poses one of the most important questions that can be asked of assimilation: Would the world have been better off, indeed would Jews have been better off, if Lauren had designed clothes to be worn only by fellow Jews from Pinsk or if Berlin, the son of a cantor, had opted for his father's career in a New York shul? Lauren's work I leave for others to judge. For me, Berlin's prodigious output and glorious music, sung by almost every popular entertainer from Fred Astaire to Linda Ronstadt, are beyond priceless. Jews have every reason to be proud that one who shares their ethnicity did so much for America. And non-Jewish Americans can take heart that celebrations of both their holidays and their country—Berlin also wrote "God Bless America"—were put to music by someone who was different from them.

Assimilation is a powerful force that disrupts all ethnic communities, not only the Jews. Because assimilation leaves few traces behind—the speed at which American Jews lost familiarity with Yiddish is astonishing—it is easy to compare it to a hurricane destroying everything in its path. The trouble with any such comparisons is that unlike hurricanes, assimilation, as Berlin's music demonstrates, does leave something valuable behind: a new generation possessing sufficient distance from worlds of dense ethnic and religious ties to explore those ties in new and more complicated ways. Despite the fears of all those worried about continuity, secularization and postethnicity do not mean religion and peoplehood disappear; when religion and peoplehood are chosen rather than ascribed, individuals must call upon powers of imagination rather than of memory. No longer able to be taken for granted, Jewishness and Judaism must be re-created.

An interesting example of such re-creation is offered in the realm of fiction. The second-generation Jews who were born and bred into Jewish-saturated environments produced novelists such as Saul Bellow, Philip Roth, and Cynthia Ozick, along with literary critics such as Alfred Kazin and Irving Howe.[63] All these writers thrived in the borderlands between the confines of their neighborhoods and the larger world visible all around them. No matter how much they rejected the religion of their parents in favor of socialism, Zionism, or in some cases neoconservatism, they looked backward for their material; the characters they so vividly brought to life—Arthur Sammler, Nathan Zuckerman, Ruth Puttermesser—were preoccupied with the tragedies of the twentieth century. They were Jewish novelists—and they wrote Jewish novels.

Ethnicity and religion may be in decline, but Jewish contributions to diasporic literature not only continue but in many ways are even more Jewish than those of previous generations. Creative British Jews like Harold Pinter once made their mark by downplaying their ethnic identity, or even becoming highly vocal critics of Israel; now, like Howard Jacobson, they make it central to everything they write. (His book *The Finkler Question* won the 2010 Man Booker Prize.) Meanwhile in the United States, for all the talk of Bellow's passing and Roth's withdrawal, novelists Michael Chabon, Nathan Englander, Jonathan Safran Foer, Allegra Goodman, and Nicole Kraus reach large numbers of readers, and behind them is an even younger group of American novelists that includes Dara Horn, Sara Houghteling, Julie Orringer, and Austin Ratner. These too are Jewish writers, and in their own way they are writing Jewish fiction, but having little or no personal memory of a Jewish golden age to sustain them, they either transform historical events in magical ways (Horn's treatment of the American Civil War) or create fantastic worlds that never existed (Chabon's Sitka and its policemen's union). Jewish fiction has been freed from the confines of ethnicity to explore the wonders of ethnic identity.

Jews can continue to think and act as a people doomed to drown in a sea filled with danger, from Christians, from secularization, and as we shall see in the next chapter, from Muslims—just as they can convince themselves that people with choices will choose something other than Judaism, either for their spouses or with respect to their god. Such fears are stoked by Jewish leaders who, as if against all hope, are convinced that every trend in the modern world is a plot against them. "I think Anglo-Jewish communal leaders need these bogey men— whether Arab terrorists and 'assimilation' and so forth," Clive Sinclair, a British novelist and short-story writer, once told an interviewer.[64] "They *do* exist, but the real question is the nature and severity of the threat. And if they didn't exist—the powers-that-be would certainly invent them." Sinclair may have been speaking about England, but his comment applies wherever Diaspora Jews live. Christians suffer from an often obnoxious tendency to want to share their good news even with people who do not share their faith. Jews suffer from rarely having any good news to share.

Perhaps a less depressing approach may be in order. The truth is that it is no longer possible, and most likely never was, for the continuity of either Jewishness or Judaism to be maintained by resisting larger changes taking place in the world around them. With so many choices to make, and so many ways to make them, continuity is not something for which exhortations can be proclaimed and plans developed. "Assimilation," Gerson Cohen informed the students he addressed in 1966, "is not a one-way street; very much like the Torah itself, it is capable of paralyzing or of energizing, depending on how we react to it."[65] The debate over Jewish continuity has featured all-too-much paralysis. Rabbi Sacks has written that "in Judaism the golden age is always in the future."[66] Speaking religiously, that glorious future will come with the arrival of the Messiah. Thinking demographically, it will come to Jews who, to one degree or another, will be mixed together with the others with whom they live.

CHAPTER 6

Anti-Anti-Semitism

I

Assimilation and anti-Semitism represent radically different responses to the conditions of diasporic life. In the former, Jews are killed with kindness, as gentiles go out of their way to recruit them into their schools, firms, and families; one reason Jews intermarry so often is because non-Jews, far from shunning them, view them as unusually desirable spouses. In the latter, Jews are simply killed, either symbolically through the deployment of crude stereotypes meant to cause them psychic pain or by far uglier means designed to take their lives. It would seem impossible for assimilation and anti-Semitism to coexist: as one goes up, the other must go down.

Despite the ongoing tendency of Jews to assimilate throughout the Diaspora in the past few decades, a number of contemporary observers are reluctant to conclude that anti-Semitism has diminished in our time; if anything, they argue, assimilation has given way for Jew hatred to express itself in an ever-wider variety of forms.[1] There is, as always, the violence that Jew haters, first Christian and now increasingly Muslim, never cease to employ. But anti-Semitism can also appear in acts of exclusion, snobbery and slights that while less deadly can cause their own kind of pain and discomfort. There is allegedly even a specifically Jewish version of anti-Semitism, especially among left-wing intellectuals who, in attacking Israel, offend all those for whom that state has become the symbol, if not the reality, of Jewish survival. It is because of lingering anti-Semitism, we are so often told, that Jews must continue to be particularist at home and Zionist abroad, as willing to call attention to the persistent prejudice against them as to defend the one state that will always take them in. Assimilate if you must, runs the message, but never drop your suspicion of those all around you. If assimilation is the fate for which particularism is the remedy, anti-Semitism is the reality that makes universalism a pipe dream.

Characterized as "the longest hatred," anti-Semitism has been a constant theme throughout Western history.[2] As one comprehensive, recent treatment documents, the Jews have long served as the alien force against which non-Jews have created their very understanding of reality.[3] Given that history, it is possible to conclude that when it comes to anti-Semitism, the primary obligation, if error be made, is to err on the side of caution: the dangers involved in finding anti-Semitism where it may not exist pale in comparison to ignoring situations that could burst out into Jew hatred with just the slightest spark. That anti-Semitism never seems to disappear completely, that these days it raises its ugly face across so much of Europe and around the world, only serves as a warning never to relax where this most insidious of poisons is concerned.

Yet a constant search for ever-fresher forms of anti-Semitism runs the risk of becoming what the British academic Neil Lazarus calls a "Jewish addiction," requiring increasingly strong doses of egregious examples to satisfy its cravings.[4] Unlike periods throughout history in which Jews were the object of so much scorn, today they both have their own state and exercise significant influence in most of the other countries in which they live. Far from representing an appeal for the rights of powerless minorities to live in dignity, repeated accusations of anti-Semitism under such conditions all too often lose their innocence. There is about them not the cry of pain associated with those minorities who face the unrelenting hostility of the majority but little more than contempt toward outsiders and manifestations of pride among insiders. As with fears for Jewish continuity, the claim of un-yielding anti-Semitism is another of those bogeymen called upon to remind Jews that Diaspora equals danger. Dangers there will always be, but the reality is that the barriers once put in place to keep Jews out of the major institutions of gentile societies have crumbled in nearly all the places in which significant numbers of Jews live. Fortunately, at least for those hopeful of a more optimistic Jewish future, as the barriers crumble, so do the last obstacles in the path of universalism's return.

II

Victor Mishcon (1915–2006), the son of a Polish rabbi, was born in Brixton, a poverty-stricken neighborhood in South London that would later erupt in violence among its Afro-Caribbean residents. His career amounted to one success story after another. Mishcon attended the City of London School; became a solicitor; founded a one-man neighborhood law firm; began to attract clients, earn significant money, and acquire political contacts; stood for Parliament; served on the Wolfenden Committee that urged the reform of Britain's harsh laws against homosexuality; acted as a secret intermediary in talks between Israel's Shimon Peres and Jordan's King Hussein; and eventually became a baron and life peer. Because he was not a member of one of the so-called noble Jewish families such as the Rothschilds or the Montefiores, Mishcon, had he been born a century earlier, would have stood little chance of obtaining such honors. His accomplishments illustrate what becomes possible in a postemancipation world in which Jews are allowed to display their full range of talents.

Mishcon's story, moreover, did not end there. After his law practice, now known as Mishcon de Reya, moved to central London and merged with parts of another firm, it became even more prestigious. (In 2010 it established an office in New York City.) The firm defended historian Deborah Lipstadt against the charge that she had libeled the Holocaust-denier David Irving. Its clients included Robert Maxwell, the publisher; the writer and disgraced politician Jeffrey Archer; and Lord Palumbo, the art collector. The most famous of them all was Diana, the Princess of Wales, who sought out Mishcon de Reya to represent her in her divorce from Prince Charles. With that, Mishcon's work had not only reached the highest levels of British public life, it had also become directly involved with the royal family.

One of Mishcon de Reya's partners, Anthony Julius, took charge of Princess Diana's legal affairs. Julius's life amounted to an impressive success story as well: although born in more prosperous circumstances than Mishcon, he was not only a highly regarded lawyer but also the author of a major study of the anti-Semitic leanings of the twentieth-century poet T. S. Eliot. A man of such noteworthy achievements might have concluded that Jews were finally welcome in the British Isles. Julius did otherwise. Yes, he had gone to Cambridge University, he mused, but only after he had been offered a reserve place, that is, a spot for a Jew he could accept only if another turned it down. To be sure, he worked for a leading law firm, but he also knew that it never would have made sense to apply to other firms known for not hiring Jews. Those events happened a few decades ago, when Britain was more parochial and Julius less well known. The real slights, in fact the only times that he had experienced anti-Semitism during his legal career, took place at what should have been its pinnacle. There were two that especially galled him. The *Telegraph*, a newspaper sympathetic to the royal family, sarcastically assigning him the last name "genius," compared his "bullish attitude" with the "softly-softly approach" of the more aristocratic divorce attorney chosen by Charles, Fiona Shackleton.[5] In addition, a pamphlet written by a notorious anti-Semite, Nick Griffin, singled him out for his "paranoid over-sensitivity" that "often creates hostility to innocent Jews where none existed before."

Such experiences, Julius wrote, "inform my own perspective on the threats that now bear down on the Jews." His effort to shed light on these threats, ranging from medieval beliefs about blood libel, through the literary figures of Shylock and Fagin, and down to the violent rhetoric of contemporary British Muslims, resulted in the publication of an 811-page book, *Trials of the Diaspora: A History of Anti-Semitism in England.* Being a public figure taught Julius that anti-Semitism took two major forms: the genteel version of the suites (the *Telegraph*) and the gutter variety of the streets (Griffin). Unlike Nazi Germany, which perfected the latter, the English were typically given to expressions of the former. The one may seem far worse than the other, but Julius nonetheless concluded that England had to be credited with major contributions to Jew hatred: "The anti-Semitism of no other country has this density of history. The anti-Semitism of no other country is so continuously innovative."

Julius had a ready method for making his case that no amount of assimilation can still the ghosts of anti-Semitism: he developed a radar apparatus so sensitive that it can detect Jew hatred in places others might never notice. Walking past a pro-Israel demonstration in London in 2009, he witnessed counterdemonstrators shouting, "How many kids did you kill today?" That slogan was taken from a rhyme originally developed by Americans protesting the Vietnam War:

Hey, hey, LBJ,
How many kids did you kill today?

For Julius, however, the words evoked the most heinous anti-Semitic trope in Western history: the medieval blood libel in which Jews were accused of murdering Christian children in order to use their blood in the making of Passover matzoh. Merely to suggest that Israel's actions may have resulted in the killing of children was taken by him as an expression of a desire to kill Jewish children in return.[6]

Trials of the Diaspora received a warm welcome, especially in the United States. Both the publication of the book and its reception, however, tells us more about ongoing Jewish discomfort in the Diaspora than about the extent of the anti-Semitism to be found there. England has changed, indeed the world has changed, since the days that marked the start of Julius's career when, fearful of Jewish entry into their professions, the leaders of major British institutions really did resort to anti-Semitism to keep them out. One has to search far and wide to find anything like that today: the two contemporary incidents that so disturbed Julius, after all, were not among the most horrible crimes committed against the Jews in their history; and in any case, the *Telegraph* almost immediately offered an apology for its words, while Griffin, for all his vile language, actually considers himself a passionate defender of Israel. Despite Julius's lawyer-like efforts to ignore the fact, far more doors are open to the Jews than at any time in their history. Now that the world has changed, the question is whether Jews have done so as well. If Julius's book is any indication, some seem not to have changed much at all.

III

The American way of welcoming Jews into society's leading institutions has its own lessons to teach. In his effort to tell a major part of that story, the historian David Hollinger reminds us that the United States was once dominated by a "generic, transdenominational Protestantism" that "had come by the end of the nineteenth century to be taken for granted by nearly all of the Americans in a position to influence the character of the nation's major institutions, including those controlling public education, the law, literature, the arts, scholarship, and even science."[7] Of all those institutions, the one that offers the best example of what Hollinger calls "de-Christianization" is the university. It is not just that once they were let in Jews made such important contributions to so many academic fields. It is also that their presence made American academic institutions more open to careers determined by talent, less narrow in outlook, and better able to absorb the findings of modern scholarship. By doing well for themselves, Jews did well for others.

So arbitrary was Jewish exclusion that the process of opening up the university is often told as one of gritty determination on the part of those American Jews, much like Mishcon and Julius in England, wanting nothing more than to reach the highest levels to which their talents could take them. There is much truth in such an account, but in telling it that way we lose sight of the fact that this academic transformation also required farsighted non-Jewish leaders willing to reject long-established practices and traditions. Protestant institutions did not become "de-Christianized" inadvertently. They took active steps to rectify past discrimination, a process that has continued to the present time with respect to other once-excluded groups.

Consider the case of Yale University. Dominated by an emphasis on athletics and gentlemanly deportment in the late nineteenth century, Yale created a culture especially comfortable for privileged WASPs. Its social pyramid, psychiatrist and author Dan A. Oren writes, "was barred to Jews. No Jew reached the top; few had even come close."[8] If the few Jewish students who managed somehow to be accepted—despite Yale's explicitly discriminatory admissions policies—felt considerable coolness, faculty faced outright exclusion. Yale would from time to time accept a Jew on the faculty of its professional schools—the first one, Lafayette B. Mendel, received a full professorship in physiological chemistry in the Sheffield Scientific School in 1903—but no Jew occupied a tenured appointment at Yale College, the true bastion of its self-satisfied Christians, until the end of World War II. Even sociology, a field known for its preponderance of Jews, did not see one in a tenured position at Yale until the end of the 1970s when Rosabeth Kanter was appointed. "By closing itself off to Jews . . . ," Oren points out, "Yale created a legacy of inhospitality that took years to expunge." All the Ivy League universities had a history of discriminating against Jews. Yale's was the worst.

In 2012 Richard Levin stepped down from Yale's presidency after serving nineteen years, the seventh longest term of any Yale president going back to 1701, longer in fact than such illustrious figures as Ezra Stiles (1778–95), Noah Porter (1871–86), and Kingman Brewster (1963–77). How did an institution move in so short a time from one that conspicuously lacked Jewish tenured professors to one that welcomed a Jew as president for so long? Part of the answer lies in the way Kanter received her appointment. In what Oren calls "an unusual move for the university" that took place in 1961, Brewster, then the provost, distraught at sociology's mediocre reputation at Yale, created a special ad hoc committee that recommended adding new strengths to the department.[9] His move broke a long-existing logjam that paved the way for new appointments, eventually including Kanter's. Change comes to American universities slowly, and when it does, it is often at the behest of administrators willing to take on the challenge.

Assuming Yale's presidency in 1963, Brewster was determined to transform other aspects of the university's culture in ways that would open it up to new talent. To do so, he turned to his inner circle of like-minded Protestant reformers, seeking advice from longtime friends such as Cyrus Vance, who would become US secretary of state under Jimmy Carter, and McGeorge Bundy, then serving as President Kennedy's national security advisor. These men not only symbolized the Protestant establishment, they more or less constituted it. Along with other prominent leaders associated with Yale such as Pennsylvania governor William Scranton; John Lindsay, who would soon become mayor of New York; and Elliott Richardson, later to be US attorney general, Brewster was surrounded by those the journalist David Halberstam would later dismiss sarcastically as "the best and the brightest."[10] The reputation of some of them was tarnished by the Vietnam War (Bundy) and the long hot summers of urban America (Lindsay). But their impact on Yale was profound.

With respect to changing Yale's culture, and especially the diversity of the student body, the most important member of that inner circle proved to be R. Inslee (Inky) Clark, selected as director of undergraduate admissions in 1965. Four years before his appointment, Clark, then serving on the admissions committee, was shocked at the anti-Semitism he had found there. "It was incredible," he later recounted. "It was deeply ingrained, more so than for other minorities. . . . One of the reasons nobody [from Yale's admissions office] wanted to go to Brooklyn Tech or Bronx Science or Stuyvesant was because those schools were where the Jews were."[11] Determined to rectify the situation when he became director, Clark bypassed the usual prep schools that had served as feeders for Yale and visited people such as Abe Lass, the principal of Brooklyn's Abraham Lincoln High School, who bluntly told him that he would send Lincoln's top Jewish students to Columbia or MIT but not to Yale.[12] In response, Clark fired most of the existing admissions staff and engaged in a series of reforms that

set off furious reactions at those prep schools. In the process he offended alumni who could not understand why their children were not
being automatically accepted and development officers who worried
that their usual donors would turn off the taps. The ugliest reactions
came from members of the university's board, the Yale Corporation.
One of them, Los Angeles attorney Herbert F. Sturdy, complained
that Clark's actions would lead to an exodus of WASP students comparable to white flight in American cities. Sturdy feared that Jews
would undermine Yale's "civilizing mission and inspiration for leadership," while another member of the corporation bluntly told Clark,
"You're talking about Jews and public school graduates as leaders.
Look around you at this table. . . . There are no Jews here."[13] Brewster
and his team obviously disagreed; from their perspective, Yale did not
educate leaders, it helped make them, and by admitting more students
from diverse backgrounds, Yale would help broaden the base from
which American leaders were chosen. By the 1970s, when Yale's Hillel
was led by Arnold Jacob Wolf, whose Chicago congregation would
later appeal to a young Barack Obama, Yale's determination to make
amends for its restrictive past could no longer be doubted, even if lingering anti-Semitism, as Wolf himself alleged, persisted throughout
the university during that decade.

The author Gregory Kabaservice, who has written a close study of
Yale under this enlightened Protestant leadership, is determined to
give such leaders their due, but precisely because he feels he has to, it
is fair to say that their contributions to American public life have been
generally underappreciated. Even before Yale's reformers had engaged
in any of their actions, they had been denounced by William F. Buckley Jr., the conservative and Catholic founder of *National Review*, as
far too liberal and secular.[14] After their reign had been established,
Buckley ran for a place on the Yale Corporation "on a platform of
undoing the works of Inky Clark," as journalist Nicholas Lehman
put it, "and establishing a policy under which any alumnus son judged
capable of graduating would automatically be admitted."[15] The liberal
Republicans among Yale's leaders, no matter how prominent a role
they may have played in the 1960s, offered the kind of policies that the

rest of the party, in the form of Barry Goldwater and Ronald Reagan, let alone the far more extreme Republicans of today, were determined to repudiate. As prominent an American conservative as Supreme Court justice Clarence Thomas, a graduate of Yale Law School, voted against the very kinds of affirmative action that Yale's leaders were instrumental in creating. Not all the opposition, moreover, came from the right. At the other end of the political spectrum, radicals active in Students for a Democratic Society and similar leftist organizations singled out those who had moved into the ranks of the "best and the brightest," including many with Yale connections, as a focus of their frequent campus-based protests. The political views of Brewster and his circle may have been progressive and their instincts inclusive, but they nonetheless constituted an establishment, and after the turmoils of the 1960s and 1970s establishments were no longer all that welcome in American life.

Jews must be included among those reluctant to show appreciation for the efforts of Brewster and the members of his inner circle to reach out to them. One such member, McGeorge Bundy, a target for protests because of his role in planning the Vietnam War, aroused intense Jewish fury when as president of the Ford Foundation he supported "community control" of the schools in the Ocean Hill–Brownsville section of Brooklyn that resulted in the firing of a number of Jewish teachers. Brewster's and Clark's commitments to affirmative action did not help in this regard, as many American Jews found themselves uncomfortable with policies that in their view bore an unpleasant resemblance to the quotas that had once kept them out of places such as Yale. Nor were matters better on other issues involving race; in an interview reflecting on his life, Yale computer scientist David Gelernter, the Unabomber victim turned neoconservative essayist, called the efforts of Brewster and Clark "a beautiful impulse with dreadful consequences," because it led to the presence of black radicals on campus, and in his view, to Brewster's naïve sympathy for them.[16] One can only wonder, moreover, what the Protestant leaders who open Yale up to Jews would have made of those Orthodox Jewish students who later were happy to attend the university but demanded special living arrangements to keep themselves segregated from other students they compared to the inhabitants of Sodom and Gomorrah.[17] Even those more open to Yale's diversification efforts, such as the Berkeley sociologist Jerome Karabel, found things to criticize in the actions of Yale's reformist leaders. Although he acknowledges that their efforts were "by any standard historic," Karabel also characterizes their work as "a preservationist impulse, dedicated to making the changes that would permit the free enterprise system to survive."[18]

Far from showing gratitude, at least one Jew who was the recipient of Inky Clark's largesse turned to accusations. In 1970 Clark left Yale to become headmaster and later president of the Horace Mann School, an elite private high school in the Bronx. Amos Kamil, an Israeli-born playwright who grew up in the same borough, recounts how Clark, an avid baseball fan, discovered him pitching at his public junior high school and brought him to Horace Mann. During his years at the school, Kamil was vaguely aware that some faculty members may have been engaged in sexual abuse. Inspired by later events at Penn State involving such abuse and cover-up, he interviewed some of his friends from his Horace Mann years and wrote an essay in the *New York Times Magazine* describing their recollections. Like all such cases, one can only feel awful for the victims and rage at the perpetrators. But that does not explain why Kamil would go out of his way to note that Clark, a bachelor, had "a noticeably closer-than-average relationship" with another bachelor, and one of the abusers, on the faculty.[19] Although Kamil later learned that Clark had financed his scholarship to Horace Mann out of his own pocket, he nonetheless found it impossible to extend his thanks: "For reasons I still can't fathom," he said of Clark, "he had gone to the effort of changing my life." It does not seem to occur to Kamil that, even if he may have been a flawed man, and there is no compelling evidence that he was, Clark wanted to do good things for people like Kamil, because he thought they deserved the chance to have the opportunities once denied to their parents and grandparents.

There can be little doubt that Brewster and his inner circle transformed Yale more out of concern for the future of their institution than out of love for the Jews. At the same time, Kabaservice is correct to conclude that "there was nothing inevitable about Yale's move toward meritocracy and diversity."[20] Yale's leaders, after all, could have listened to the advice offered by Buckley and turned their institution into even more of a gentlemen's club. Yet while an Internet search for the words "Kingman," "Brewster," and "gratitude" yields an expression of thanks from an Irish-Italian Catholic from Newark, Richard Conniff, a writer on human and natural behavior,[21] I can find precious little thanks anywhere else, save for one student recruited from Brooklyn's Poly Prep who published his gratitude in the *Yale Alumni Magazine* after an excerpt from Kabaservice's book appeared there.[22] Jews were so convinced that they deserved a place at Yale, a conviction no doubt justified, that they seemed to assume that such places would be granted.

Many reasons exist for Jews not to express appreciation for those who opened up once-exclusive institutions to them, but one stands out. Were prominent Jews to conclude that their success, however much due to their own efforts, also required help from gentiles, they could no longer maintain, as Anthony Julius insists, that anti-Semitism is always and everywhere on the march. Doing so would therefore require them to drop the defensive stance that every insult they may encounter—and who does not at times encounter an insult?—is just the latest form taken by an unbroken chain of hostility directed against them going back thousands of years. The United States, lacking a snobbish and historically exclusive aristocracy, is no doubt better in this regard than the England of which Julius wrote; in a 2010 review of *Trials of the Diaspora*, Harold Bloom, another distinguished Jewish scholar who had found a place on the Yale faculty, gave thanks that his Odessa-born father, after making his way to London, had the good fortune to continue on to the United States.[23] Yet even in America, if the case of Yale is any indication, Jews seem lacking in the confidence that would enable them to become a little more appreciative of just how securely this one part of the Diaspora has offered them a home.

IV

"If I'm confronted by anti-Semitism in my face," said the New York–based financial representative Jeffrey Wiesenfeld to the *Atlantic's* Jeffrey Goldberg, "I'm going to call it out."[24] Like Julius, Wiesenfeld is quick to spot accusations of blood libel all around him, although unlike the British lawyer, he especially finds such charges uttered by Jews themselves: Let any Jew accuse Israel of ethnic cleansing, and Wiesenfeld is certain that he or she is in the same business as those medieval peasants who spread rumors about why Jews were duty bound to kill Christian children. "You've crossed the line if you've said that," he explained to Goldberg. "It's Darfur, Bosnia, Nazi Germany. If you say the Jewish people engaged in ethnic cleansing, then you put them in the class of the Nazis." Wiesenfeld was not speaking hypothetically; he had in mind the well-known playwright Tony Kushner, author of *Angels in America* and, a year after the interview with Goldberg took place, the screenplay of Steven Spielberg's *Lincoln*. Is Kushner, Goldberg followed up, an anti-Semite? "My mother would call Tony Kushner a kapo," Wiesenfeld responded proudly, referring to those concentration camp guards recruited as trustees from among the victims. It was on this basis that Wiesenfeld, a trustee of the City University of New York, worked to deny Kushner an honorary degree from one of its component colleges, even if unsuccessfully.

Wiesenfeld was not exploring new territory when he labeled Kushner anti-Semitic. That ground was prepared in 2006 when the American Jewish Committee sponsored the publication of "'Progressive' Jewish Thought and the New Anti-Semitism," an essay written by Indiana University's Alvin Rosenfeld. Rosenfeld read through the writings of a number of contemporary Jewish left-wingers in an effort to prove that their writings on Israel were tainted with contempt for the Jews. Merely criticizing Israel is not by itself anti-Semitic, he was careful to point out, but anyone who goes beyond what he called "legitimate" criticism of its policies is entering dangerous territory.[25] Left-wing Jewish critics of Israel, he charged, do so in two ways. One is by using such terms as *apartheid, genocide,* and, once again, *ethnic cleansing,* which are meant to convey that Israel is engaged in heinous political evil or in the most egregious cases, in acts comparable to those carried out by Hitler and his henchmen. The other is by questioning Israel's "origins and essence," either by claiming that it came into being through inhumane or criminal acts or by implying that it has no right to exist in the future as a Jewish state.

Rosenfeld included one Israeli among his "progressive" Jews, the philosopher Yeshayahu Leibowitz, an odd choice given that Leibowitz, called the "conscience of Israel" by his fellow Latvian Isaiah Berlin,[26] was Orthodox in his faith and objected to the corruption of his country by both its militarism and its watering down of the Torah, the latter being a position not usually identified with the left.[27] But with this one exception, Rosenfeld found this "new" Jewish anti-Semitism throughout the English-speaking Diaspora, starting in Great Britain (Jacqueline Rose), continuing on to Canada (Michael Neumann), stopping for a short stay with a British American historian of France who had served in the Israeli Army (the late Tony Judt), before turning to a host of Americans including Alisa Solomon, Daniel Boyarin, Joel Kovel, and, it goes almost without saying, Tony Kushner.

Rosenfeld treats these Jewish critics of Israel with a scorn usually reserved for history's worst bigots. For one thing, they are not in his view all that different from them. "The fact that anti-Zionism—understood as the rejection of the long-established right of Jews to a secure national homeland in Israel—shares common features with anti-Jewish ideologies of the past either eludes or fails to trouble Jews who identify with these political tendencies," he wrote. "That is more than just a pity—it is a betrayal. Over the decades, elements within the left stood as principled opponents of anti-Semitism and fought against it. To witness some of their heirs today contributing to a newly resurgent anti-Zionism that, in many ways, recalls older versions of anti-Semitism is dismaying as well as disheartening." For another, the only proper response, once such an equation is established, is not to express disagreement with their views but to dismiss them as too tortured to be worth serious rebuttal. "The extreme anti-Zionism exhibited in the quotations above is not driven by anything remotely like reasoned historical analysis," as Rosenfeld describes the writings of those upon whom he focused, "but rather by a complex tangle of psychological as well as political motives that subvert reason and replace it with something akin to hysteria." Rosenfeld does not call these Jews self-hating in the way such charges have been leveled against Elmer Berger, Philip Weiss, and Judith Butler; given his language, he does not have to.

Jewish anti-Semitism is not, unfortunately, a contradiction in terms: read through what Karl Marx had to say about the Jews and weep. But never in the writings of all those cited by Rosenfeld does one hear of anyone being called a "Jewish nigger," as Marx described the German socialist Ferdinand LaSalle in an 1862 letter to Friedrich Engels,[28] let alone the emphasis on "haggling" that framed one section of his "On the Jewish Question."[29] Nor, for that matter, do any of these Jewish critics of Israel come close to the very paragon of Jewish anti-Semitism, the twisted Austrian Otto Weininger, who in 1903 at the age of twenty-three wrote *Sex and Character*, a book filled with venom against both women and Jews, and then less than four months later killed himself.[30] (Weininger, wrote Amos Elon, "inspired the typically Viennese adage that anti-Semitism did not really get serious until it was taken up by the Jews.")[31] Far from casting aspersions on their fellow Jews in the way Marx and Weininger did, Kushner, for one, is quite capable of saying positive things about them, even ones with whom he strongly disagrees; Roy M. Cohn, the facilitator of Senator Joseph McCarthy's smear tactics who was also gay, is given a surprisingly sympathetic treatment in *Angels in America*. Jewish anti-Semitism has a history, but it is a sparse one. The nineteenth-century German and Austrian Jews, perhaps the worst offenders, were participating in an assimilation process that left them filled with guilt and confusion. Those accused of Jewish anti-Semitism today, by contrast, are fully assimilated, evidently not suicidal, and proud to self-identify. Reading them, one has the sense that they are more critical of Israel than of other countries, not because they are anti-Semites but because they expect so much more from the Jewish state.

One of the most interesting aspects of this relentless search for Jewish anti-Semitism is that it is has been taking place during a period in which the Christian variety has substantially declined.[32] So dramatic has been that decline that the organization whose purpose is to find and publicize examples of anti-Semitism whenever and wherever they take place, the Anti-Defamation League, has had difficulty doing so. In 2011 the ADL uncovered 1,080 such incidents that took place in the United States, a drop from 1,239 in the previous year, broken down into physical assaults (19), threats and cases of harassment (731), and instances of vandalism (330).[33] Given its mission, the ADL expressed its share of caveats: anti-Semitic incidents may be declining as a whole, but acts of vandalism are holding steady; bullying among schoolchildren is all too common; and no count was taken of blogs and websites that might contain anti-Semitic material. One nonetheless cannot help but conclude that numbers such as these are astonishingly small for a country with a total population of 311,000,000.

Those convinced of the unending persistence of Jew hatred nonetheless must have targets, and if real ones are increasingly in short supply, newer ones can always be invented. Adding Jews to the mix of those presumed to be carriers of the anti-Semitic virus accomplishes this task in three ways. First, it shifts the focus from the right to the left. Anti-Semitism has become increasingly marginal on the political right, in large part because conservatives have learned that traces of the overt religious prejudice that were once part of their worldview would stand in their way of their new-found influence. Into the resulting vacuum can be poured left-wingers whose writings can be combed for examples of presumed Jew hatred. Jewish academics, second, are not known for engaging in vandalism—a typical example cited by the ADL is an egg thrown from a passing pickup truck at a Jew in a synagogue parking lot—but they do produce a great deal of words, ever more of them, it would seem, as Israel's actions become increasingly controversial, and adding words to deeds greatly expands the number of targets available to anti-Semitism detectives. Conflating anti-Zionism with anti-Semitism is the third such method of expansion: if it is increasingly difficult to find gross stereotyping of the Jews as people, criticisms of the actions of the Jewish state are made all the time. (This difference matters because criticism of a state is constitutionally protected speech, while criticism of a people can easily turn into stereotyping and bigotry.) If all this is a far cry from the Jewish anti-Semitism of a Marx or a Weininger, it is even further from *anti-Semitism* as the term was coined by the German Jew-hater Wilhelm Marr in 1879. Yet to hunters after anti-Semitism, hatred of the Jews, Proteus-like, is capable of taking insidious forms wherever it appears, and all its forms are viewed as variations on the same theme.

The oddest aspect of this search for anti-Semitism among Jews is that it overlooks the one place in American life where more traditional forms of anti-Semitism still retain their appeal: in the realm of religion itself. In the 1930s and 1940s, the ranks of conservative Christianity were open to Jew haters of many stripes: Gerald L. K. Smith and Gerald Winrod were especially fervent among Protestant preachers, for example, while Father Charles Coughlin was the best known, but far from the only, anti-Semite in the Catholic Church. Although much of this faith-based hostility toward the Jews has withered away, every now and then a public figure from the conservative Christian community is revealed to have expressed views similar to those of a Smith or a Winrod. Two prominent examples can be cited; the Reverend Billy Graham complained privately to Richard Nixon about the Jewish influence on America in the early 1970s, and the Rev. John Hagee, in his book *Jerusalem Countdown*, wrote that Hitler, descended from Esau, was "part Jewish" and that the Jews through their "own rebellion" had "birthed the seed of anti-Semitism that would arise and bring destruction to them for years to come."[34] If one believes, as so many evangelical Christians do, that only by accepting Jesus can salvation be achieved, Jews will always be viewed as needing the correction that only a conversion to a new faith can bring.

Rather than condemning such expressions of contempt for the Jews, however, major Jewish organizations in the United States have welcomed those who utter them. The most striking example is offered by the case of Hagee, whose charge that the Jews brought on the hatred against them through their own acts is as classic an anti-

Semitic trope as one can find, but who nonetheless was invited to address the 2007 convention of the American Israel Political Action Committee, and one year later was given a clean bill of health by the ADL after he pledged "to express my faith in a way that is sensitive to and respectful of others."[35] It may seem odd for Jewish organizations to reach out to right-wing Christians, but once the criterion for finding anti-Semitism becomes not what one thinks of the Jews but how much one supports Israel, Christians who dislike Jews but love Israel are preferable to those cite the Hebrew prophets as forerunners but are critical of the Jewish state. Hagee has his own reasons for considering himself pro-Zion. For him, support for Israel is premised on a theological doctrine that the creation of the Jewish state is a necessary step before the rapture, which will save those true Christians able to survive Armageddon. For others such as Billy Graham's son Franklin, the Jews, although not Christian, are clearly preferable to members of that other monotheistic non-Christian faith, Islam. None of this matters to those who believe that Kushner is far more dangerous to the Jews than Hagee. To avoid the scourge of anti-Semitism, one must welcome anti-Semites into the ranks.

Throughout their history, Diaspora Jews did face the fact of relentless anti-Semitism. The last thing they need, now that non-Jews have finally learned the art of living peacefully and respectfully alongside them, are accusations from other Jews that they are today's equivalents of Hitler and Hamas. When it comes to the question of Israel, political debate, even if not especially contentious political debate, is a healthy sign. Accusations of "betrayal" and "hysteria"—terms employed by Rosenfeld—are not. The bizarre quest to uncover examples of anti-Semitism among Jewish critics of Israel will surely go down as one of the oddest chapters in their long history in the Diaspora.

V

"How did the Jews get back at Hitler?" run the words of what one presumes to be a joke. "They sent him back the gas bill."[36] So spoke a British Muslim cleric, Abdullah al-Faisal, to appreciative laughter at a 2001 event in the English city of Luton. One of his listeners then posed some questions: "Should we hate Jews, and when we see them on the street, should we beat them up?" To which the good cleric replied, "You have no choice but to hate them. How do you fight the Jews? You kill the Jews." These horrific sentiments are cited by Julius toward the end of *Trials of the Diaspora*. If Christian anti-Semitism is no longer as powerful as it once was, and if Jewish anti-Semitism is a far-fetched charge, then the most important source of diasporic anti-Semitism may well be the rancid language and all-too-frequent violent deeds emanating from the world's ever-growing Muslim community, especially, as the Luton story suggests, in Europe, where tensions between these two faiths have been palpable.

In a 2008 report, the highly reputable Pew Research Center found disturbing trends in xenophobia and anti-Semitism throughout much of the European continent.[37] Not all such Jew hatred originates with Muslims. Neo-Nazi and ultranationalist parties, such as Golden Dawn in Greece, Jobbik in Hungary, and Svodoba in the Ukraine, while clearly anti-Semitic, contain more than their fair share of native-born Europeans who in all likelihood hate Muslims as well as Jews. But all too much of it does. France in particular has witnessed serious Islamic-based violence against Jewish targets. Toulouse, for example, was not only where four Jews, including three children, were killed by a French Muslim in 2012, but it has also been the scene of repeated anti-Semitic vandalism since.[38] Saudi-run schools in Great Britain, according to the BBC program Panorama, rely on textbooks filled with anti-Semitic words and pictures, including descriptions of Jews as "monkeys and pigs."[39] Malmö, Sweden's third largest city, which has one of the largest percentages of Muslims anywhere on the continent and whose mayor once suggested that Jews bring hatred on themselves, has experienced record-breaking numbers of attacks, including an explosive placed in front of a Jewish Community Center.[40] A survey conducted by the Belgian sociologist Mark Elchardus found that half of the Muslim schoolchildren in Brussels hold anti-Semitic views.[41] One can argue about why these things are happening. But that they are indeed happening is obvious. Had large numbers of Muslims not made Europe their home over the past decades, anti-Semitism would no doubt still exist there. That so many have only adds to a potentially combustible mix.

For some writers, Muslim hostility against European Jews is just the latest chapter in a long history of Islamic intolerance.[42] Islam, they contend, has always been a violent faith, shaped above all by its fascination with holy war. Jews, from such a perspective, offer an opportunity for hatred Muslims simply never have been able to resist. The Prophet himself, according to this line of thinking, expelled the Jews from Medina. In subsequent years, for example, during the eighth- and ninth-century Abbasid caliphates of Harun al-Rashid and al-Mutawakkil, Jews were forced to wear distinctive markings, setting a precedent for the Nazis to follow centuries later with their yellow stars. Even during the so-called Spanish Golden Age of interfaith coexistence, they were nonetheless *dhimmis*, or second-class citizens. Throughout the rest of the Middle Ages they were forced either to convert or to face death in Yemen, Morocco, and what we now call Iraq. They were subject to the charge of blood libel in Damascus in the nineteenth century. In the twentieth, the Nazi campaign against them was cheered along by figures such as Haj Amin al-Husseini (1897–1974), the grand mufti of Jerusalem, who lived in Germany, helped the Nazis with their genocidal efforts in Bosnia, urged on them the need to find a solution, any solution, that would prevent Jews from emigrating to Palestine, and then spread his anti-Semitic poison throughout the Middle East after Israel came into existence. His work was carried on by Hasan al-Banna, the founder of the Muslim Brotherhood in Egypt; Sayyid Qutb, whose writings inspired the attacks on the World Trade Center; and in our time by the terrorists associated with Hamas and Hezbollah. "The totalitarianism—and the evil—of Islamic Jihadism," writes David Patterson of the University of Texas at Dallas, whose book *A Genealogy of Evil* is only one of many that promotes such a point of view, "exceeds even that of National Socialism, extending as it does not only throughout this world but also into the next."[43]

History rarely unfolds in quite so consistent a manner, however, and many of the incidents that constitute this presumably unbroken chain of Jew hatred, especially in more modern times, do not quite fit the role assigned to them. It is true, for example, that Damascus became obsessed with charges of blood libel in 1840. But since, as Rabbi Sacks points out, "the Blood Libel makes sense only to those who believe in transubstantiation," it was the Christians in that city, especially those associated with the French consulate, and not the Muslims, who were the most engaged with it.[44] Along similar lines, the fact that the Holocaust extended its reach to Muslim Bosnia overlooks that it was even more prevalent in predominantly Christian countries such as Poland and Romania. (Bulgaria, which also has a significant Muslim population, was one of the only European countries whose Jews for the most part survived.) The truth is that the history of Islamic-Jewish relations is far from one of nonstop conflict. "There is nothing in Islamic history," Bernard Lewis has written, "to parallel the Spanish expulsion and Inquisition, the Russian pogroms, or the Nazi Holocaust."[45] Among Arab countries, moreover, the same pattern held until the twentieth century: "Despite ominous developments in the wider world," the historian Martin Gilbert explains, "the life of the Jews in some Muslim countries was never better than in the 1920s."[46] Such coexistence continued into the next, and most horrific, decade. When Hitler assumed power in Germany, the Iraqi Jewish community, 120,000 strong, was not threatened; and in North Africa a ruler such as Ahmed Pasha, Bey of Tunis, Gilbert continues, "showed his contempt for Vichy's anti-Jewish laws by granting exemptions to several leading Jews." (Never mentioned by those who insist on the unshakable hostility of Muslims toward Jews is that North African leaders frequently resisted the determined efforts of officials in Vichy France to persecute Jews of North African origin living there.) Along similar lines, Si Kaddour Benghabrit, rector of the Grand Mosque of Paris, as the film *Les Hommes Libre* shows, provided refuge to a small number of French Jews.[47] Contemporary Muslim-inspired anti-Semitism in Europe, in short, runs against, not with, the historical record.

Of all the points in what is offered as unforgiving Muslim anti-Semitism, the most crucial role is generally assigned to al-Husseini.

No one can doubt the mufti's vile anti-Semitism. Yet the idea that he acted as the transmission belt responsible for shifting anti-Semitism from war-torn Europe to the war-plagued Middle East cannot stand close examination. Al-Husseini was widely distrusted by other Palestinian and Arab leaders who found his demagoguery and extremism counterproductive to the cause of Palestinian nationalism. (For the same reason, he was a godsend to the Zionist revisionists, his views and actions serving as confirmation of their argument that the Arab problem could be solved only through violence.) However important he may have been during the 1930s, moreover, his influence waned after the state of Israel came into existence: although popular in the Arab world because of his militancy, he played little role in the emergence of the Palestine Liberation Organization and Fatah, its political offshoot. Controversy will always surround this man. Still, one thing about him is indisputable: more attention is paid to him by supporters of Israel than by its critics: Peter Novick pointed out that the article on him in the *Encyclopedia of the Holocaust*, published by Yad Vashem in Israel, was longer than the articles devoted to Goebbels, Goring, Himmler, and Heydrich,[48] while Gilbert Achcar, a Beirut-born French scholar, found ten times as many mentions of his name on English-language websites as on Arabic-language ones.[49]

If the example of the mufti teaches anything, it is that Muslim-inspired anti-Semitism is very real—and that far from being a constant, unvarying, phenomenon, it breaks out due to particular contexts and situations. Two words of caution are therefore in order before concluding that the current situation in Europe proves that Jews, once again, will never be safe in the Diaspora. One is that we should not become so preoccupied with Islamic anti-Semitism that we ignore ongoing efforts at cooperation between the two faiths. The other is that precisely because Islamic-inspired anti-Semitism in Europe has been so very real, special care should be taken not to repeat the mistake of conflating genuine race-based hatred of Jews with political criticism of Israel.

In the United States, Christians, Jews, and Muslims, for all the differences between them, have from time to time identified a common enemy in secularism. Much the same is true in Europe, where Judaism and Islam are minority faiths united by the conviction that they are outnumbered not only by Christians but even more so by nonbelievers. At an interfaith parlay held in Paris in 2012, for example, Viatcheslav Moshe Kantor, president of the European Jewish Congress, pointed to bans on ritual slaughter as an issue that united Jews and Muslims, and he issued a call for unity between the two faiths that was endorsed by Mustafa Ceríc, the grand mufti of Sarajevo.[50] Head coverings, holiday observance, cemetery burials, military chaplains, women's clothing, circumcision—all offer opportunities for leaders of both faiths to claim that their religious freedoms are being violated. As religious minorities, Jews and Muslims find themselves in a similar position, and in that way will always to some degree be tied together. This is even more so because they represent only two of the many minority religions that now exist on the once predominantly Christian European continent. In the French city of Bussy Saint-Georges outside Paris, where secularism has long been a way of life, land was set aside to house not only a mosque and a synagogue but also a Laotian Buddhist pagoda and a Taiwanese Buddhist temple, all of them within view of a Roman Catholic church. Asked about his relations with the other faiths, Farid Chaoui, a leading Muslim in the town, replied that "we're for cohabitation, and we're very optimistic."[51] Chaoui specifically included the Jews among those with whom he would be living.

It is not just among the most devout that efforts such as these take place. Ethnicity characterizes Muslims as it does Jews, and like numerous immigrants before them, European Muslims find themselves simultaneously wanting to preserve traditional ways of life while integrating themselves into a new world. Having negotiated the same difficult terrain before them, Jews offer a model of how Turks, Moroccans, and Pakistanis might proceed. For every fiery cleric there are thousands of ordinary people learning a new language, being exposed to customs with which they are unfamiliar, and adjusting to the demands of work and family life. It is true that second-generation European Muslims, often depicted as seething with anger, tend to be more attracted to radical religious and political movements than their parents.[52] Not only was the same thing true of many a second-generation New York Jew, even if it took more political than religious form, but radicalism, to the degree it represents a voluntary choice, is itself a step away from the more circumscribed traditional ways of life. Assimilation in one form or another is the ultimate fate of all ethnic groups, which is one reason European governments are working actively to support policies and programs designed to smooth the path toward greater integration of their Muslim communities. In return, Muslim leaders, for the most part, have toned down the rhetoric. "Even more than street protests," writes the political scientist Jonathan Laurence, a close student of these trends, "Islamic activism increasingly takes the form of institutional consultation, lobbying, and lawsuits."[53] Those are not venues in which overt displays of anti-Semitism are welcome.

Overlooking such examples of cooperation between Muslims and Jews, European anti-Semitism watchdogs, like their American counterparts, are quick to exaggerate the extent of Jew hatred by finding instances of anti-Semitism on the part of anyone who has critical things to say about the Jewish state. Not surprising, Jewish critics of Israel whose views they deem illegitimate offer one inviting target. The British journalist Robin Shepherd, for example, calls such left-wing Jews self-negating rather than self-hating.[54] That would be too kind a characterization for the Kazakhstan-born, English historian Robert Wistrich, currently living and teaching in Israel. He writes of such historians as Oxford's Avi Shlaim and the late Tony Judt that they "continue to rationalize terrorism, trivialize anti-Semitism, and demonize Israel in a shameful manner" and that "they can match and often surpass the most anti-Semitic Gentiles in their demonization of the Jewish state."[55] The United States clearly has no monopoly when it comes to conflating Israeli critics who are Jewish with the world's worst haters.

Unlike in the United States, which has such a large number of Jewish public intellectuals, the bulk of European attention on this matter is paid to non-Jewish writers and thinkers. Because he is German, and charges of anti-Semitism take on a special meaning given

Germany's Nazi history, the views of the journalist and blogger Jakob Augstein are especially noteworthy. (Augstein is the adopted son of the founder of the widely read weekly *Der Spiegel,* and his biological father, according to his mother, is the prominent German novelist Martin Walser.) For a series of statements criticizing Israel's nuclear weapons, influence in Washington, actions in Gaza, and reliance upon the ultra-Orthodox, Augstein was named number nine in a list of the world's "top ten" anti-Semites by the Los Angeles–based Simon Wiesenthal Center in 2012. But that was just the start of the controversy: the Polish-born German Jewish writer Henryk Broder, often compared to Christopher Hitchens because of his provocative essays, followed up by denouncing Augstein as a "pure anti-Semite" and "little Streicher," a reference to Julius Streicher, one of the ugliest anti-Semites of the Nazi era, "who only missed the opportunity to make his career with the Gestapo because he was born after the war."[56] If assimilation inevitably invites comparisons to the Nazi era, so do charges of anti-Semitism. Are such charges fair? By almost any objective criteria, they are not; Augstein's views, certainly strongly stated, bear no relation at all to *Der Stürmer,* the outlet for Streicher's bile. In any case, all this name-calling takes place at far remove: Augstein was more than willing to defend himself publicly against the Wiesenthal Center's case against him, but the organization refused an invitation to debate him, insisting that he apologize first.

Muslims, rather than Christians, offer a final target for those unprepared to accept that people may criticize Israel for the simple reason that they object to its policies. Whatever the original national background of many European Muslims, including those not from the Middle East, support for the Palestinian cause tends to be strong. Consequently, so are the words they choose to condemn Israel's actions. The 2004 remarks of Sir Iqbal Sacranie, at the time secretary general of the Muslim Council of Britain, are fairly typical. "Now the evidence is incontrovertible," he declared on that occasion. "What we are seeing is a creeping genocide of the Palestinian people. It is palpably clear that the Israeli campaign is calculated and deliberate."[57] In so doing, Sacranie violated one of the rules established by those who make distinctions between legitimate and illegitimate criticism: he used the term *genocide*, even if modified, to characterize the actions of the Israeli state. "To compare Israel's treatment of the Palestinians with the Holocaust and to call it genocide is abhorrent," Shepherd responded. "It could also be construed as diminishing the Holocaust by equating it with antiterrorist measures. Such statements are deeply insulting to the Jewish people and are an affront to civilised values." That Sacranie was knighted by Queen Elizabeth did not deter Shepherd from his attack; on the contrary, it fueled it. Because Jews were the victims of horrific evil, Shepherd and those of similar views were claiming, no use of a term conveying horrific evil can be used against Israel.

Europeans have their own reasons for collapsing the distinction between anti-Zionism and anti-Semitism. Unlike in the United States, where support for Israel is strong, negative stereotypes about the Jews in Europe, they believe, may well worsen a situation in which anger at Israel is already deeply entrenched. In addition, they tell us, Europeans are too comfortable in their lifestyles to denounce the evil of radical Islamism and too pacifist in their views to support Israel's campaigns against it, breeding a kind of fashionable left-wing criticism that is unwilling to confront Europe's sizable Muslim populations, even at the cost of offending its far smaller Jewish ones. Shepherd is illustrative of those who argue from such a vantage point. For him, life in modern Europe "offers up a vision of civilisational exhaustion: a continent not so much energised by tolerance, pluralism, and peaceful coexistence as one of energised by nothing at all." The Jews, he reminds us, were the victims of the Holocaust. Just as naïve Europeans turned their backs on the Jews then, an all-too-decadent Europe is ignoring the plight of the Israelis now.

The exact opposite may well be closer to the truth: because anti-Semitism is more evident in Europe than in the United States, it is all the more important to separate criticism of Israel from hatred of the Jews. As the British commentator Jonathan Freedland has written, "distinctions matter" when it comes to this subject. Distinctions are precisely what are ignored when Jews believe that "the calendar might say 2013 but the year is forever 1930, with the Jews of Europe on the verge of another catastrophe—and once again too blind to see it coming," as Freedland puts it.[58] Once one assumes catastrophe is just around the corner, it becomes impossible to recognize that the criticisms made of Israeli policies by Sacranie and Augstein, no matter how vehemently expressed, are worlds apart from the bigotry and violence-promoting preachings of Luton's al-Faisal. (Reading Julius's description of al-Faisal's recommendation to kill all the Jews chilled my blood.) Thus is reinforced one of the oddest features of contemporary efforts to identify and condemn anti-Semitism: persistent efforts to deflect attention from the ugliest expressions of sheer hatred by equating them with what are, in the end, disagreements that constitute the very stuff of ordinary political life. Jews have sufficient enemies in Europe; they do not need to add gratuitously to their number. Creating new enemies out of whole cloth can only benefit those who want to collect as many anti-Semites as possible to provide justification for Israel to do anything it considers necessary.

Freedland, who was criticized from a wide variety of quarters for his relatively optimistic take on these matters,[59] is clear that anti-Semitism very much exists in Europe; he wrote a positive review of *Trials of the Diaspora* for the *New Republic*.[60] What he does not understand are those Americans who take every example of anti-Semitism recounted to them, true or not, as proof that a new Nazi era in Europe is about to make its appearance. Yet this presumed reappearance of Hitler has been all too common a feature of diasporic life in the years after Hitler's death. Unaccustomed to being welcomed into institutions that once excluded them, convinced that their own ranks are filled with fellow Jews so perverse that they fail to love Israel with all their hearts, willing to overlook the virulent anti-Semitism existing among Israel's supporters in the Christian right, these Diaspora Jews cannot help but feel that Muslims around the world, and especially in Europe where the Jews once came so close to being destroyed, must be brimming with hatred toward them. Some indeed are. The tragedy lies in failing to recognize that not all feel the same way. Every Jew ought to want to ensure that whatever anti-Semitism remains in the world gets consigned to the same burial grounds as the anti-Semitisms of the past. That goal cannot be achieved when those who engage in the worst forms of anti-Semitism, such as al-Faisal, are told that they are not alone, that in fact there are ever-growing numbers of people just like them, some of whom are themselves Jewish. Real anti-Semites should be fought, not offered comfort.

VI

The University and College Union (UCU) is a trade union representing teachers throughout the United Kingdom. It is also an organization that has called for academics to boycott Israel. One of the UCU's most controversial actions involved the European Union's working definition of anti-Semitism. That definition included as examples of Jew hatred attempts to "target the state of Israel as a Jewish collectivity," for example, by "denying the Jewish people their right to self-determination, e.g., by claiming that the existence of a State of Israel is a racist endeavor" or by "applying double standards by requiring of it a behavior not expected or demanded of any other democratic nation."[61] Arguing that such a definition "confuses criticism of Israeli government policy and actions with genuine antisemitism, and is being used to silence debate about Israel and Palestine on campus,"[62] the UCU in May 2011 passed Resolution 70/2011 dissociating itself from the EU's approach. Academics should feel free to criticize Israel strongly, the union claimed, without facing the charge that in doing so, they were engaging in Jew hatred.

The UCU contains a number of Jewish members, and one of them, Ronnie Fraser, a mathematics instructor and the director of Academic Friends of Israel, did believe that criticism of Israel too often becomes indistinguishable from anti-Semitism. Fraser decided to fight back against the leaders of his organization by filing a lawsuit against them. To help him in his efforts, he hired Anthony Julius, who by then had become deputy chairman of Mishcon de Reya. On July 1, 2011, Julius wrote a three-page letter to Sally Hunt, general secretary of the UCU, in which he charged that the UCU was "not a place that is hospitable to Jews" and that his client faced an environment that was "humiliating," "hostile," "degrading," and "offensive."[63] Julius demanded the repeal of Resolution 70/2011 and called for "an open and unqualified acknowledgment by the UCU that it has been guilty of institutional anti-Semitism, and a public apology in this regard both to its Jewish members and ex-members, and those other members and ex-members who have complained about or who otherwise deprecate this anti-Semitism." The resulting lawsuit received the strong support of most of the major British Jewish organizations and featured an impressive array of witnesses claiming that they too felt demeaned by the UCU's words. With the UCU on one side and much of official British Jewry on the other, the case offered the British judiciary a chance to pass judgment on the notion, firmly held by so many Diaspora Jews, that criticism of Israel amounts to hatred of them.

As fine a scholar of T. S. Eliot as Julius may be, he is not, if this particular case is cited as evidence, an especially effective lawyer: in April 2013 a three-person employment tribunal, chaired by Judge A. M. Snelson, rejected nearly all the claims made by Julius on Fraser's behalf. As if annoyed that anyone could take seriously the idea that the expression of public positions on Israel could be confused with institutional discrimination, the tribunal declared that "a belief in the Zionist project or an attachment to Israel or any similar sentiment cannot amount to a protected characteristic. It is not intrinsically a part of Jewishness."[64] There is no equivalent in the United Kingdom to the First Amendment of the US Constitution, which guarantees freedom of speech; courts there are thus more inclined than those in the United States to the view that words found to be hurtful can indeed degrade and humiliate individuals. But in this case the judges found absurd the idea that criticism of another country amounted to discrimination against Fraser and other British Jews.

One could, of course, interpret the court's actions as proof positive of Julius's thesis that anti-Semitism in England is still alive and well: one can hear those offended by the decision asking themselves, how can non-Jews possibly understand the close identification with Israel that Diaspora Jews feel? The irony in thinking this way, however, is rich. Throughout their long history in the Diaspora, Jews, very much including Julius himself, understood themselves as fully capable of living up to the talents they knew they possessed. Now that their virtues finally have been recognized and their careers ensured, a determined effort to insist that they are still hated, still the victims of intentional discrimination, and still second-class citizens who will never be fully accepted comes across as little more than what Jews call kvetching. Anti-Semitism, Julius wrote in *Trials of the Diaspora*, "permits the luxury of self-pity, and the moral status associated with being a victim, without any of the perils that define that condition."[65] A better description of Julius's own outlook would be difficult to find.

CHAPTER 7

The End of Exilic History?

I

In 2010 Thilo Sarrazin, a German politician and banker, published a book, *Deutschland schafft sich ab*, or *Germany Does Away with Itself*, so critical of Muslim immigrants that it easily spilled over into the ugliest of racial and religious stereotyping. When the Social Democrats refused to expel Sarrazin, Sergey Lagodinsky, founder of a Jewish-oriented group within the party, resigned. "As a Jewish person," he declared, "I had seen a possibility to revive Germany's long Jewish tradition together with other minority and majority groups in our country. That hope is now dashed."[1] An immigrant who arrived in Germany at the age of eighteen—he was born in Astrakhan, then part of the Soviet Union, in 1975—Lagodinsky had moved to a country that had become visibly, and unalterably, multicultural. It was therefore unacceptable, he believed, to hang out a sign saying "'The party is closed for Easter; Muslims and non-believers wait outside."[2] Like his fellow Jews arriving in Germany from the former Soviet Union, Muslim immigrants had unpacked and stored away their suitcases. Because Germany had become the home to both communities, their representatives were under an obligation to become involved in

German politics; for his part, Lagodinsky shifted his allegiance to the Greens.

Lagodinsky belongs to a generation of Jews that no longer lives in the direct shadow of the Holocaust and the birth of the Jewish state. Unlike so many who left the Soviet Union, he did not move to Israel, or for that matter to the United States, but to a country that earlier generations of Jews refused to visit, let alone make their home. He was, in addition, born at a time when Israel had already established itself as a successful state; the War of Independence (1948), the Sinai campaign (1956), the Six-Day War (1967), and the Yom Kippur War (1973) all preceded his entry into the world. Lagodinsky is fully aware that he represents a new generation of Jews: one of his major goals is to gain recognition, especially from established German Jewish organizations, of those who like him are both secular and born abroad. In his words and actions, it is as if we are back in the 1940s when so many American Jewish organizations responded to the Holocaust by urging action against all forms of injustice and not just those directed against the Jews. The question with which this book concludes is whether the kind of universalist sensibility Lagodinsky represents will increasingly become typical of the generation to which he belongs.

II

In discussing the prospects of a revival of Jewish universalism, one cannot ignore that Lagodinsky is European. Europe occupies a unique position in the Diaspora. It is, for one thing, the place where most of the world's Jews survived their long history in exile; as the writers Sandra Lustig (Germany) and Ian Leveson (the United Kingdom) point out, "Haskalah, Ladino, klezmer, Reform Judaism, Yiddish, Bundism, Hasidim, gefilte fish, and the Frankfurt School were all created in Europe."[3] But Europe, of course, was also where so many millions of Jews met their deaths at the hands of not one but two totalitarian dictators. Because the horror of the latter so outweighed the benefits of the former, some predicted that there would be no place for European Jews in a postwar world in which Israel offered pride and the

United States opportunity. "The problem is that there is little evidence that in the conditions of the contemporary European Diaspora, Jews have, any longer, the minimal internal resources to respond effectively to the challenge and the potentialities of a genuine cultural pluralism," wrote the British-born, University of Chicago historian Bernard Wasserstein in 1997. "Slowly but surely they are fading away. Soon nothing will be left save a disembodied memory."[4]

In retrospect, Wasserstein's account of this "vanishing Diaspora," like fears for Jewish continuity in the United States, proved exaggerated. Although it is difficult to obtain precise figures, according to one compilation France, the destination of twin streams of immigrants from both Eastern Europe and North Africa, in 2012 contained more Jews (480,000) than all the states of the former Soviet Union plus all the Eastern European satellites that once defined the Soviet bloc combined (382,500).[5] Despite Anthony Julius's warnings about the pervasiveness of English anti-Semitism, it is fair to say, as the historian Todd Endelman has, that "at the end of the twentieth century, despite its declining numbers, Anglo-Jewry exhibited greater liveliness, self-confidence, and diversity than at any time before."[6] Everyone knows that Anne Frank was unable to survive World War II in her secret Amsterdam hiding place, but few know that two postwar mayors of that city, Ivo Samkalden and Job Cohen, shared her faith. Sweden's Jewish population is higher now than it was before the Holocaust.[7] The place that once welcomed Jews and then notoriously expelled them, Spain, is friendly once again: "Nowadays Jews, both individually and collectively enjoy a richer and more prosperous life in Spain than at any time during the past century," writes Raanan Rein, vice president of the University of Tel Aviv, and coauthor Martina Weisz of the Vidal Sassoon International Center for the Study of Anti-Semitism at the Hebrew University of Jerusalem.[8] Most remarkable of all is the country that attracted Lagodinsky, which now has well over 100,000 Jews. Reflecting on the work that Lagodinsky and similarly minded younger German Jews have undertaken, Y. Michal Bodemann, a sociologist at the University of Toronto, concluded that "today, German Jewry is the most dynamic Jewish Diaspora in Europe and worldwide."

The "astonishing reemergence of Berlin Jewry," as Bodemann describes it, suggests that there is a future, and a potentially vital one, for European Jews after all.[9]

We are used to hearing that Europe today continues to be haunted by the poison of Jew hatred brought to its ultimate expression in the horrors of twentieth-century totalitarianism. As I suggested in the previous chapter, it is not difficult to find examples of anti-Semitism on the continent that serve as all too unfortunate reminders of that history: physical and verbal attacks on Jews have always existed and, alas, are unlikely ever to disappear, especially in Eastern Europe and, as some recent events suggest, France. In focusing so much on the continuity of such a hateful past, however, we lose sight of how much has changed in a positive direction; the European Diaspora is being transformed more than it is vanishing.

In one way, European Jewry is like its American counterpart; Jews in both places have chosen not to live in Israel. But European Jews also find themselves in countries whose Jewish population is neither as large nor as influential as the one in the United States. (French Jews, the largest such community in Europe, represent .07 percent of the total French population.) At one level this renders Europe's Jewish population politically weak; in a democratic age, where numbers count, the numbers simply are not there. But in another sense their low numbers make them typical of Jews throughout their history. If being in a minority teaches the blessings of exile, European Jews are doubly exiled: from both their American and their Israeli counterparts.

One thinker who has assumed a special prominence in working toward a rebirth of European Jewry is a woman who has been called "the grand lady of optimism" on this issue, Diana Pinto.[10] A Parisian born to Italian parents and educated at Harvard, Pinto believes that only in the past couple of decades has it become possible to create a genuine European Jewish identity. Throughout the postwar decades, she has written, the Holocaust was displaced from Europe as American Jews found in its memory a sense of victimhood and Israelis a justification for statehood; the result was that European Jews came to be viewed as "second class assistants in the great Jewish play unfolding in Israel and in America, with the added misfortune of performing on a lateral and badly lit stage with an indifferent public."[11] All this changed as the twentieth century came to an end. The collapse of communism in 1989 was a crucial moment: those East European Jews who stayed on the continent, having done so by choice, broke the pre-Shoah pattern of Jewish life in which an elite monopolized whatever possibilities for assimilation existed, leaving either Orthodoxy or Zionism to appeal to the more oppressed Jews of the Pale. In addition, movements toward a more unified Europe made it increasingly possible to speak of European rather than English, German, or French Jews. Jews everywhere faced challenges in the twenty-first century, but "in Europe, perhaps because they are spelled out for the first time across the continent, they take on a special significance and even symbolism."

Pinto views European Jewry as constituting the third side of a triangle, with Israel and the United States forming the other sides. American Jews, she believes, are not only engaged in a quest to recall a European past with which European Jews are all too familiar, they have also become too obsessed with their own survival. Meanwhile Israel, widely believed to be the instigator of so many injustices against the Palestinians, alienates those European Jews who view the United States as too supportive of Israel to criticize what they believe to be its repeated violations of human rights. "In the future," Pinto concludes, "European Jewry may well end up being a point of equilibrium between the Israeli and the American poles of world Jewry." To the latter it can offer real history instead of nostalgia. To the former, it serves as a reminder of the pluralism that a society increasingly unable to escape the grip of the ultra-Orthodox requires if it is ever to have a more democratic future.

A number of thinkers and activists are already filling the role that Pinto holds out for European Jews. One, Tamarah Benima, a Dutch journalist, columnist, and rabbi, proposed a useful metaphor. "The Holocaust," she told the British writer Nick Lambert, who had written a book based on interviews with many like her, "functioned rather like a neutron bomb: it left the Dutch buildings and general social, political, and economic institutions intact, but the Jews were wiped out, and the holes were filled again with non-Jews."[12] The others with whom Lambert spoke were trying to refill those holes, some by identifying with the social movements of the 1960s, others by becoming deeply engaged with their professions. These Jews by no means share the same political views; on the question of European integration, for example, some view it as the fulfillment of Jewish universalistic values while others are put off that so many of the advocates for a united Europe had been Christian and spoke in Christian terms. At the same time, Lambert uncovered few exponents of particularism among them; instead, they view their commitments to social justice, respect for the natural environment, and support for governmental reform as expressions of their chosenness as Jews. Benima's attitude toward the Israelis exemplifies this sense of diasporic universalism; using the German term for soil, as well as the one for an admirable person, she says, "I think Diaspora is good not only for Jews but for everyone. It makes you more of a *Mensch* if you are not defined by *Boden*."

Of the organizations that have taken upon themselves the task of creating a new European Jewish consciousness, one of the most interesting is Paideia, the European Institute for Jewish Studies, which is located in Stockholm. Begun in 2000 with support from the Swedish government and the Wallenberg Foundation, its most important activity is an annual one-year fellowship devoted to the interpretation of Jewish texts, from the Bible and the Torah to modern Jewish philosophy, using the hevruta methodology in which a pair of participants reflect on what they have read, and in that sense create a new text out of the old one. (English is the official language of the programs but students also make use of *ulpan*, the deep Hebrew immersion program developed in Israel for new immigrants.) As of 2013, 192 individuals from 32 countries had completed the program; slightly over half of them then went on to work in or for Jewish organizations, among them the vice president of the youth department of the Jewish community of Sarajevo, an analyst on Czech radio of Jewish and Israeli affairs, a Jewish tour guide in Budapest, and a Turkish woman helping recent immigrants to Israel.[13]

Paideia is the inspiration of Barbara Lerner Spectre. Born in Madison, Wisconsin, in 1942 and educated at Barnard and New York University, Spectre made aliyah and spent much of her adult life in Israel, where she was affiliated with the Shalom Hartman Institute, the Melton Center for Jewish Studies at the Hebrew University of Jerusalem, and the Yellin College of Education. In 1999 she and her husband moved to Sweden, he to become the rabbi of Stockholm's Great Synagogue and she to start her new effort. Sweden does not contain large numbers of Jews, and those that are there tend to be so eclectic that the social psychologist Lars Dencik calls them practitioners of "*smörgåsbord* Judaism."[14] But it does, especially when compared to neighboring Denmark, hold out a welcome sign for immigrants, rendering its demographic composition more multicultural than the older Scandinavian image of all-white and culturally homogeneous societies. Like Lagodinsky, Spectre believes that Jews can play a crucial role in the inevitable European transition to multiculturalism. That was enough to bring down the wrath of the Jew haters; citing an innocent comment of hers making this point, anti-Semites, including Kevin MacDonald, the psychologist about whom the anti-Zionist Philip Weiss had expressed mixed feelings, accused her of advocating the cultural genocide of white people.[15]

Away from the fervid imaginations of the conspiracy minded, Spectre is actually reaching out to those she calls "unexpected Jews," exemplified by Eastern Europeans who learned of their Jewish roots only after the Iron Curtain fell. (Former US secretary of state Madeleine Albright offers an especially prominent example of such hiddenness.) Generally not religious, but curious about their backgrounds, they more than any other Jews in Europe are the victims of the neutron bomb that left buildings standing while depriving people of their identity. At a time when so many other Jews are assimilating, moreover, these unexpected Jews offer a major opportunity for Jewish revival. Spectre's role is to introduce them to the guiding principles of Jewish peoplehood that emerge out of the texts that all Paideia fellows read. In her view, those principles lean in a universalist direction; they teach that "the world as it is does not have to be accepted," insist on "a profound trust in the human mind as an instrument to perfect the world," and uphold "a fierce, irrepressible faith in the Jewish people at the crux of this journey leading toward the improvement of human existence."[16] The enthusiasm of those who have participated in Paideia's programs has led Spectre to conclude that the European Diaspora is alive and well. To the United Jewish Appeal–Federation of New York in 2006, she said, "It behooves the world Jewish community to be cognizant of what is transpiring in Europe—the remarkable phenomenon of dis-assimilation that is taking place there could well inform and expand our notions of Jewish peoplehood and Jewish vitality."

It is helpful to compare this Swedish-based effort at Jewish revival with a country with a comparatively large, and historically well-organized, Jewish community: Great Britain. Established organizations such as the Board of Deputies of British Jews and the Zionist Federation, like their counterparts in the United States, had developed in a particularist direction in the years after World War II, emphasizing both the persistence of British anti-Semitism and the need for strong identification with Israel.[17] Also, as with the situation in America, British Jewish leaders became concerned with the problem of continuity in the early 1990s; as I discussed in chapter 5, the chief rabbi at the time, Sir Jonathan Sacks, wondered in print whether his generation would produce Jewish grandchildren. Although the position of chief rabbi is always filled with someone from within the Orthodox tradition, the organization Sacks created to deal with the problem, Jewish Continuity, as if reflecting the wide gap between this Jewish community and the one across the Atlantic, was designed to contain "fresh faces" and "to be big and bold, and shift the community's agenda toward issues of education and community development," its first executive director wrote.[18] Practicing both inreach and outreach simultaneously, Jewish Continuity was in an ambiguous position. On the one hand, as its statement of objectives put it, its aim was "to secure the future of British Jewry by creating a vibrant community of proud, knowledgeable and committed Jews."[19] On the other, it would undertake "initiatives in fields that other pre-existing organisations cannot or have not pursued ... that might enhance the prospects of Jewish continuity." Jewish Continuity was an establishment organization seeking credibility among those outside the establishment.

That first executive director was Clive A. Lawton, whose shoulder-length white hair and capacious beard make a striking contrast with the wealthy and meticulously groomed figures who once led British Jewry. Lawton was in an ideal position to address the issue of Jewish continuity. A former head teacher at the King David High School in Liverpool and education officer at the Board of Deputies, he was and is widely experienced in the world of Jewish education; in 2013 the New York–based website Algemeiner.com, the *Huffington Post* for all things Jewish, named him to its top one hundred people influencing Jewish life.[20] His major contribution to the revival of European Jewish identity, however, came not from his work with Jewish Continuity but with Limmud (Hebrew for "learning"), which he helped start in 1980. Limmud was necessary because British Jewry, in Lawton's view, "was neither a dynamic, educated, nor exciting community.... The vast majority of Jews in Britain did not know and did not want to know that there were Jews anywhere else—or if they knew they were pretty sure they couldn't learn anything from them."[21] No one could have imagined that by the second decade of the twentieth century, Limmud would become the most celebrated and successful effort at Jewish education anywhere in the world and that its impact would be felt even among more establishment-oriented Jews in the United States.

Feeding off the energy of young Jews in search of more authentic roots, Limmud quickly evolved into something, as many of its attendees described it, of a Jewish Woodstock; music, food, Torah study, book discussion groups, film, dancing, hiking in the woods—all could be found at a typical Limmud conference. It also began to spread from its base in Great Britain. Local Limmuds can now be found all over the world; in May 2013, to cite only one example, Limmud FSU (former Soviet Union) convened in Vitebsk, Belarus, a part of the world that had produced two Israeli prime ministers (Shimon Peres and Menachem Begin), as well as two great artists (Marc Chagall and Chaim Soutine). "I've become a Limmud addict," said Vasilisa

Smirnova, a cosmetics business developer from Moldova who was attending her seventh Limmud event. "For me, this is important because I find Jewish culture very deep and very wise, and because I am young and looking for answers. I have found that Jewish culture helps me find answers to questions like, 'Who I am in this world?' and 'What I should do?'"[22]

Limmud seeks to be inclusive of all ways of being Jewish; Lawton himself identifies as modern Orthodox. Still, an organization so shaped by the sensibility of the 1960s that it rejects hierarchy and encourages pluralism will not be acceptable to everyone; Orthodox British rabbis who attend its conferences do so in the face of official disapproval, and right-wing Zionists have never been happy with the participation of left-wing activists. Given its approach, the young people attracted to Limmud are unlikely to possess a self-protective mentality that views Jews as constantly in danger and support for the Jewish state as necessary for survival. In a comparative study of attendees, for example, Steven M. Cohen and Ezra Kopelowitz found that participants from Britain expressed weaker communal ties, attached less importance to being Jewish, and were far less emotionally attached to Israel than those from the United States and Israel.[23] (British attendees were also less likely than their counterparts in the two other legs of the global Jewish triangle to express support for repairing the world.) This can all be taken as evidence of how inhospitable Britain is to Judaism, but another explanation seems more compelling. Limmud arrived at a time when multiculturalism was becoming the norm in Europe, and multiculturalism, as the scholars Ben Gidley and Keith Kahn-Harris have emphasized, changed the whole stance of British Jewry.[24] No longer just a minority group struggling to survive in a majority culture that was not their own, younger British Jews began to view themselves not as an earlier generation did, as Anglo-Jewish, but as one minority among others in societies in which what once passed for a dominant culture was becoming contested. Taking pains to separate their Judaism from what might pass as ethnic chauvinism, they are universalist in spirit if not always in self-identification.

Readers should not get the impression from all this activity that some sort of Jewish utopia is under construction in Europe. Not all European Jewish thinkers, for one thing, are universalist; the continent contains its share of intellectuals who question the benefits of assimilation, fear for the future of European Jewry, and especially call attention to expressions of hostility emanating from Muslims. France, given the persistence of its anti-Semitism, is especially noteworthy in this regard. Earlier French intellectuals who fled to that country from Eastern Europe brought universalism with them; perhaps the most interesting, at least with respect to the subject of this book, was the Polish-born Shakespeare scholar Richard Marienstras (1928–2011), whose writings on the Jewish question, strongly influenced by Simon Dubnow, "sought to revive the concept of minority culture as a viable basis for Jewish identity in the Diaspora, and therefore in France," in the words of the late historian Paula Hyman.[25] In more recent years, by contrast, not only are Ashkenazi Jews such as Alain Finkielkraut (b. 1948) known for their strong pro-Israel views, but a significant number of French intellectuals of North African origin, lacking much appreciation for the European enlightenment, have also been quite public in their search for a more particularist Jewish identity. The Egyptian-born Benny Lévy (1945–2003), a former Maoist revolutionary and secretary to Jean Paul Sartre turned Orthodox Jew, was one, while Shmuel Trigano (b. 1948), Algerian by birth and a scholar of Jewish political philosophy, is another.[26] Neoconservatism with a strong particularist bent is by no means only an American phenomenon.[27]

It is not, moreover, only intellectuals in Europe who are attracted to a more self-protective outlook. As if to match the fears of so many French thinkers, a small but significant number of French Jews from all walks of life have been leaving for places such as New York City's Upper East Side and Israel; by one estimate, some two thousand French make aliyah every year,[28] the wealthier among them buying homes in the old "German Colony" in Jerusalem.[29] Along similar lines, Riccardo Pacifici, the president of Rome's lively fifteen-thousand-member Jewish community, calls aliyah an "insurance policy" against

Muslim intolerance and the recent economic slowdown.[30] Unlike most younger Jews who attend Limmud conferences, a growing number of ultra-Orthodox Jews in Europe are made uncomfortable by a trend toward secularism; proposed bans on circumcision or restrictions on ritual slaughter lead them as well to think of living elsewhere. Jews have always been a mobile people, and in an era of globalization, it can hardly come as a surprise that just as some Jews are arriving in Europe in search of a better life, others are leaving in search of a safer one.

Whether attributable to age-old Jewish pessimism, lack of economic opportunity, or warranted insecurity, this out-migration has been taken as evidence that the ever-vanishing Diaspora is vanishing ever more rapidly. In just one month, March 2013, for example, blog entries popped up on the Web with titles such as these: "Will the Last Jew Leaving Europe . . . Please Turn Out the Lights?," "A Jew-Free Europe," "Europe: The Submission That Dare Not Speak Its Name," "The Decline of the Jewish Presence in Europe," "Europe Acquiesces While Jews Are Threatened and Killed," and "A Jewish Exodus from Europe?"[31]

Despite both the number of these warnings and their alarmist tone, however, they should not be taken as the final word, and not only because the author of one of them, Guilio Meotti, was discovered to have been a longtime plagiarist.[32] The most significant aspect of the Jewish presence in Europe is not whether it is growing; an aging population, it is in fact losing numbers. More important is the kind of Jews young people in Europe are becoming. And here the irony is unavoidable: it is where the Holocaust happened that such significant steps to overcome particularism are being taken. What Milan Kundera wrote of one half of Europe could also be said of the other: "Aliens everywhere and everywhere at home, lifted above national quarrels, the Jews in the twentieth century were the principal, cosmopolitan, integrating element in central Europe: They were its intellectual cement, a condensed version of its spirit, creators of its spiritual unity."[33] It seems somehow fitting that universalism should flourish where universalism was invented.

III

No movement toward universalism can have much of an impact unless it spreads across the Atlantic. There, the reception is proving to be mixed. Many more countries, of course, can be found on the American side of the ocean than the United States: Argentina contains more Jews than Germany, while Canada has more than England. For reasons peculiar to the history of each, however, neither is likely to serve as the source of a universalist revival; if one is to take place, the burden is on younger generations of Jews from the United States.

Argentina has had some experience with diasporic universalism: both Jacobo Timerman, the human rights activist, and Daniel Barenboim, the Israeli musician and peace campaigner, were born there. Still, a long history of domestic anti-Semitism, the welcome offered to prominent Nazis by the country's leaders, and two major terrorist attacks against Jewish targets combined to produce a Jewish community that traditionally leans either toward Orthodoxy or toward secularism. It is true that Congregation B'nai Jeshurun in New York, which was discussed earlier in this book, was given new life by rabbis from Argentina, but it is also the case that their leader, Rabbi Marshall Meyer (1930–93), was a New York–born Jew who had moved to Buenos Aires in 1958. Limmud is active in Argentina, as it is throughout Latin America, which suggests that some efforts at the revival of universalism may be taking place. But pressures to survive as a Jewish community are so strong there, and in other countries in Latin America that have significant Jewish communities, that opportunities to reach out to others around the world are limited.

Canada ought to be a major player in any revival of universalism because of its ties to Europe. There exists some evidence of just such a connection: Independent Jewish Voices (IJV), the left-wing British organization, has a Canadian branch that remains active; Naomi Klein, a well-known antiglobalization campaigner, addressed its first congress in 2008.[34] (Klein's American-born parents moved to Canada during the Vietnam War years.) Along similar lines, Sheryl Nestel, who serves on the steering committee of IJV, Canada, believes that her work in solidarity with the Palestinians could, as she told the 2012 an-nual general meeting of the organization, serve the cause of "opening up new, politically and socially inclusive forms of Jewish identity and ethically and humanly responsible forms of Jewish communal life."[35] In chapter 4 I made a distinction between two kinds of Jewish uni-versalism, one of which objects to the very idea of a Jewish state while the other seeks to improve it. Many of Canada's most visible Jewish political activists belong in the former camp rather than the latter.

If left-wing Canadian Jews tend to be more radical than their American counterparts, Canada's traditional Jews tend to be more conservative. It is not just that a number of prominent Jewish conser-vatives, such as Saul Bellow, Ruth Wisse, David Frum, and Charles Krauthammer, were either born in Canada or lived there as children. (*National Review*'s Mark Steyn, also Canadian, one of whose mater-nal great-grandparents was Jewish, was baptized Catholic and later confirmed as an Episcopalian.) Unlike in the United States, a sig-nificant number of refugees from the Holocaust found welcome in Canada, and their experience has given Canadian Jewry a more par-ticularist outlook ever since. Statistics bear this out: 40 percent of Canadian Jews are Orthodox and only 20 percent are Reform, twice as many Canadian Jews have visited Israel than their counterparts in the United States, and almost twice as many Canadian children at-tend Jewish schools.[36] This particularist outlook is true of both the Toronto and the Montreal Jewish communities: the latter became more self-protective, and more willing to leave Canada, as Quebec's majority, also leaning in a particularist direction, began to insist on the use of French, while Toronto Jews have never been all that attracted to melting-pot versions of assimilation, in part because Canada gives of-ficial state recognition to religion. (Other cities, especially Winnipeg, Vancouver, and Ottawa, contain smaller Jewish communities than those found in Canada's two major urban centers.) A universalism emerging out of the Jewish tradition but seeking to speak in the name of all seems unlikely to arise in a country whose Jewish left and right are, in contrast to the rest of Canada's political culture, so polarized.

What, then, about the United States? Even here, and especially among younger generations of American Jews, signs are beginning to appear suggesting that the movement in Europe toward universalism is winning adherents in the largest diasporic Jewish home in the world. One such sign involves Limmud. Interestingly enough, there is no need for American-based organizations to copy Limmud's model because, as part of its global reach, Limmud itself is active in roughly eight US cities. Those who participate, whether in Denver, Atlanta, or on the two coasts, experience the same kinds of social, educational, and artistic forms of expression that have made Limmud so popular everywhere else.

Although all facets of Jewish life are included in a Limmud conference, Americans who go to them are typically more interested in those that bring out Judaism's more capacious side. Attending one such conference, the writer Abigail Pogrebin, for example, recalls in her diary that she no sooner got out of her car at the site near New Paltz, New York, than she attended a presentation "Creating an Egalitarian Day for G-d."[37] Impressed by how many participants were younger than her own cohort of forty- and fifty-year-olds, she joined a session on sexuality, made her own presentation on "Bored Jews in Synagogue," and skipped morning services to practice yoga. Some of the sessions to which she went had a clear religious component and one was devoted to "Zionism and Messianism." But it is difficult to read her account of the whole experience without concluding that everything that took place there was a far cry from the protective particularism of the generation of American Jews that preceded her. Even if one wishes to be particularist in this environment, one has to do it in a way that appreciates that "true leaders are those who can find a 'grain of good'—some 'mitzvah'—in every human being," as one presenter, Rabbi Shai Held, from Manhattan's Mechon Hadar yeshiva put it.

Mechon Hadar, along with the older Kehilat Hadar out of which it grew, is also a component of the new landscape being shaped by younger American Jews seeking more authentic outlets for their religious expression. These are minyanim, or prayer groups, that, much like Limmud, rely on the voluntary enthusiasm of those who attend. Although both are committed to fiercely egalitarianism methods of prayer, Kehilat Hadar includes among its activities efforts to make society at large more egalitarian as well: it has engaged in a partnership with the Interfaith Assembly on Homelessness and Housing, for example, and it has urged its members to protest New York City's efforts to reduce the number of rent-regulated apartments in the city.[38] Such prayer groups are not limited to Manhattan; just about every American city with a sizable Jewish population has one, and they have also begun to spring up in college towns such as Palo Alto, California, Princeton, New Jersey, and Charlottesville, Virginia. Jack Wertheimer of the Jewish Theological Seminary notes that these minyanim "are not inhabited by people who wanted to reform existing congregations but by those who sought an entirely different model of community, prayer, and learning."[39] They are organizations searching for authentic identities and composed of individuals doing the same thing. In his book *The Crisis of Zionism*, Peter Beinart cites Shai Held as a perfect example of someone who believes that younger Diaspora Jews must be as concerned with Israel as their parents, even if that concern, rather than offering robotic support, takes the form of asking the Jewish state to do a better job living up to Jewish principles.[40]

For Wertheimer, both Limmud and Mechon Hadar are part of a new "nonestablishment" Judaism, as he and his colleagues call it. Establishment Judaism refers to the institutions created during the post–World War II growth years, anchored by a Jewish version of the trilogy: synagogues sustained by active attendance; federations supported by philanthropy; and national organizations defending the interests of Jews and the state of Israel. For better or worse, no longer are these kinds of organizations at the center of American Jewish life: "It seems reasonable to assume," Wertheimer wrote in this context, "that we are watching the American Jewish communal structure change before our eyes. . . . The communal system is changing and all players will have to be mindful that the system we have known since World War II is rapidly reconfiguring."[41] The reasons for this are not difficult to discern. Younger Jews tend to be mobile and distrustful of organized religion. To the extent that they have philanthropic means, they are more likely to give to environmental or social justice causes than Jewish ones. And they are far less likely to advance uncritical support for Israel. Unless such patterns change, and it would take a massive move on the part of city-dwelling young people to replicate the suburban, upwardly mobile, and child-centered lifestyles of their parents, the future of American Judaism belongs with this new sector.

No single political or denominational orientation covers all these nonestablishment Jewish organizations. This sector, for example, includes explicitly pro-Israel groups such as Boston's David Project, which seeks to help young Zionists especially on college campuses make the case for Israel among their peers. Other efforts are inspired by Orthodox, and in some cases ultra-Orthodox, Jews hoping to bring those who have lapsed back into the fold. There are even nonestablishment groups catering to the needs of those born abroad; Limmud, for example, held a well-attended 2013 conference for Russian-speaking Jews in Princeton, New Jersey, and Israeli-born Jews have groups of their own.

But the great bulk of movements and organizations that constitute the nonestablishment sector lean toward such liberal values as pluralism and inclusion. The Seattle-based Kavana Cooperative, for example, which combines Danish-inspired cohousing living arrangements with campus-inspired Hillel educational programs, reflects an openness toward personal choice by insisting that "there is no one right way" to lead a proper Jewish life.[42] Other groups focus on explicit commitments to social justice causes, such New York City's J Corps and the Progressive Jewish Alliance based in California. The burning question for so many of the upcoming generation is not whether Jews should intermarry but whether gays and lesbians will be able to marry anywhere they please; it comes as no surprise that the nonestablishment sector includes Nehirim, a community of LGBT Jews. The same is true on the foreign policy front: taking a far more balanced view of the Middle East than the David Project, there is Encounter, which characterizes itself as "a conflict transformation organization, equipping influential Jewish leaders from across the political and ideological spectra with access to Palestinian perspectives and claims on the ground."[43] These examples show that universalism is built into the DNA of the nonestablishment sector; as Wertheimer observes, "Some important actors in this area are receptive to criticism of Israeli policies and some take quite radical stances on the matter," while "more broadly, non-establishment leaders tend to favor social justice with a universal mission over narrower Jewish ones."[44]

Wertheimer writes with mixed feelings about the groups and organizations he so effectively describes. He was, the reader may recall, an active participant in the American debate over continuity that produced *A Statement on the Jewish Future* in the early 1990s. Like the other signatories to that document, Wertheimer then believed that the best way to ensure Jewish continuity lay in appealing inward to those who were already committed to Jewish life rather than reaching outward to those whose commitments followed from personal choice or inclination. This explains why he became an advocate for boundaries, both between Judaism and other religions and within Judaism itself. The success of the nonestablishment sector has given Wertheimer second thoughts about his earlier convictions. "The ways young leaders think about the relationship between Jews and non-Jews, their desire to include the latter in programs, and their openness to intermarried Jews suggest a major shift in how Jews think about the boundaries of Jewish life," he now concedes. "Indeed, the very notion that boundaries ought to exist may further erode."[45] As much as he may long for the old days, it has become clear to Wertheimer that they are unlikely to return. In this he is no doubt correct. Young Jews do not want to be hectored on their failings or confined to one way of life. They want a Jewish world that fits the open world in which they live.

Those attracted to nonestablishment efforts at prayer and Jewish education, it is important to point out, remain a minority among Jews in general. But this is not because more traditional Jews outnumber them. It is instead because so many American Jews are secular, or as they are sometimes called, cultural; according to the 2013 study conducted by the Pew Research Center, 22 percent of American Jews now characterize themselves as having no religion.[46] Some of these secular Jews may admire those attracted to Limmud and similar organizations for their commitment. Others may wonder what in the world young people could find attractive about ancient texts and outmoded practices. But in either case it would never dawn on nonreligious Jews to become active in movements for Jewish revival no matter how universalistic they may be. Secular Jews are more interested in Jewishness than Judaism: living in a society in which all groups are expected to have at least some ethnic pride, and fully aware that if they had been in Europe a generation or two earlier they would likely be among the dead, they are in general unwilling to drop their Jewishness completely. In a study of "unsynagogued" Jews in Providence, Rhode Island, for example, the sociologist Lynn Davidman discovered that her respondents adapted Jewish rituals and practices to fit contemporary secular conditions, by making Friday night dinners a special occasion (even when serving nonkosher pizza) or by transforming sacred Jewish holidays into celebrations of the natural environment.[47] Even gestures such as these may be too religious for others who nonetheless identify as Jews: for them, appreciating the humor of a Sarah Silverman or a Larry David may express one's Jewishness more appropriately than lighting Sabbath candles. (The 2013 Pew study found that just as many young Jews say that having a good sense of humor is as essential to being Jewish as caring about Israel.)

If secular Jews, who tend to be politically liberal, are added to the picture, the prospects for a revival of universalism brighten considerably. Should they be? For the more traditionally minded, *secular Judaism* is a contradiction in terms; if you do not practice Judaism, you are not a Jew. This is not a position held only by Jews on the more conservative end of the spectrum. The prominent Reform rabbi Eric Yoffie, for example, whose views on the methods needed to revive Jewish worship were discussed in a previous chapter, shares such a view.[48] Secular or cultural Jews may think they have liberated themselves from belief in God and that they are no longer slaves to tradition, he has written, but in doing so they are under an illusion: one cannot pick and choose from Judaism, rejecting all the God talk while holding on to their cultural ties.

In one sense, Yoffie has a point: it is by no means clear what is specifically Jewish about those who never go to synagogue, marry outside the faith, and just have a vaguely defined sense that being from a Jewish background means that one must be liberal in outlook or attracted to a life of the mind. (I include myself in such a category, for reasons I explain in the personal afterword that follows.) Yet the fact remains that there is something decidedly Jewish about secular Jews, many of whom retain the stories of oppression and heroism they learned as children and then are influenced by those stories the rest of their lives, even as the beliefs and practices of religious Judaism no longer appeal to them. If Yoffie does not find such individuals sufficiently Jewish, others do. A surprise among them is Steven M. Cohen, who, like his colleague Jack Wertheimer, has shifted his views since the publication of *A Statement on the Jewish Future*. Along with the former editor of *Moment*, Leonard Fine, Cohen has written that he now prefers "to give primacy to Judaism's wonderful varied branches," including, the authors specifically suggest, its secular ones.[49] Yoffie fails to recognize, Fine and Cohen maintain, that Jewish values such as decency and social justice "have momentum on their own, that their derivation may be interesting to historians and theologians, but are of very little interest to their practitioners, including the thousands of Jewish social activists who champion the social and economic justice causes of labor, civil rights, peace, freedom, human rights, feminism and, most recently, environmentalism." There is surely a sea change taking place in American Judaism when those who once hoped to shrink the circle back in a particularist direction have become so willing to expand it forward in a universalist one.

In 2010 the former editor of *Commentary*, Norman Podhoretz, published a book called *Why Are Jews Liberal?* Like so many of the neoconservative particularists of his generation, he could not understand the determination of Jews to remain on the left side of the political spectrum. It may have made sense during the New Deal to vote for FDR, he maintained, but in more recent times, when Jews had become so prosperous and Israel had become so worthy of support, the failure of Jews to change political positions at first glance appeared inexplicable. Nonetheless determined to find a reason, Podhoretz came up with an ingenious one: "These supposed secularists," he wrote of the universalist Jews with whom he had such political disagreements, "none less than the Jewish liberals who speak in the name of Judaism, transfer and apply the faith that the Torah of Judaism inspired in their forbears to the Torah of Liberalism, and to this new Torah they give a like measure of steadfast devotion and scrupulous obedience."[50] In this, I think Podhoretz is essentially correct: no matter how conservative the United States becomes, the overwhelming majority of American Jews retain a commitment to social justice in ways that resemble a biblical commandment. Religious or secular, universalism is part of who they are.

The question contained in the title of Podhoretz's book was primarily addressed to the generation that came immediately after him: those Jews so marked by the events of 1968 that they never fully lost their youthful radicalism. At a time when the members of that generation are now collecting social security, one can only wonder what Podhoretz would think of the even younger Jews of the nonestablishment sector for whom gay marriage is long overdue, respect for the environment a given, and criticism of Israel second nature. These Jews are liberal because they believe that being liberal helps them be more Jewish. The Jews of the postwar period, it turns out, did have Jewish grandchildren. They simply have turned out to be far more inclined toward universalism than those who came before them.

IV

Every decade or so, an academic will write an essay so provocative in its argument that debates surrounding it can last for decades. Such was the case of a 1989 article, afterward expanded into a book, called "The End of History?" Influenced by philosophers such as Georg Wilhelm Friedrich Hegel and Alexandre Kojève, the political scientist Francis Fukuyama argued that history can have a direction ultimately resulting in a final resting place.[51] The two major ideological movements that had challenged Western liberalism, fascism and communism, he argued, had both proven to be dead ends. Liberalism, understood broadly as freedom in the economy and democracy in politics, had won out over all of its rivals. Ideologically speaking, there was no other place to go.

Without entering into the debate over whether he was correct,[52] it is worth pointing out that neither in the original article nor in the book did Fukuyama ever mention an ideology that very much shared the conviction that its triumph would also bring history, at least of a particular sort, to an end: Zionism. Although nearly all forms of Zionism were secular, they were nonetheless shaped by the messianic tradition within Judaism: just as the arrival of the Messiah would redeem the Jewish people, the state of Israel would end that form of Jewish history known as the *galut*. A long history of anti-Semitism would, alas, continue, directed against not only the Jews as a people but the new state that spoke in their name. But by returning to the very place from which they were so long ago expelled, the Jews had at long last closed the chapter in which statelessness was always associated with powerlessness.

History, we now know, did so such thing. Despite considerable efforts at enticement, many of the world's Jews chose to remain behind in the Diaspora. This is a reality difficult for passionate Zionists to accept, but over time a way was nonetheless found to hold fast to the idea that the weakness induced by exile was still a thing of the past: Israel would protect itself through its military might while Jews in the Diaspora, and especially in United States, would protect themselves as well as Israel by offering the latter their full support. Whatever else this was, it was not the powerless Judaism of the dispersion. Even those who remained outside the state knew where their hearts, if not always their bodies, ought to belong, and it was no longer in a dream called Zion but in the reality of an actual place on the map. No one could have said the same of the Jews of the Spanish Golden Age, the Polish and Lithuanian Council of the Four Lands, early twentieth-century Odessa, or even the United States in the 1920s and 1930s. Statehood changed the powerlessness of exile by giving it a purpose. So long as some were engaged in the struggle to realize that purpose, all would have a home.

There is no more important lesson for contemporary Jews to learn

than that "there is no end to history, no solution by fiat to future conflicts between human beings," Göran Rosenberg, Swedish editor and
writer, has observed.[53] Letting go of messianism, secular or religious,
will help Jews recall that they were and are an exilic people—and that
exile is good for the Jews. For those who remain scattered around the
world, exile keeps alive a tradition far older than Zionism: a people
who live among others not like themselves, conscious of their status as
a minority, will inevitably develop a sympathy for the underdog. Exile,
like Zionism, once contained its own messianic elements: political
philosopher Michael Walzer reminds us that it was the story of the
expulsion from Egypt that did so much to frame ideas of freedom
from oppression that have attracted so many Jews throughout the
centuries. At the same time, exile, by bringing Jews in contact with
other faiths (or no faith at all), brought messianism down to earth. "It
was in Christian, and then later in secular, cities and states that the
radical potential of Exodus was realized," as Walzer puts it. "The story
provided its readers with an alternative to the Apocalypse, a narrative
frame within which it was possible to think about oppression and liberation in this-worldly terms. It suggested—and still suggests—that
there might be a great day that wasn't the Last Day."[54]

This meaning of exile is what has been all too often submerged by
the creation of a Jewish state that has lost the universalism attractive
to both its critics and its founders. In our time, the remembrance of
exile is what the Jewish state most needs, and the Diaspora is the
place that can offer it. Although negation of the Diaspora retained its
popularity from the early Zionist pioneers down to contemporary intellectuals such as A. B. Yehoshua, Israel has always depended on Jews
living abroad for money and political support. All the more reason,
then, that Diaspora Jews who care for Israel's future offer universalism
instead. Anti-Zionists, who believe that Zionism represents "the sub-
version of Jewish culture and not its culmination," as Jonathan Boyarin and Daniel Boyarin have put it, are in no position to be helpful in
this regard.[55] Far more meaningful would be the advice of Gershom
Gorenberg, the liberal Zionist from Israel, who has written that "the
most basic Jewish memory is that 'we were strangers,' we were the

minority and were badly done by. . . . The most basic Jewish aspiration should be to do better as a majority when we have the opportunity."[56] What Zionism once negated is what Zionism now most needs.

Do Diaspora Jews possess sufficient standing to offer Israelis a way out of the cul-de-sac to which their alienation from universalism has led them? At least one prominent labor Zionist has said no. "For all of Diaspora Jewry's affinity to Israel," the Israeli political scientist Shlomo Aveneri believes, "the tough political decisions must be ours—and ours alone—to make, and it isn't fitting for noncitizens to have any part and parcel in those decisions."[57] Technically speaking, Aveneri is correct. Diaspora Jews, the Israelis among them excepted, are not citizens of the Jewish state. Nor have they gone through the process of building a new society, as older Zionists have done, or serving in the Israeli military, as current generations are doing. If being Israeli is a precondition for speaking out, they have no grounds to do so.

But it is also true, as the educator Alex Sinclair wrote in response to Aveneri, that "if we want the Jewish people to be connected to Israel, then Israel has to be connected to and considerate of the Jewish people."[58] Born in London three years before Lagodinsky was born in Russia, educated at Oxford and at the Hebrew University, and currently director of the Kesher Hadash, or "New Connections" (a semester-in-Israel program at the Jewish Theological Seminary in Jerusalem), Sinclair is also from a younger generation that did not directly experience either the Holocaust or the creation of the state of Israel. He describes himself as "a committed liberal Jew . . . deeply attached to certain core Jewish practices, traditions, [and] lifestyles" as well as "a universalist and pluralist, deeply influenced by social constructionist views of religion, and suspicious (to put it mildly) of fundamentalist religious approaches."[59] The program he directs aims to challenge the relationship between the Diaspora and Israel that has dominated Jewish life in the post–World War II period. "Israeli education," he explains, "should put American Jews and Israelis in positions where they have to engage in conversation about diverse issues, including some of the weighty questions about the future of Israel and its relations with the Diaspora: the peace process; the character of Jerusalem; religion and state; egalitarian Judaism."[60] If Sinclair is any example, the urge that has led Jews outside Israel to think in new ways about how and where Jews should live has been at work among those inside the Jewish state as well.

Those younger Jews who are leaning in a more universalist direction—whether by participating in the politics of their home country, rediscovering where their parents and grandparents came from, proposing new approaches to Jewish education, or remaining secular in outlook and universal in inclination—have sufficient distance from the events that made Israel possible to offer Israel's current Jewish population just such a needed perspective. There remain large sections of world Jewry convinced that the linked memories of the destruction caused by the Holocaust and salvation offered by statehood must never be forgotten: the memories that ought to tie all Jews together, at least in our day and age, they insist, are memories of the hatred always directed against this innocent people. For them, a younger generation of new, more universalistic Jews will be written off as too narcissistic, too unwilling to face the reality of evil, and too concerned with their personal advancement to recognize why Israel always must remain at the center of everything Jewish. But the events of the 1930s and 1940s are not the only events constituting Jewish memory. The blessings of exile are older, and more enduring, than the evils of statelessness. By bringing back to life the universalist ideals developed during their long residency in exile, a new generation of Jews can offer the best hope for a revival of the Jewish future.

PERSONAL AFTERWORD

This book is the first I have written dealing exclusively with my own tradition. For that reason, I feel that I should say something about how I came to be interested in the question of where and how Jews live.

Once a conventional political scientist interested in elections, presidents, and policies, I began to pay attention to religion when, in 1976, the Democratic Party nominated Jimmy Carter for president. Who was this man? I recall asking myself. Why is he talking about being "born-again" or, in that astonishing interview with *Playboy*, confessing to having lust in his heart? I had no idea. Especially on both coasts, commentators on US politics were familiar with the mainline Protestant denominations such as Episcopalians and Methodists, as well as with the Roman Catholic Church. But conservative Protestant denominations such as Southern Baptists were generally a mystery to them, and certainly to me. If Americans were willing to elect Carter as their leader, I quickly realized, I would have to learn more about the evangelical world in which he had been raised.

I began reading in the field and even doing a little writing, and then, after some time had passed, I was invited to be a member of the Lilly Seminar on Religion and Higher Education. Funded by the Lilly Endowment, a foundation that supports the study (and practice) of

religion from funds generated by the eponymous pharmaceutical gi-
ant, the seminar met twice a year between January 1997 and October
1999, once at a university, once at a resort.[1] The president of America's
largest seminary, two or three of the leading historians of American
evangelicalism, a smattering of Catholic intellectuals, and even (like
me) a couple of skeptics—there we were, exploring such issues as how
theology should be taught or whether colleges and universities have
a special mission to help form the moral outlooks of their students.
I gobbled it all up. For someone who grew up barely knowing any
Christians, this was new territory. By understanding more about religion, I concluded, I had begun to understand more about America.

Back in those days I wrote frequently for the *New Republic*. One of
its former editors, Michael Kelly, had moved to Boston to take over
the *Atlantic Monthly*, and we arranged to have lunch. Michael, who
not long after would become one of the first American journalists to
die while embedded with US troops in Iraq, asked me if I had any
ideas the magazine might publish, and I started telling him about
my discovery of evangelicals who could think. He could barely contain his enthusiasm, and before long I was traveling to one evangelical college after another, sitting in on classes, interviewing presidents
and provosts, and attending chapel. My resulting cover story, "The
Opening of the Evangelical Mind," received a good deal of attention.[2]
Liberal and secular writers thought I had gone soft in the head—one
of them, the journalist Judith Shulavitz, accused me of turning evangelical, evidently because I did not discuss creationism.[3] (At the time I
visited some of these colleges, creationism was taught as a controversy
in English departments, not as a scientific theory in biology departments.) Evangelicals, by contrast, were generally pleased, although
some did not like my charge that they were as attracted to goofy forms
of postmodernism as academic leftists. The most unexpected reaction
of all came a few years later when I published *The Transformation of
American Religion*, a book arguing, in part, that America's therapeutic
and inclusive culture had influenced evangelical Protestantism more
than the latter had reformed American culture.[4] Some of the most
prominent right-wing Christians in the country—the late Watergate

operative and reformed felon Chuck Colson, conservative columnist Cal Thomas, Baptist seminar president Albert Mohler—loved it. It is one thing for them to make the charge that too many evangelicals were no longer committed to the old-time religion. But when a secular, East Coast liberal of Jewish background did so, it is as if their critique was confirmed.

My interest in evangelical Protestantism stemmed from a desire to understand a group that had come to play such a prominent role in American politics, especially but not exclusively in the Republican Party. But I also found myself fascinated by people who welcomed Jesus into their hearts and who also believed, even if they rarely if ever said so directly, that anyone who did not, myself most definitely included, could never truly achieve salvation. None of it was anything I could accept. But at least it was a belief. Don't get me wrong: I am not saying that I would prefer an alcohol-free dinner at a Wheaton or Calvin College to a cabernet-laden party in Manhattan or Cambridge. But I did have the chance to meet, and to know well, people very different from me and from those in my circle.

Not long after the Lilly seminar ended, I moved from Boston University to Boston College, the former originally Methodist but now overwhelmingly secular, the latter Catholic and Jesuit. Here I found people preoccupied with matters of belief to a far greater degree than anything taking place in the evangelical world. (Theology, in the mind of many an old-time conservative Protestant, is unnecessary, indeed suspiciously Catholic, since the plain words of the Bible teach us all we need to know.) There is a species of conservative Catholic for whom Boston College (BC), and other Catholic universities like it, no longer has any true connection to the Roman Catholic Church; after all, as the late Father Richard John Neuhaus, a leader of this way of thinking, once pointed out, in hiring me BC was creating "a supportive ambiance for Alan Wolfe's project of reconstructing religion, including Catholicism, in the image of American liberalism."[5] BC, however, influenced me more than I changed it; it was a place that took theology seriously, and theology, I learned, can be an especially absorbing subject, even for a nonreligious person. Catholic institutions of higher learning are not going to be the kinds of place that disparage Western civilization; throw out the thoughts of all those dead white males, and you would pretty well be doing away with the entire Catholic intellectual tradition. It did not take long before I found myself teaching St. Augustine, rereading *Brideshead Revisited*, and writing a book on the problem of evil. The Jewish intellectual who once turned evangelical was clearly moving in another direction.

Once I established a center dealing with issues of religion and public life at BC, my fate, evidently, had been sealed: I would be the secular Jew teaching at a Catholic university while writing about conservative Protestants. Let my nonbelieving friends scoff, but I had found my niche. I still worry that at some point evangelicals will retreat to an earlier period in US history in which they avoided political engagement, perhaps a good development for America, but one that would deprive me of much of my subject matter. I also worry that the Catholic hierarchy, no great friend of the intellectual openness I have found at Boston College, will continue to close its graduation platforms to speakers who disagree with it on matters of sexual reproduction; condemn the wonderful charitable work carried out by nuns around the world; and insist that the idea of religious freedom gives it permission to control the sex lives of people who work in Catholic institutions. (The remarkable statements of Pope Francis suggest that a dramatic change from that way of thinking about the church may, at long last, reach its long overdue end; the intransigence of the Vatican bureaucracy suggests it may take time.) At some point, I tell each year's version of the class I teach on religion and politics, American public life will once again be preoccupied by issues involving economics and foreign policy. But nothing, not even the collapse of communism or the recession that lasted into the second decade of the twenty-first century, can deter at least some American politicians from their determination to condemn gay marriage, see the hand of a beneficent God in acts of rape, or call attention to the ongoing power of Satan. The issues I had carved out to study, both to my pleasure and my regret, will evidently always be there to study. My decision to focus more on American religion, and to make Christianity central to nearly everything I wrote and taught, turned out to be the best career move I had ever made.

One thing I had noticed about the academic study of religion is that scholars invariably study their own. I do not just mean that Mormons write books about Mormons or Catholics about Catholics. It goes deeper than that: mainline Protestants typically observe people much like themselves, as do Orthodox Jews. My membership in none of the above, it turned out, had given me something of an academic advantage. I may have lacked the insights that come from lifelong involvement with one particular faith. But in return I was widely viewed as someone writing about religion with no particular axe to grind. When a referee was needed, there I was. Those I studied generally treated me as an outsider but also as one making a special effort to understand them. Far from feeling excluded from their world, I felt, if anything, a bit wary about the warm embrace they offered.

Yet the fact that I had spent so much time among deeply religious Christians made me increasingly aware of two ways in which my differences with them were insurmountable: I was Jewish by background and nonreligious by conviction. For me, the two had always been intertwined. My parents were not themselves religious, nor for that matter strongly committed to any ideology. (I recall my father telling me that when he grew up, everyone he knew was either a socialist, a communist, or a Zionist, but that he had managed to avoid all such identification.) Nonetheless my parents felt Jewish enough to arrange a bar mitzvah for me, and so without much conviction on their part or mine, I did my religious duty at the age of thirteen. That has pretty much been it. I do at times read the Old Testament—the prophets in particular appeal to me—but I cannot say that the angry God pictured therein is one I find especially attractive. It is not just that I have a hard time envisioning God creating the world and then meddling with it when we human beings displease him. The religious side of

Judaism is as much about practice as it is about belief, and even in this realm I feel no urge to honor the tradition by following rules that at best seem arbitrary and at worst absurd. Although I know my share of rabbis, and even though I admire their learning and commitments to social justice, I cannot bring myself to regularly attend the synagogues of any of American Judaism's major branches. The only times I enter a shul are when I am invited to speak in one. I study religion but do not practice it, not even the one in which I was ostensibly raised.

If people who write about religion tend to write about their own, perhaps the time had come for me to write about mine: those who take pride in being Jewish while having little interest in the beliefs and practices that make one Jewish. Put that way, it sounds so ungrateful, taking from a tradition without giving anything back. I do not think this is a fair charge, and I urge the reader to consider this book an attempt to return the favor that growing up Jewish offered me. Judaism, after all, is not just a religion: it is also a way of thinking that can take secular as well as religious form, and it is the latter that has inspired me the most. David Goldberg, the London-based Liberal rabbi I mentioned in my introduction, does not know me, nor I him, but I felt he had me in mind when he wrote that "irreligious, non-believing doctors, scientists, social workers, teachers, artists, actors, tradespeople who still respond in however attenuated a fashion to some echo of their Jewish heritage and try, in however modest a way, to make the world a slightly better place for their being in it are in my view as much part of the wide campus of Jewish culture as the most devoutly observant Talmud scholar."[6]

The historian David Biale makes a distinction between two different varieties of Jewish secularism.[7] One is represented by the biographer of Leon Trotsky, Isaac Deutscher, who called attention to the non-Jewish Jew: thinkers such as Karl Marx and Sigmund Freud (as well as Baruch Spinoza and Rosa Luxemburg) who because they "dwelt on the borderlines of various civilizations, religions, and national cultures" could "rise in thought above their societies, above their nations, above their times and generations, and . . . strike out mentally into wide new horizons and far into the future."[8] The other secular tradition, according to Biale, involves thinkers who, however much they rejected Judaism as a religion, were steeped in Jewish history, identified with Jewish suffering, or were inevitably shaped by everything from which they had hoped to escape. In this latter category, Biale includes figures such as the poet of the Statue of Liberty Emma Lazarus, a Jew of Sephardic background, as well as nearly all the leading Zionists of the late nineteenth and early twentieth century, for whom nationalism rather than faith became their creed and cause.

Biale does not want to conflate these two categories; calling thinkers Jewish just because of their background strikes him as verging on "a kind of racial determinism."[9] As someone who does not consider himself as alienated as those in one of his categories or as conversant with Jewish sources as those in the other, I am not convinced that Biale is correct. For one thing, it is almost impossible to assign some key thinkers to either category; Freud, by example, is included by Deutscher as a non-Jewish Jew but also discussed by Biale because he wrote a book about Moses. In addition, times have changed, severing secular Jewish intellectuals, especially in the United States, from the immigrant experience that had once kept Hebrew and Yiddish culture alive. The most important reason, however, is that both kinds of secularism, at least before Israel came into existence, were shaped by the experience of exile they shared, as Deutscher so strongly emphasized. In the absence of boundaries within which membership is defined by a state, exilic people such as the Jews honored remembrance—or Zakhor, as they call it—by clinging to their history.[10] They also attached special importance to the written word while tolerating a certain amount of ambiguity in the meaning of those words. Lacking armies, they came to appreciate that arguments were more likely to be settled by winning others over to your ideas than by taking over their land. Whatever one's level of identification with matters Jewish, these were the traits that tied all Jewish secularists together in the absence of a unified political collectivity.

All this helps explain why those who have never read the Talmud can be so influenced by all those Jews of yore who did little else. The great Hebrew scholars of the past bequeathed to us who live in more fortunate times the opportunity to build upon their tradition and push it into territory that has little to do with how God's commands ought to be interpreted or what holidays should be celebrated and why. This Talmudic heritage, I believe, explains how I can feel Jewish without in any deep sense being Jewish. There was a time when religious Jews believed in God and argued furiously about him. There is now a time when huge numbers of fully assimilated Jews do not believe in God—and argue about everything anyway, including God. If the Jewish religion has been one long argument, I am home in that faith however much I fall short on knowledge of Hebrew, trips to Israel, or attendance at services.

As with religion, so with ethnicity. I take great pride in the accomplishments of particular Jews. Some of my friends consider it odd that I seem always to know that a composer, writer, or politician is Jewish, even when their name, such as Lorenzo Da Ponte, gives no hint that he or she might be. (Da Ponte not only wrote the libretti to the great Mozart trilogy of *The Marriage of Figaro, Don Giovanni,* and *Cosi Fan Tutte,* he also became, in turn a Roman Catholic priest, a grocer in Pennsylvania, and a professor of Italian at Columbia University.) If I learn that the first Lord Snowdon, Anthony Armstrong Jones, the husband of Princess Margaret, was descended from a German Jewish financer, or that the actress Gwyneth Paltrow comes from a long line of rabbis and publishes her seder recipes online, those facts stick with me, seemingly forever, just as I happen to know the number of Boston Red Sox players of Jewish background in 2006 (four: Kevin Youkilis, Gabe Kapler, Craig Breslow, and Adam Stern).[11] Other people collect china or stamps; I collect ethnicities. For all my belief that I am who I am because of what I have done, there lingers a sense that what I have done is at least partially explained by who my ancestors were.

At the same time that I am fascinated by the accomplishments of individual Jews, however, I bristle at the idea of Jewishness as a fixed category. Liberal universalism, in my view, should have little to do with tribalism; the whole point of there being ethnic groups is so that people can pick and choose between the best and worst of all of them. There was a time in my life when I was attracted to the idea that unencumbered selves, lacking strong ties to community, were incomplete, isolated, and therefore alienated from the society around them. But then I saw how quickly groups can become self-protective entities, requiring their members to suspend critical judgment in solidarity with what is, in the final analysis, an abstraction. For the same reason I so strongly disliked the statements of faith required by evangelical colleges, I reject the loyalty oath that says anyone who criticizes his or her group is disloyal to it.

This overall fascination with ethnicity during the past few decades, I believe, has produced too much interest in the group and too little in the individuals who compose it. The past three or four decades have witnessed the creation of numerous departments of Jewish studies. While such departments attract people with all kinds of views, including those quite critical of Zionism, and even though I have relied on their research in writing this book, too many of them promote a self-defensive mentality in which anti-Semitism is all too often portrayed as never ending and Jews are held innocent for whatever transpires in the Middle East. Outside academia, it especially concerned me that the *New Republic*, a magazine I loved and that had honored me by naming me a contributing editor, and to which I was attracted because it was so critical of the trend toward identity politics of other groups, published the anti-Arab mutterings of its former editor-in-chief Martin Peretz. (My relationship with *TNR* ended in 2013.) Special pleading, and of the nastiest sort, had not only won out in the field of politics, it had also become prominent in the world of letters. The wishy-washy Judaism in which I had been raised was neither devout nor observant. But at least it wasn't ugly.

Although I wrote this book against this tendency for Jews to put Jews first, I do not think of myself as a lonely dissenter confronting all the forces of the Jewish establishment, and not just because that establishment, as I have argued in this book, is beginning to crumble. In truth, there are many Jews like me. We have our own identity, so to speak, one in part shaped by Jewish history, culture, and faith, but one also influenced by the special privilege of living among others with different faith traditions. When I think of what being Jewish means to me, neither the Maccabees nor the Anti-Defamation League come first to mind. What does instead is the world of the Haskalah. It goes without saying that, in Amos Elon's words, it was a "pity" that it all came to an end, and in so brutal a manner. But there is no reason why enlightenment cannot live once again, if not in precisely the form it did then.[12]

Call this book, written in what used to be called old age, a return to what was around me but not especially visible to me when I was young. Not especially concerned with Jewish life in the glorious years when Israel came into being, I find myself preoccupied with Jewish matters when Israel is losing so many friends. My aim is not to add my name to its enemies list; I hope I have made clear throughout that for all Israel's problems, it is an established state that came into existence for justifiable reasons, and it ought to be allowed to find its way to a better future. Instead, I merely want to make my voice heard. Like so many others concerned about where Jewish nationalism has led, I prefer a Judaism that is special but not chosen to one that is chosen but not special. Jews survive best, for themselves and for the gentile world around them, when they do more than live but live up to an ideal.

ACKNOWLEDGMENTS

The original inspiration for this book came when I served as the John Winant Professor of American Government at the University of Oxford. I want to thank those at Balliol College and the Rothermere American Institute for providing such a stimulating home.

As usual, the staff at the Boisi Center at Boston College gave me support and encouragement. Thanks to Susan Richard, Erik Owens, Yael Levin Hungerford, and Ben Miyamoto in particular.

My agent, Andrew Stuart, and my editor, Amy Caldwell, were indispensable to the book's completion. Ruth Langer provided feedback on one key chapter, as did Benjamin C.I. Ravid on another. Ellen Messer's help was huge. Paideia, the European Institute for Jewish Studies in Stockholm, served as the perfect place to try out the themes of this book.

NOTES

INTRODUCTION. DIASPORA'S DESTINY

1. David Landau, "Alive and Well," *Economist*, July 28, 2012, http://www.economist.com/node/21559464.

2. David J. Goldberg, *The Divided Self: Israel and the Jewish Psyche Today* (London: I. B. Taurus, 2011), 47–48.

3. Todd M. Endelman, *The Jews of Britain: 1656 to 2000* (Berkeley: University of California Press, 2002), 169.

4. Cited in "Jewish State and Jewish World," The Jewish Agency website, http://www.jafi.org.il/JewishAgency/English/Jewish+Education/Compelling+Content/Worldwide+Community/Connecting+to+Community/Jewish+State+And+Jewish+World.htm. For more on his views, see Jacob Neusner, *Stranger at Home: "The Holocaust," Zionism, and American Judaism* (Chicago: University of Chicago Press, 1981).

5. *A Portrait of Jewish Americans: Findings from a Pew Research Survey of American Jews* (Washington, DC: Pew Research Center, 2013), 57, 59, 93.

6. Theodore Sasson, *The New American Zionism* (New York: New York University Press, 2013).

7. Alvin H. Rosenfeld, *The End of the Holocaust* (Bloomington: University of Indiana Press, 2011).

8. Philip Roth, *Operation Shylock: A Confession* (New York: Simon and Schuster, 1993), 104.

9. Ibid., 170.

CHAPTER I. WE'LL ROT TILL WE STINK

1. Simon Rawidowicz, "Only from Zion: A Chapter in the Prehistory of Brandeis University," in *State of Israel, Diaspora, and Jewish Continuity: Essays on the "Ever-Dying People,"* ed. B. Ravid (Hanover, NH: Brandeis University Press, 1986), 240, 41.

2. Jehuda Reinharz, *Chaim Weizmann: The Making of a Zionist Leader* (New York: Oxford University Press, 1985), 87–89.

3. Rawidowicz, "Only from Zion," 240.

4. PoemHunter.com website, http://www.poemhunter.com/poem/return-36.

5. On this point, see J. J. Goldberg, "Kishinev 1903. The Birth of a Century: Reconsidering the 49 Deaths that Galvanized a Generation and Changed Jewish History," *Forward*, April 4, 2003, http://www.kishinevpogrom.com/narratives1 .html.

6. Walter Laqueur, *A History of Zionism* (New York: Schocken Books, 2003), 61, 286.

7. The first part of the quote is from Laqueur, *History of Zionism*, 61. The second is cited in Zeev Sternhell, *The Founding Myths of Israel: Nationalism, Socialism, and the Making of the Jewish State*, trans. David Maisel (Princeton, NJ: Princeton University Press, 1998), 47.

8. Jacob Klatzkin, "A Nation Must Have Its Own Land and Language," in *The Zionist Idea: A Historical Analysis and Reader*, ed. Arthur Hertzberg (Philadelphia: Jewish Publication Society, 1997), 319.

9. Jacob Klatzkin, "The Galut Must Be Preserved Long Enough to Be Transcended," in Hertzberg, *Zionist Idea*, 325.

10. Laqueur, *History of Zionism*, 61.

11. Cited in Bernard Wasserstein, *On the Eve: The Jews of Europe before the Second World War* (New York: Simon and Schuster, 2012), 57.

12. The quotations in this paragraph come from Heinrich Graetz, *History of the Jews*, vol. 5 (Philadelphia: Jewish Publication Society of America, 1895), 417, 419, 421, 583.

13. The quotations in this paragraph can be found in Amos Elon, *The Pity of It All: A Portrait of Jews in Germany, 1743–1933* (New York: Penguin Books, 2004), 268.

14. Peter Pulzer, *Jews and the German State: The Political History of a Minority, 1848–1933* (Detroit: Wayne State University Press, 2003), 171.

15. Cited in Amnon Rubinstein, *From Herzl to Rabin: The Changing Image of Zionism* (New York: Holmes and Meier, 2000), 10.

16. Anita Shapira, *Land and Power: The Zionist Resort to Force, 1881–1948*, trans. William Templer (New York: Oxford University Press, 1992), 155.

17. Cited in Yuval Elizur and Lawrence Malkin, *The War Within: Israel's Ultra-Orthodox Threat to Democracy and the Nation* (New York: Overlook Press, 2013), 55.

18. Shapira, *Land and Power*, 332.

19. The quotations in this paragraph, unless otherwise noted, are cited in Tom Segev, *The Seventh Million: Israelis and the Holocaust*, trans. Haim Watzman (New York: Hill and Wang, 1993), 44, 100, 109.

20. This quotation and those in the next paragraph, unless otherwise noted, are from Rubenstein, *From Herzl to Rabin*, 85, 35, 13.

21. Sternhell, *Founding Myths of Israel*, 49.

22. Nir Kedar, "Ben Gurion's *Mamlakhtiyut*: Etymological and Theoretical Roots," *Israel Studies* 7, no. 3 (2002): 117–33.

23. Segev, *Seventh Million*, 97.

24. Bernard Wasserstein, *Vanishing Diaspora: The Jews in Europe Since 1945* (London: Penguin Books, 1997), 4.

25. For examples, see David J. Goldberg, *The Divided Self: Israel and the Jewish Psyche Today* (London: I. B. Taurus, 2011), 136.

26. Segev, *Seventh Million*, 183.

27. Ibid., 206.

28. Cited in Zvi Ganin, *An Uneasy Relationship: American Jewish Leadership and Israel, 1948–1957* (Syracuse, NY: Syracuse University Press, 2005), 36.

29. A frequent source of confusion for those who do not follow the ins and outs of Zionist politics in the United States is that there exist three organizations using the same three letters in their abbreviations: the American Jewish Committee, which raised serious questions about Zionism but eventually became a strong supporter of Israel; the American Council for Judaism, which was known for its fervent anti-Zionism; and the American Jewish Congress, associated with liberal rabbis such as Stephen Wise, which was consistently pro-Zionist.

30. Charles S. Liebman, "Diaspora Influence on Israel: The Ben-Gurion–Blaustein 'Exchange' and Its Aftermath," *Jewish Social Studies* 36, nos. 3–4 (July–October 1974): 275. For more on this agreement, see Ganin, *Uneasy Relationship*, 87–100, and Ariel L. Feldenstein, *Ben-Gurion, Zionism, and American Jewry, 1948–1963* (London: Routledge, 2006), 33–39.

31. Liebman, "Diaspora Influence on Israel," 277.

32. Deborah E. Lipstadt, *The Eichmann Trial* (New York: Schocken, 2011), 195.

33. Ibid., 196.

34. Segev, *Seventh Million*, 330.

35. I am indebted to the historian Deborah Hertz for this information.

36. Rubenstein, *From Herzl to Rabin*, 88.

37. Barbara Amiel, "Without Israel, Judaism Is Pointless," *Jerusalem Post*, February 23, 2001.

38. Joshua J. Adler, "Negate the Diaspora," *Jerusalem Post*, September 6, 2006.

39. The quotations in this and the next paragraph come from Hillel Halkin,

Letters to an American Jewish Friend: A Zionist's Polemic (Philadelphia: Jewish Publication Society of America, 1977), 24, 59, 111, 112, 134–35.

40. "Appendix: A. B. Yehoshua's Comments at the AJC Centennial Symposium," in *The A. B. Yehoshua Controversy: An Israel-Diaspora Dialogue on Jewishness, Israeliness, and Identity* (New York: American Jewish Committee, 2006), 63, http://www.ajc.org/atf/cf/%7BF56F4495-CF69-45CB-A2D7-F8ECA17198 EE%7D/ Yehoushua_Controversy_2006.pdf.

41. The quotations in this paragraph, unless otherwise noted, are from A. B. Yehoshua, "The Meaning of Homeland," in *A. B. Yehoshua Controversy*, 9.

42. Hillel Halkin, "More Right Than Wrong," in *A. B. Yehoshua Controversy*, 42.

43. "Novelist Yehoshua Labels American Jews 'Partial Jews,'" JTA Jewish News Archive, March 18, 2012, http://www.jta.org/news/article/2012/03/18/3092202/ novelist-yehoshua-calls-american-jews-partial-jews.

44. Revital Blumenfeld, "A B. Yehoshua: Americans, Unlike Israelis, Are Only Partial Jews," *Ha'aretz* (Israel), March 18, 2012.

45. Karl Marx, *Eighteenth Brumaire of Louis Napoleon* (New York: International Publishers, 1994), 2.

46. Pierre Birnbaum, *Geography of Hope: Exile, the Enlightenment, Disassimilation*, trans. Charlotte Mandell (Stanford, CA: Stanford University Press, 2008), 36–37.

47. Yehuda Kurtzer, "A. B. Yehoshua Should Pipe Down," *Tablet*, April 6, 2012, http://www.tabletmag.com/jewish-arts-and-culture/books/96231/yehoshua.

48. The first official is Mort Mandel and the second is Martin Citrin. See Jonathan Woocher, *Sacred Survival: The Civil Religion of American Jews* (Bloomington: University of Indiana Press, 1986), 78–79.

49. Shlomit Levy, Hannah Levinsohn, and Elihu Katz, "A Portrait of Israeli Jewry: Beliefs, Observances and Values among Israeli Jews 2000," 12, http:// avichai.org/knowledge_base/a-portrait-of-israeli-jewry-2000/.

50. Woocher, *Sacred Survival*, 77.

51. Cited in J. J. Goldberg, *Jewish Power: Inside the American Jewish Establishment* (Reading, MA: Addison-Wesley, 1996), 347.

52. Noa Levanon, "Anti-Zionism by 'Progressive' Jews," YnetNews.com, July 16, 2007, http://www.ynetnews.com/articles/0,7340,L-3425687,00.html.

53. For making this point, I am grateful to my colleague Kevin Kenny of the Boston College History Department. See also Kevin Kenny, *Diaspora: A Very Short Introduction* (New York: Oxford University Press, 2013).

CHAPTER 2. DEFENDERS OF DIASPORA

1. Saul Friedländer, *The Years of Extermination: Nazi Germany and the Jews, 1939–1945* (New York: Harper Collins, 2007), 247, 262.

2. Arie M. Dubnov, *Isaiah Berlin: The Journey of a Jewish Liberal* (New York: Palgrave Macmillan, 2012), 34. Dubnov, who teaches history at Stanford University, is a descendant of Simon Dubnow.

3. *Jewish Life in Kovno, Riga and Lwów, 1939*, YouTube.com, http://www.youtube.com/watch?v=xzrilp-b4tY.

4. For biographical details, see Kristi Groberg, "The Life and Influence of Simon Dubnow (1860–1941)," *Modern Judaism* 13, no. 1 (February 1993): 71–93; and Sophie Dubnov-Erlich, *The Life and Work of S. M. Dubnov*, trans. Judith Vowles (1950; repr., Bloomington: University of Indiana Press, 1991).

5. Cited in Koppel S. Pinson, "Simon Dubnow: Historian and Political Philosopher," in Simon Dubnow, *Nationalism and History: Essays on Old and New Judaism*, ed. Koppel S. Pinson (New York: Athenaeum, 1970), 33.

6. Ruth R. Wisse, *Jews and Power* (New York: Schocken, 2007), 7.

7. Simon Dubnow, "Autonomism, the Basis of the National Program," in Pinson, *Nationalism and History*, 134.

8. Simon Dubnow, "The Doctrine of Jewish Nationalism," in Pinson, *Nationalism and History*, 85.

9. Charles King, *Odessa: Genius and Death in a City of Dreams* (New York: Norton, 2011), 170.

10. Simon Dubnow, "The Survival of the Jewish People," in Pinson, *Nationalism and History*, 335.

11. Simon Dubnow, "The Ethics of Nationalism," in Pinson, *Nationalism and History*, 123.

12. Yehudah Mirsky, "The Non-Zionist," *Jewish Ideas Daily*, November 8, 2010, http://www.jewishideasdaily.com/content/module/2010/11/8/main-feature/1/the-non-zionist.

13. Simon Dubnow, "A Historic Moment," in Pinson, *Nationalism and History*, 195.

14. Simon Dubnow, "The Emancipation Movement and the Emigration Movement," in Pinson, *Nationalism and History*, 239.

15. Such is the conclusion of Friedländer, *Years of Extermination*, 262.

16. Dubnow, "Doctrine of Jewish Nationalism," in Pinson, *Nationalism and History*, 91.

17. Simon Dubnow, *Jewish History: An Essay in the Philosophy of History* (1903; repr., Freeport, NY: Books for Libraries Press, 1972), 37.

18. Steven J. Zipperstein, *Elusive Prophet: Ahad Ha'am and the Origins of Zionism* (Berkeley: University of California Press, 1993), 224–25.

19. Simon Dubnow, "Reality and Fantasy in Zionism," in Pinson, *Nationalism and History*, 164.

20. Simon Dubnow, "Letters of Old and New Judaism," in Pinson, *Nationalism*

and History, 74, and "'The Affirmation of the Diaspora," in Pinson, *Nationalism and History*, 182.

21. Simon Dubnow, "The Affirmation of the Diaspora," in Pinson, *Nationalism and History*, 190.

22. To S. Dubnow, September 27, 1919, in Ahad Ha'am, *Essays, Letters, Memoirs*, trans. Leon Simon (Oxford, UK: East and West Library, n.d.), 267.

23. Ha'am, "Zionism and Jewish Culture," in *Essays, Letters, Memoirs*, 91.

24. To S. Dubnow, *Essays, Letters, Memoirs*, 268.

25. Ahad Ha'am, "Slavery in Freedom," in *Selected Essays*, trans. Leon Simon (Philadelphia: Jewish Publication Society of America, 1912), 170–94.

26. Ha'am, "Zionism and Jewish Culture," in *Essays, Letters, Memoirs*, 86.

27. Ha'am, "Pinsker and Political Zionism," in *Essays, Letters, Memoirs*, 188.

28. To A. Druyanov, Odessa, September 16, 1906, in *Essays, Letters, Memoirs*, 263.

29. To S. Dubnow, December 18, 1907, in *Essays, Letters, Memoirs*, 309.

30. Cited in Antony Polonsky, *The Jews in Russia and Poland*, vol. 2, *1881 to 1914* (Oxford, UK: Littman Library of Jewish Civilization, 2010), 229.

31. David H. Weinberg, *Between Tradition and Modernity: Haim Zhitlowski, Simon Dubnow, Ahad Ha'am, and the Shaping of Modern Jewish Identity* (New York: Holmes and Meier, 1996), 277.

32. Zipperstein, *Elusive Prophet*, 202–3.

33. Cited in Weinberg, *Between Tradition and Modernity*, 282.

34. Ha'am, "A Spiritual Center," in *Essays, Letters, Memoirs*, 204.

35. On this point, see Weinberg, *Between Tradition and Modernity*, 283.

36. Ha'am, "Jewish and Christian Ethics," in *Essays, Letters, Memoirs*, 132.

37. Cited in Zipperstein, *Elusive Prophet*, 133.

38. Ha'am, "Moses," in *Essays, Letters, Memoirs*, 114.

39. The quotations from Chomsky in this paragraph can be found in "Q and A: Noam Chomsky Interviewed by David Samuels," *Tablet*, November 12, 2010, http://www.chomsky.info/interviews/20101112.htm.

40. Zipperstein, *Elusive Prophet*, 226.

41. "Q and A," *Tablet*.

42. This quotation and those that follow in this paragraph are from Alan Dowty, "Much Ado about Little: Ahad Ha'am's 'Truth from Eretz Yisrael,' Zionism, and the Arabs," *Israeli Studies* 5, no. 2 (Fall 2000): 162. This article contains an English translation of Ha'am's 1891 essay.

43. Zipperstein, *Elusive Prophet*, 246.

44. Dowty, "Much Ado about Little."

45. Avraham Burg, *The Holocaust Is Over; We Must Rise from Its Ashes* (New York: Palgrave MacMillan, 2008).

46. A complete English translation of the interview can be found at the *Peace-*

palestine blog, http://peacepalestine.blogspot.com/2007/06/complete-abraham-burg-interview-leaving.html.

47. David Remnick, "The Apostate," *New Yorker*, July 30, 2007, http://www.newyorker.com/reporting/2007/07/30/070730fa_fact_remnick.

48. *Peacepalestine* blog, http://peacepalestine.blogspot.com/2007/06/complete-abraham-burg-interview-leaving.html.

49. J. J. Goldberg, "Avraham Burg's New Zionism," *Jewish Daily Forward*, June 15, 2007, http://forward.com/articles/10943/avraham-burg-s-new-zionism/.

50. Zipperstein, *Elusive Prophet*, 300.

51. The details of Rawidowicz's life can be found in "Introduction: The Life and Writings of Simon Rawidowicz," in Simon Rawidowicz, *State of Israel, Diaspora, and Jewish Continuity*, ed. B. Ravid (Hanover, NH: Brandeis University Press, 1986), 13–50; David N. Myers, *Between Jew and Arab: The Lost World of Simon Rawidowicz* (Hanover, NH: Brandeis University Press, 2008), 1–134; and Noam Pianko, *Zionism and the Roads Not Taken: Rawidowicz, Kaplan, Kohn* (Bloomington: Indiana University Press, 2010), 61–93.

52. See Jonathan Sacks, *Future Tense: A Vision for Jews and Judaism in the Global Culture* (London: Hodder, 2010), 54.

53. The quotations in this paragraph unless otherwise noted are from Simon Rawidowicz, "Israel: The Ever-Dying People," in *State of Israel, Diaspora, and Jewish Continuity*, 53–63.

54. Salo Wittmayer Baron, "Ghetto and Emancipation: Shall We Revise the Traditional View?" in *The Menorah Treasury: Harvest of Half a Century*, ed. Leo Schwartz (Philadelphia: Jewish Publication Society of America, 1973), 63. The same tendency to recount the history of the Jews as the history of disaster has been called the "Oy Vey" approach by the British Jewish educator Clive Lawton; see Clive A. Lawton, "European Models of Community: Can Ambiguity Help?" in *Turning the Kaleidoscope: Perspectives on European Jewry*, ed. Sandra Lustig and Ian Leveson (New York: Berghan Books, 2006), 42.

55. The quotations in this paragraph unless otherwise noted are from Simon Rawidowicz, "On the Concept of *Galut*," in *State of Israel, Diaspora, and Jewish Continuity*, 96–117.

56. Pianko, *Zionism and the Roads Not Taken*, 67.

57. Personal interview with author, Newton, Massachusetts, summer 2012.

58. Simon Rawidowicz, "Jewish Existence: The End and the Endless," in *State of Israel, Diaspora, and Jewish Continuity*, 89–90.

59. Simon Rawidowicz, "Two That Are One," in ibid., 159.

60. Simon Rawidowicz, "Israel: The People and the State," in ibid., 192.

61. The two quotations from Ben-Gurion in this and the next paragraph are from Ben-Gurion to Rawidowicz, November 24, 1954, in ibid., 197.

62. Myers, *Between Jew and Arab*, 6. The term *cruel Zionism* was invented by

the Zionist militant Avraham Sharon (*nè* Schwardon, 1878–1957). Regarding "pseudo-Nietzscheans," see Rawidowicz, "On the Concept of *Galut*," 115.

63. Rawidowicz, "Jewish Existence," 86.

64. Cited in Pianko, *Zionism and the Roads Not Taken*, 83.

65. Simon Rawidowicz, "Jerusalem and Babylon," in *State of Israel, Diaspora, and Jewish Continuity*, 230.

66. Cited in Myers, *Between Jew and Arab*, 59.

67. Rawidowicz, "Jerusalem and Babylon," 231.

68. The quotations in this paragraph are from Myers, *Between Jew and Arab*, 142, 145, 164, 173.

69. The quotations in this paragraph are from Simon Rawidowicz, "Libertas Differendi: The Right to Be Different," in *State of Israel, Diaspora, and Jewish Continuity*, 124–25, 126.

70. The quotations in this paragraph are from Myers, *Between Jew and Arab*, 152, 164.

71. Allan Arkush, "State and Counter-State," *Jewish Review of Books* (Summer 2011), http://www.jewishreviewofbooks.com/publications/detail/state-and-counterstate.

72. "Report: Future of Judaism Studies at Risk," *Ynet*, March 9, 2011, http://www.jidaily.com/BG8uG. See also Alex Joffe, "Jewish Studies in Decline?," *Jewish Ideas Daily*, March 26, 2011, http://www.jewishideasdaily.com/851/features/jewish-studies-in-decline/.

73. Abram Sachar, *Brandeis University: A Host at Last* (Hanover, NH: Brandeis University Press, 1976), 247.

CHAPTER 3. THE SECULARIZATION OF PARTICULARISM

1. Sharon Otterman, "Therapist Sentenced to 103 Years for Child Sexual Abuse," *New York Times*, January 22, 2013.

2. Svante Lungren, *Particularism and Universalism in Modern Jewish Thought* (Binghamton, NY: Academic Studies in the History of Judaism, 2001), 10.

3. Yehuda Halevi, *The Kuzari: In Defense of the Despised Faith*, trans. and annot. N. Daniel Korobkin (Northvale, NJ: Jason Aronson, 1998), 220.

4. Hillel Halkin, *Yehuda Halevi* (New York: Schocken, 2010), 296.

5. Maimonides, *Laws of Kings and Wars: Translated from the Rambam's Mishne Torah*, trans. Reuven Brauner (Raanana, Israel: Reuven Brauner, 2012), 10.7, p. 30, http://halakhah.com/rst/kingsandwars.pdf.

6. For background, I found very helpful Kenneth Seeskin, *Maimonides: A Guide for Today's Perplexed* (Springfield, NJ: Behrman House, 1991).

7. Lundgren, *Particularism and Universalism*, 38.

8. Victoria Bekiempis, "Does Talmudic Law Require Jews to Report Sex Crimes?," *Village Voice*, May 18, 2012, http://blogs.villagevoice.com/runninscared/2012/05/jews_sex_crimes_talmud.php.

9. Rachel Elbaum, "Hail to the Chief: Americans Eyed in Search for Britain's Top Rabbi," *World News*, November 8, 2012, NBC.com, http://worldnews.nbcnews.com/_news/2012/11/08/14966142-hail-to-the-chief-americans-eyed-in-search-for-britains-top-rabbi?lite.

10. The quotations in this paragraph are from Michael J. Broyde, "Jewish Law and American Public Policy: A Principled Jewish Law View and Some Practical Jewish Observations," in *Religion as a Public Good: Jews and Other Americans on Religion in the Public Square*, ed. Alan Mittleman (Lanham, MD: Rowman and Littlefield, 2003), 168, 170. See also Michael J. Broyde, "The Obligation of Jews to Seek Observance of Noachite Laws by Gentiles: A Theoretical Review," *Jewish Law*, n.d., http://www.jlaw.com/Articles/noach2.html.

11. Cited in Marc Dollinger, *Quest for Inclusion: Jews and Liberalism in Modern America* (Princeton, NJ: Princeton University Press, 2000), 57.

12. Ibid., 112.

13. Peter Novick, *The Holocaust in American Life* (Boston: Houghton Mifflin, 1999), 114.

14. Cited in Stuart Svonkin, *Jews Against Prejudice: American Jews and the Fight for Civil Liberties* (New York: Columbia University Press, 1997), 81.

15. Ibid., 20.

16. Clayborne Carson, "Black-Jewish Universalism," in *Struggles in the Promised Land: Toward a History of Black-Jewish Relations in the United States*, ed. Jack Salzman and Cornel West (New York: Oxford University Press, 1997), 192, cited in Dollinger, *Quest for Inclusion*, 201.

17. Dollinger, *Quest for Inclusion*, 221.

18. Donald Downs, *Nazis in Skokie: Freedom, Community, and the First Amendment* (Notre Dame, IN: University of Notre Dame Press, 1985), 53.

19. Svonkin, *Jews Against Prejudice*, 178.

20. Aryeh Neier, *Defending My Enemy: American Nazis, the Skokie Case, and the Risks of Freedom* (New York: Dutton, 1979), 4.

21. Downs, *Nazis in Skokie*, 23.

22. Phillipa Strum, *When the Nazis Came to Skokie: Freedom for Speech We Hate* (Lawrence: University Press of Kansas, 1999), 67, 71.

23. Novick, *Holocaust in American Life*, 226.

24. "2012 Election Results," Cook County Clerk website, http://electionnight.cookcountyclerk.com/summary.aspx?eid=110612.

25. I have in mind the blogger M. J. Rosenberg, who has used the term "Israel Firster." See "The Israel Firster Brouhaha & Why I Left Media Matters,"

Huffington Post, April 7, 2012, http://www.huffingtonpost.com/mj-rosenberg/the-israel-firster-brouha_1_b_1409931.html.

26. Irving Kristol, "Why Religion Is Good for the Jews," in *The Neo-Conservative Persuasion: Selected Essays, 1942–2009* (New York: Basic Books, 2011), 286.

27. Kristol, "Liberalism and American Jews," in ibid., 279.

28. Kristol, "The Political Dilemma of American Jews," in ibid., 264.

29. Kristol, "Christianity, Judaism, and Socialism," in *Neo-Conservatism: The Autobiography of an Idea; Selected Essays 1949–1995* (New York: Free Press, 1995), 430.

30. Ibid., 429.

31. Meir Soloveichik, "Irving Kristol, Edmund Burke, and the Rabbis," *Jewish Review of Books* (Summer 2011), http://www.jewishreviewofbooks.com/publications/detail/irving-kristol-edmund-burke-and-the-rabbis.

32. Elbaum, "Hail to the Chief."

33. Kristol, "The Future of American Jewry," in *Neo-Conservatism*, 450.

34. Kristol, "Christianity, Judaism, and Socialism," in ibid., 432.

35. Kristol, "A Note on Religious Tolerance," in *The Neo-Conservative Persuasion*, 297.

36. The quotations in this paragraph and the next are from Kristol, "The Future of American Jewry," in *Neo-Conservatism*, 453, 454.

37. Kristol, *The Neo-Conservative Persuasion*, 301–14.

38. For the details see Ami Pedahzur, *The Triumph of Israel's Radical Right* (New York: Oxford University Press, 2012).

39. Wisse describes her relationship with Howe in "The Socialist," *Tablet*, March 18, 2011, http://www.tabletmag.com/jewish-news-and-politics/60829/the-socialist.

40. The quotations in this and subsequent paragraphs are from Ruth Wisse, *Jews and Power* (New York: Schocken, 2000), 76, 85, 86, 96.

41. Ibid., 176.

42. Ibid., 162.

43. "Cynthia Ozick Accepts Jewish Book Council's Lifetime Achievement Award," *The ProsenPeople*, March 11, 2011, Jewish Book Council website, http://www.jewishbookcouncil.org/.

44. Joseph Lowin, "Cynthia Ozick," Jewish Women's Archive, http://jwa.org/encyclopedia/article/ozick-cynthia.

45. Cynthia Ozick, *The Shawl* (New York: Knopf, 1989) and *The Puttermesser Papers* (New York: Knopf, 1997).

46. The quotations in this paragraph are from Cynthia Ozick, "Where Hatred Trumps Bread: What Does the 'Palestinian Nation' Offer the World?," *Wall Street Journal*, June 30, 2003.

47. Ozick, *Puttermesser Papers*, 215.

48. Irving Howe, *Politics and the Novel* (Cleveland: World Publishing, 1957).

49. For examples, see Pamela Geller, *Freedom or Submission: On the Dangers of Islamic Extremism and American Complacency* (Seattle: CreateSpace Independent Publishing Platform, 2013); Melanie Phillips, *The World Turned Upside Down: The Global Battle over God, Truth, and Power* (New York: Encounter Books, 2010); Daniel Pipes, *Militant Islam Reaches America* (New York: Norton, 2002); and David Horowitz, *Unholy Alliance: Radical Islam and the American Left* (New York: Regnery, 2006). Phillips acknowledges using the term "Jews for Genocide" in "Why Jonathan Freedman Is Wrong," *Jewish Chronicle*, April 6, 2007; also published at Phillips's website, http://melaniephillips.com/why-jonathan-freedland-is-wrong.

50. The quotations in this paragraph come from David Horowitz, "Reflections of a Diaspora Jew on Zionism, America, and the Fate of the Jews," *Frontpage Magazine*, September 7, 2012, http://frontpagemag.com/2012/david-horowitz/reflections -of-a-diaspora-jew-on-zionism-america-and-the-fate-of-the-jews/.

51. Ibid.

52. Halevi, *Kuzari*, 51.

CHAPTER 4. A TALE OF TWO RABBIS

1. The quotations in this paragraph are from Eliezar Segal, "The Concept of Diaspora in Talmudic Thought," in *Encyclopedia of the Jewish Diaspora: Origins, Experience, and Culture,* ed. M. Avrum Erlich (Santa Barbara, CA: ABC Clio, n.d.), 1:5.

2. This quotation and the one that follows in the next paragraph are from Amos Elon, *The Pity of It All: A Portrait of Jews in Germany, 1743–1933* (New York: Penguin Books, 2004), 66, 127.

3. See Antony Polonsky, *The Jews in Poland and Russia*, vol. 1, *1350 to 1881* (Oxford: Littman Library of Jewish Civilization, 2010), 259, 294.

4. A summary of Einhorn's theology can be found in "David Einhorn," in *Encyclopedia of American Jewish History*, ed. Edward L. Queen, Stephen R. Prothero, and Gardiner H. Shattuck, vol. 1 (New York: Facts on File, 1996), 359.

5. Michael A. Meyer, *Response to Modernity: A History of the Reform Movement in Judaism* (New York: Oxford University Press, 1988), 247.

6. Cited in Michael Goldfarb, *Emancipation: How Liberating Europe's Jews from the Ghetto Led to Revolution and Renaissance* (New York: Simon and Schuster, 2009), 129.

7. The Pittsburgh Platform can be found at the Jewish Virtual Library, http:// www.jewishvirtuallibrary.org/jsource/Judaism/pittsburgh_program.html.

8. Meyer, *Response to Modernity*, 270.

9. The Columbus Platform can be found at the Jewish Virtual Library, http:// www.jewishvirtuallibrary.org/jsource/Judaism/Columbus_platform.html.

10. See Alan Silverstein, *Alternatives to Assimilation: The Response of Reform*

Judaism to American Culture, 1840–1930 (Hanover, NH: University Press of New England for Brandeis University Press, 1994).

11. Marc Dollinger, *Quest for Inclusion: Jews and Liberalism in Modern America* (Princeton, NJ: Princeton University Press, 2000), 89.

12. The facts and quotations in this paragraph unless otherwise noted come from Jack Ross, *Rabbi Outcast: Elmer Berger and American Jewish Anti-Zionism* (Washington, DC: Potomac Books, 2011), 37.

13. For a history of its early years, see Thomas A. Kolsky, *Jews Against Zionism: The American Council for Judaism, 1942–1948* (Philadelphia: Temple University Press, 1992).

14. Ross, *Rabbi Outcast*, 49.

15. Ibid., 138.

16. Hugh Wilford, *The Mighty Wurlitzer: How the CIA Played America* (Cambridge, MA: Harvard University Press, 2008), 126–27; and Robert Moats Miller, *Harry Emerson Fosdick: Preacher, Pastor, Prophet* (New York: Oxford University Press, 1985), 192.

17. Ross, *Rabbi Outcast*, 153.

18. Deborah Lipstadt, *Denying the Holocaust: The Growing Assault of Truth and Memory* (New York: Penguin, 1994), 41.

19. Samuel G. Freedman, "American Jews Who Reject Israel Say Events Aid Cause," *New York Times*, June 25, 2010, http://www.nytimes.com/2010/06/26/us/26religion.html/.

20. The most comprehensive biography is Melvin L. Urofsky, *A Voice That Spoke for Justice: The Life and Times of Stephen S. Wise* (Albany: State University of New York Press, 1982).

21. Henry Morgenthau Sr., first president of the Free Synagogue, quoted in David W. Dunlap, *From Abyssian to Zion: A Guide to Manhattan's Houses of Worship* (New York: Columbia University Press, 2004), 265.

22. Urofsky, *Voice That Spoke*, 63. On the relationship between Wise and Hirsch more generally, see Tobias Brinkmann, *Sundays at Sinai: A Jewish Congregation in Chicago* (Chicago: University of Chicago Press, 2012).

23. See Carl Hermann Voss, *Preacher and Minister: The Friendship of Stephen S. Wise and John Haynes Holmes* (Buffalo: Prometheus Books, 1980).

24. Mark A. Raider, "Idealism, Vision, and Pragmatism: Stephen S. Wise, Nahum Goldmann, and Abba Hillel Silver in the United States," in *Nahum Goldmann: Statesman Without a State*, ed. Mark A. Raider (Albany: State University of New York Press, 2009), 144.

25. For the material discussed in this paragraph I am indebted to Silverstein, *Alternatives to Assimilation*, 156–66.

26. Urofsky, *Voice That Spoke*, 215.

27. The quotations in this paragraph are from ibid., 280, 281.

28. Richard Hofstadter, *The Age of Reform: From Bryan to FDR* (New York: Vintage Books, 1955), 204.

29. Elizabeth Ann Bryant, "Moses Did It, Why Can't You?," PhD diss., Department of History, Florida State University, September 2012.

30. Richard Breitman and Allan J. Lichtman, *FDR and the Jews* (Cambridge, MA: Harvard University Press, 2013), 322.

31. From remarks at the 2004 conference of the American Jewish Historical Society, http://www.wymaninstitute.org/press/2004–06–09.php.

32. Urofsky, *Voice That Spoke*, 280.

33. On the rivalry between these two men, see Ofer Shiff, "Abba Hillel Silver and David Ben Gurion: A Diaspora Leader Challenges the Revered Status of the 'Founding Father,'" *Studies in Ethnicity and Nationalism* 10, no. 3 (December 2010): 391–412.

34. Philip Weiss, "Zionism as a Political Movement Is Dead," July 11, 2012, *Mondoweiss*, http://mondoweiss.net/2012/07/zionism-as-a-political-movement-is-kaput.html.

35. Cited in Michelle Goldberg, "Mondoweiss," *Tablet*, January 20, 2011, http://www.tabletmag.com/jewish-news-and-politics/56447/mondo-weiss.

36. Hermann Cohen, *Religion of Reason: Out of the Sources of Judaism* (1919; repr., New York: Praeger, 1972), 14.

37. Judith Butler, *Parting Ways: Jewishness and the Critique of Zionism* (New York: Columbia University Press, 2012), 15.

38. Armin Rosen, "A Reminder That Anti-Semitism Has No Place in Debates over Israel," July 14, 2012, http://www.theatlantic.com/international/archive/2012/07/a-reminder-that-anti-semitism-has-no-place-in-debates-over-israel/259830/; and "The Mainstreaming of Anti-Semitism: Salon Partners with Mondoweiss," *The Elder of Ziyon* blog, http://elderofziyon.blogspot.com/2012/07/mainstreaming-of-anti-semitism-salon.html.

39. Cited in Benjamin Weinthal, "Frankfurt to Award Advocate of Israeli Boycott," *Jerusalem Post*, August 26, 2012, http://www.jpost.com/International/Article.aspx?id=282583.

40. "Judith Butler and the Politics of Hypocrisy," *Jerusalem Post*, August 30, 2013, *The Warped Mirror* blog, http://blogs.jpost.com/content/judith-butler-and-politics-hypocrisy.

41. Philip Weiss, "Jack Ross's Glorious Biography of the Prophetic Anti-Zionist Elmer Berger," *Mondoweiss*, July 1, 2011, http://mondoweiss.net/2011/07/jack-rosss-glorious-biography-of-the-prophetic-anti-zionist-elmer-berger.html.

42. E-mail to author, September 6, 2012. See also Sheldon Richman,

"Libertarian Left," *American Conservative*, February 3, 2011, http://www.the americanconservative.com/articles/libertarian-left/.

43. "Kevin MacDonald," Southern Poverty Law Center website, http://www .splcenter.org/get-informed/intelligence-files/profiles/kevin-macdonald.

44. Philip Weiss, "Kevin MacDonald and the Politics of WASP Resentment," *Mondoweiss*, December 18, 2007, http://mondoweiss.net/2007/12/kevin-mac donald.html.

45. Hannah Arendt, "Can the Jewish-Arab Question Be Solved?," in *The Jewish Writings*, ed. Jerome Kohn and Ron H. Feldman (New York: Schocken Books, 2007), 194.

46. The quotations in this paragraph are from Butler, *Parting Ways*, 4, 49, 215.

47. Gershom Gorenberg, *The Unmaking of Israel* (New York: Harper Collins, 2011), 13.

48. Gershom Gorenberg, *The Accidental Empire: Israel and the Birth of the Settlements, 1967–1977* (New York: Holt, 2007).

49. The quotations in this paragraph are from Peter Beinart, *The Crisis of Zionism* (New York: Henry Holt, 2012), 36.

50. Ibid., 79–99.

CHAPTER 5. THE LOST JEWS, THE LAST JEWS

1. Jacques Kornberg, *Theodor Herzl: From Assimilation to Zionism* (Bloomington: Indiana University Press, 1993), 24–25, 41.

2. Amos Elon, *The Pity of It All: A Portrait of Jews in Germany, 1743–1933* (New York: Penguin Books, 2004), 285.

3. Walter Laqueur, *A History of Zionism: From the French Revolution to the Establishment of the State of Israel* (1972; repr., New York: Schocken, 2003), 170.

4. "The Holocaust Is Killing American Jews," *Los Angeles Times*, April 28, 1992, at NJOP website, http://njop.org/resources/publications-archive/articles/the -holocaust-is-killing-americas-jews/.

5. Yair Ettinger, "Israeli Justice Minister: Assimilation of Diaspora Jews Fulfills Hitler's Vision," *Ha'aretz* (Israel), June 26, 2011, http://www.haaretz.com/print -edition/news/israeli-justice-minister-assimilation-of-diaspora-jews-fulfills -hitler-s-vision-1.369613.

6. Barry Rubin, *Assimilation and Its Discontents* (New York: Times Books, 1995), 158.

7. Cited in Kornberg, *Theodor Herzl*, 26.

8. The Cohen quotations in this paragraph are from Gerson Cohen, "The Blessings of Assimilation in Jewish History," in *Jewish History and Jewish Destiny* (New York: Jewish Theological Seminary of America, 1997), 152, 155. For an effort to bring Cohen's perspective up to date, see David N. Myers, "The 'Blessings of

Assimilation' Reconsidered: An Inquiry into Jewish Cultural Studies," in *From Ghetto to Emancipation: Historical and Contemporary Reconsideration of the Jewish Community*, ed. David Myers and William Rowe (Scranton: University of Scranton Press, 2005), 1–35.

9. For the results of the survey, see Barry A. Kosmin et al., *Highlights of the CJF National Jewish Population Survey* (New York: Council of Jewish Federations, 1991). For background and context, see Sidney Goldstein, "Profile of American Jewry: Insights from the 1990 National Jewish Population Survey," North American Jewish Data Bank, Occasional Paper No. 6, May 1993.

10. Jonathan D. Sarna, *American Judaism: A History* (New Haven, CT: Yale University Press, 2004), 361.

11. Krugman has used this term in a number of his columns. For a typical one, see Paul Krugman, "Hawks and Hypocrites," *New York Times*, November 11, 2012.

12. "Historical Inflation Rates: 1914–2014," US Inflation Calculator, http://www.usinflationcalculator.com/inflation/historical-inflation-rates/.

13. "Brides, Grooms Often Have Different Faiths," June 4, 2009, Pew Research Religion and Public Life Project, http://www.pewforum.org/Brides-Grooms-Often-Have-Different-Faiths.aspx.

14. Wendy Wang, "The Rise of Intermarriage: Rates, Characteristics Vary by Race and Gender," Pew Research Social and Demographic Trends, February 16, 2012, http://www.pewsocialtrends.org/2012/02/16/the-rise-of-intermarriage/.

15. Dennis Papazian, "Armenians in America" webpage, http://www.umd.umich.edu/dept/armenian/papazian/america.html. From Papazian's article in *Het Christelijk Oosten* 52, nos. 3–4 (2000): 311–47. Figures on Armenian intermarriage are difficult to come by; Papazian's estimate from 1980 found rates as high as 80 percent in some locations.

16. American Jewish Committee, *A Statement on the Jewish Future: Text and Responses* (New York: American Jewish Committee, n.d.), 41. The statement is available at http://www.kintera.org/atf/cf/%7B42D75369-D582-4380-8395-D2 5925B85EAF%7DStatementJewishFuture.pdf.

17. The founding text is Mordecai M. Kaplan, *Judaism as a Civilization: Toward a Reconstruction of American-Jewish Life* (1934; repr., Philadelphia: Jewish Publication Society, 2010).

18. The quotations from Moore are from the American Jewish Committee, *Statement on the Jewish Future*, 24–27.

19. For background on the reassessment of the 1990 findings, see Nacha Cattan, "New Population Survey Retracts Intermarriage Figure," *Jewish Daily Forward*, September 13, 2003, http://forward.com/articles/8112/new-population-survey-retracts-intermarriage-figur/.

20. *The National Jewish Population Survey 2000–01: Strength, Challenge, and*

Diversity in the American Jewish Population (A United Jewish Communities Report in Cooperation with the Mandell L. Berman Institute—North American Jewish Data Bank, September 2003, updated January 2004), 16.

21. Pew Research Center, *A Portrait of Jewish Americans: Findings from a Pew Research Survey of American Jews* (Washington, DC: Pew Research Center, 2013), 35. The other figures cited in this paragraph are found on pages 7–8. The entire report can be found at http://www.pewforum.org/2013/10/01/jewish-american -beliefs-attitudes-culture-survey/.

22. Paul Krugman, "Not Enough Inflation," *New York Times*, April 5, 2012.

23. *Le Monde*, February 23, 1990, cited in Bernard Wasserstein, *Vanishing Diaspora: The Jews in Europe Since 1945* (London: Penguin Books, 1997), 286.

24. Sergio DellaPergola, *Jewish Demographic Policies: Population Trends and Options in Israel and in the Diaspora* (Jerusalem: Jewish People Policy Institute, n.d.), 24.

25. "Vital Statistics: Jewish Population in the United States, Nationally," Jewish Virtual Library, http://www.jewishvirtuallibrary.org/jsource/US-Israel/ usjewpop1.html.

26. Sarna, *American Judaism*, 364.

27. Sylvia Barack Fishman, *Double or Nothing? Jewish Families and Mixed Marriage* (Hanover, NH: Brandeis University Press, 2004), 165.

28. The quotations in this paragraph are from Keren R. McGinity, *Still Jewish: A History of Women and Intermarriage in America* (New York: New York University Press, 2009), 193, 194–95.

29. Elihu Bergman, "The American Jewish Population Erosion," *Midstream* 23 (October 1977): 9–19, cited in Dana Evan Kaplan, *Contemporary American Judaism: Transformation and Renewal* (New York: Columbia University Press, 2009), 167.

30. Alan Dershowitz, *The Vanishing American Jew: In Search of Jewish Identity for the Next Century* (Boston: Little, Brown, 1997), 24, cited in McGinity, *Still Jewish*, 215.

31. Calvin Goldscheider, *Studying the Jewish Future* (Seattle: University of Washington Press, 2004).

32. Cited in Sarna, *American Judaism*, 276–77.

33. Ibid., 275.

34. The quotations in this paragraph are from Jonathan Sacks, *Future Tense: A Vision for Jews and Judaism in the Global Culture* (London: Hodder, 2010), 45, 46.

35. Daniel J. Elazar, "The Jewish People as the Classic Diaspora: A Political Analysis," Daniel Elazar Papers, Jerusalem Center for Public Affairs, http://www .jcpa.org/dje/articles2/classicdias.htm.

36. Marshall Sklare, *America's Jews* (New York: Random House, 1971), 117.

37. Will Herberg, *Protestant, Catholic, Jew: An Essay in American Religious Sociology* (Garden City, NJ: Doubleday, 1955).

38. Marshall Sklare, with Joseph Greenblum, *Jewish Identity on the Suburban Frontier: A Study of Group Survival in the Open Society* (Chicago: University of Chicago Press, 1979).

39. Daniel Hillel Freelander, "Why Temples Look the Way They Do," *Reform Judaism*, Fall 1994, http://www.synagogue3000.org/printpdf/60.

40. David Kaufman, *Shul with a Pool: The Synagogue Center in American History* (Hanover, NH: University Press of New England, 1999).

41. Jonathan Woocher, *Sacred Survival: The Civil Religion of American Jews* (Bloomington: Indiana University Press, 1986), 20–21.

42. Deborah Dash Moore, *To the Golden Cities: Pursuing the American Jewish Dream in Miami and L.A.* (Cambridge, MA: Harvard University Press, 1994).

43. Uzi Rebhun, *The Wandering Jew in America* (Boston: Academic Studies Press, 2011), 117.

44. Haviv Rettig Gore, "Two Centuries after the Death of Its Founder, Chabad Launches Year-Long Celebration with Re-Issue of His Works," *Times of Israel*, January 7, 2013, http://www.timesofisrael.com/two-centuries-after-the-death -of-its-founder-chabad-launches-year-long-celebration-with-reissue-of-his -works/.

45. Sharon Otterman and Joseph Berger, "Cheering U.N. Palestine Vote, Synagogue Tests Its Members," *New York Times*, December 4, 2012.

46. Caryn Aviv and David Shneer, *New Jews: The End of the Jewish Diaspora* (New York: New York University Press, 2005), 22.

47. Jonathan D. Sarna, "From World-Wide People to First-World People: The Consolidation of World Jewry," unpublished paper.

48. Christopher Hitchens, *Hitch-22: A Memoir* (London: Atlantic Books, 2011), 383.

49. The quotations in this paragraph are from Eric H. Yoffie, "The Worship Revolution," *Reform Judaism Online* (Spring 2000), http://reformjudaismmag .org/Articles/index.cfm?id=2193. See also the discussion in Kaplan, *Contemporary American Judaism*, 341.

50. For a helpful overview, see Aviva Ben-Ur, *Sephardic Jews in America: A Diasporic History* (New York: New York University Press, 2009).

51. See, for example, Ben Birnbaum, "Brownsville, Revisited," *Tablet*, August 2, 2006, http://www.tabletmag.com/jewish-arts-and-culture/books/871/browns ville-revisited. For views of Brownsville from a woman's perspective, see Carole Ford Bell, *The Girls: Jewish Women of Brownsville, Brooklyn, 1940–1995* (Albany: State University of New York Press, 2000).

52. Deborah Dash Moore, *At Home in America: Second Generation New York Jews* (New York: Columbia University Press, 1981), 77.

53. The quotations in this paragraph are from Nathan Glazer, *American Judaism*, 2nd ed. (1957; repr., Chicago: University of Chicago Press, 1972), 85, 88.

54. Cited in Moore, *To the Golden Cities*, 96.

55. Sacks, *Future Tense*, 60–61.

56. Jonathan Sacks, *Will We Have Jewish Grandchildren? Jewish Continuity and How to Achieve It* (London: Vallentine Mitchell, 1994), 102.

57. American Jewish Committee, *Statement on the Jewish Future*, 12.

58. The quotations in this paragraph are from Jack Wertheimer, "Whatever Happened to the Jewish People?," *Commentary*, June 2006.

59. Herbert J. Gans, "Symbolic Ethnicity: The Future of Ethnic Groups and Cultures in America," *Ethnic and Racial Studies* 2, no. 1 (1979): 1–20; Mary Waters, *Ethnic Options: Choosing Identities in America* (Berkeley: University of California Press, 1990); Richard D. Alba, *Ethnic Identity: The Transformation of White America* (New Haven, CT: Yale University Press, 1990); David Hollinger, *Post-Ethnic America: Beyond Multiculturalism* (New York: Basic Books, 2005).

60. Shaul Magid, "Be the Jew You Make: Jews, Judaism, and Jewishness in Post-Ethnic America," *Sh'ma*, March 1, 2011, http://www.shma.com/2011/03/be-the-jew-you-make-jews-judaism-and-jewishness-in-post-ethnic-america/. See also Shaul Magid, *American Post-Judaism: Identity and Renewal in a Post-Ethnic Society* (Bloomington: University of Indiana Press, 2013).

61. Steven M. Cohen and Jack Wertheimer, "What Is So Great about 'Post-Ethnic Judaism'?," *Sh'ma*, March 1, 2011, http://www.shma.com/2011/03/what-is-so-great-about-%E2%80%9Cpost-ethnic-judaism%E2%80%9D/.

62. Marc Gellman, "Joe Lieberman as Rorschach Test," *First Things*, December 2000, http://www.firstthings.com/article/2007/01/joe-lieberman-as-rorschach-test-16.

63. These themes are explored in Eli Lederhendler, *New York Jews and the Decline of Urban Ethnicity, 1950–1970* (Syracuse, NY: Syracuse University Press, 2001).

64. Cited in Nick Lambert, *Jews and Europe in the Twenty-First Century: Thinking Jewish* (London: Vallentine Mitchell, 2008), 83.

65. Cohen, "Blessings of Assimilation," 155.

66. Sacks, *Future Tense*, 241. The original text is in italics.

CHAPTER 6. ANTI-ANTI-SEMITISM

1. Some of the more prominent forms are collected in Alvin H. Rosenfeld, ed., *Resurgent Anti-Semitism: Global Perspectives* (Bloomington: University of Indiana Press, 2013).

2. Robert S. Wistrich, *Antisemitism: The Longest Hatred* (New York: Pantheon Books, 1991).

3. David Nirenberg, *Anti-Judaism: The Western Tradition* (New York: Norton, 2013).

4. Neil Lazarus, "The Jewish Addiction," in *Israel, the Diaspora, and Jewish Identity*, ed. Danny Ben-Moshe and Zohar Segev (Eastbourne, UK: Sussex Academic Press, 2007), 22–27.

5. The quotations in this and the next paragraph can be found in Anthony Julius, *Trials of the Diaspora: A History of Anti-Semitism in England* (Oxford, UK: Oxford University Press, 2010), xxxiii, xxxv, xlii.

6. Ibid., 476–77.

7. David A. Hollinger, *Science, Jews, and Secular Culture: Studies in Mid-Twentieth-Century American Intellectual History* (Princeton, NJ: Princeton University Press, 1996), 20.

8. The quotations and information in this paragraph come from Dan A. Oren, *Joining the Club: A History of Jews and Yale*, 2nd ed. (1985; repr., New Haven, CT: Yale University Press, 2000), 40, 121, 128.

9. Ibid., 432.

10. David Halberstam, *The Best and the Brightest* (New York: Random House, 1972).

11. Cited in Jerome Karabel, *The Chosen: The Hidden History of Admission and Exclusion at Harvard, Yale, and Princeton* (Boston: Houghton Mifflin, 2005), 331.

12. Gregory Kabaservice, *The Guardians: Kingman Brewster, His Circle, and the Rise of the Liberal Establishment* (New York: Henry Holt, 2004), 266.

13. Oren, *Joining the Club*, 272; Karabel, *The Chosen*, 375. A slightly different version of the same incident is offered in Nicholas Lehman, *The Big Test: The Secret History of the American Meritocracy* (New York: Farrar, Straus and Giroux, 2000), 150.

14. William F. Buckley Jr., *God and Man at Yale: The Superstitions of Academic Freedom* (Chicago: Regnery, 1951).

15. Lehman, *Big Test*, 150.

16. Kathryn Lopez, "NRO Interview with David Gelernter," July 18, 2012, *Ruthfully Yours*, http://www.ruthfullyyours.com/2012/07/18/nro-interview-with-david-gelernter-by-kathryn-lopez/.

17. William Glaberson, "Five Orthodox Jews Spur Moral Debate over Housing Rules at Yale," *New York Times*, September 7, 1997, http://www.nytimes.com/1997/09/07/nyregion/five-orthodox-jews-spur-moral-debate-over-housing-rules-at-yale.html?pagewanted=all&src=pm.

18. Karabel, *The Chosen*, 536, 542.

19. Amos Kamil, "Pre-School Predators: The Horace Mann School's Secret History of Sexual Abuse," *New York Times Magazine*, June 6, 2012, http://www.nytimes.com/2012/06/10/magazine/the-horace-mann-schools-secret-history-of-sexual-abuse.html?pagewanted=all.

20. Kabaservice, *The Guardians*, 289.

21. Richard Conniff, "Personal Heroes: Inky Clark," *Strange Behaviors* blog, http://strangebehaviors.wordpress.com/2012/05/30/personal-heroes-inky -clark/.

22. "The Birth Goes On," letter to the editor, *Yale Alumni Magazine*, March 2000, http://archives.yalealumnimagazine.com/issues/00_03/letters.html.

23. Harold Bloom, "The Jewish Question: British Anti-Semitism," *New York Times Book Review*, May 9, 2010, BR1.

24. The quotations in this paragraph come from Jeffrey Goldberg, "Wiesenfeld: 'My Mother Would Call Tony Kushner a Kapo,'" *Atlantic*, May 6, 2011, http:// www.theatlantic.com/national/archive/2011/05/wiesenfeld-my-mother-would -call-tony-kushner-a-kapo/238478/.

25. The quotations and information in this and the next two paragraphs, unless otherwise noted, are from Alvin H. Rosenfeld, *Progressive Jewish Thought and the New Anti-Semitism* (New York: American Jewish Committee, 2006), 8, 21, 25.

26. Cited in Avishai Margalit, "Prophets with Honor," *New York Review of Books*, November 4, 1993, http://www.nybooks.com/articles/archives/1993/nov/ 04/prophets-with-honor/?pagination=false.

27. See the essays in Yeshayahu Leibowitz, *Judaism, Human Values, and the Jewish State*, ed. Eliezer Goldman (Cambridge, MA: Harvard University Press, 1992).

28. "Marx to Engels in Manchester," July 30, 1862, *MECW [Marx/Engels Collected Works]*, 41, no. 388, http://www.marxists.org/archive/marx/works/1862/ letters/62_07_30a.htm.

29. Karl Marx, "On the Jewish Question," in *Karl Marx: Selected Writings*, ed. David McLellan (Oxford, UK: Oxford University Press, 1977), 58.

30. Otto Weininger, *Sex and Character*, auth. trans. from 6th ed. (New York: G. P. Putnam and Sons, 1906).

31. Amos Elon, *The Pity of It All: A Portrait of Jews in Germany, 1743–1933* (New York: Penguin Books, 2004), 237.

32. The story of how traditional anti-Semitism slowly disappeared in the years after World War II is told in Leonard Dinnerstein, *Antisemitism in America* (New York: Oxford University Press, 1994).

33. "2011 Audit of Anti-Semitic Incidents," Anti-Defamation League website, October 29, 2012, http://www.adl.org/assets/pdf/anti-semitism/2011-Audit-of -Anti-Semitic-Incidents.pdf.

34. The quotations in this paragraph can be found in John Hagee, *Jerusalem Countdown* (Lake Mary, FL: Frontline, 2006), 57, 149.

35. Letter from Hagee to ADL, June 13, 2008, Anti-Defamation League website, http://archive.adl.org/PresRele/HolNa_52/5299_52.htm.

36. Julius, *Trials of the Diaspora*, 543.

37. Andrew Kohut and Richard Wike, "Xenophobia on the Continent," *National Interest* 98 (November–December 2008).

38. "Swastika, Anti-Semitic Slogans Spray-Painted on Toulouse House," *Times of Israel*, January 3, 2013, http://www.timesofisrael.com/swastika-anti-semitic-slogans-spray-painted-on-toulouse-building/.

39. David Goldberg, "Saudi Arabia's Intolerable Antisemitic Textbooks," *Guardian (UK)*, November 24, 2010, http://www.guardian.co.uk/commentisfree/belief/2010/nov/24/saudi-arabia-antisemitic-textbooks.

40. "Malmo Anti-Semitic Crimes Go Unpunished: Report," *Jewish Daily Forward*, January 9, 2013, http://forward.com/articles/168985/malmo-anti-semitic-crimes-go-unpunished-report/.

41. "Helft Brusselse moslimleerlingen is antisemitisch [Half the Muslim students in Brussels are anti-Semitic]," *HLN.BE*, May 12, 2011, http://www.hln.be/hln/nl/957/Binnenland/article/detail/1263064/2011/05/12/Helft-Brusselse-moslimleerlingen-is-antisemitisch.dhtml.

42. For a sampling, see David D. Dalin and John F. Rothman, *Icon of Evil: Hitler's Mufti and the Rise of Radical Islam* (New Brunswick, NJ: Transaction Books, 2009); Chuck Morse, *The Nazi Connection to Islamic Terror: Adolf Hitler and Haj Amin al Husseini* (Lincoln, NE: iUniverse, 2003); Edwin Black, *The Farhud: Roots of the Arab-Nazi Alliance in the Holocaust* (Washington, DC: Dialog Press, 2010); Klaus-Michael Mallman and Martin Cüppers, *Nazi Palestine: The Plans for the Extermination of the Jews in Palestine* (2005; repr., New York: Enigma Books, 2010); Jeffrey Herf, *Nazi Propaganda for the Arab World* (New Haven, CT: Yale University Press, 2010); Klaus Gensicke, *The Mufti of Jerusalem and the Berlin Years*, trans. Alexander Fraser Gunn (2007; repr., Middlesex, UK: Middlesex House, 2011).

43. David Patterson, *A Genealogy of Evil: Anti-Semitism from Nazism to Islamic Jihad* (Cambridge, UK: Cambridge University Press, 2010), 71. Similar kinds of arguments can be found in Andrew G. Bostom and Ibn Warraq, eds., *The Legacy of Islamic Anti-Semitism: From Sacred Texts to Solemn History* (Buffalo: Prometheus Books, 2008); Walter Laqueur, *The Changing Face of Anti-Semitism: From Ancient Times to the Present Day* (New York: Oxford University Press, 2008); Bat Ye'or, *Eurabia: The Euro-Arab Axis* (Madison, NJ: Farleigh Dickinson University Press, 2005); Neil J. Kressel, *"The Sons of Pigs and Apes": Muslim Anti-Semitism and the Conspiracy of Silence* (Dulles, VA: Potomac Books, 2012); Yehuda Bauer, "Beyond the Fourth Wave: Contemporary Anti-Semitism and Radical Islam," *Judaism* 55 (Summer 2006): 55–62.

44. Jonathan Sacks, *Future Tense: A Vision for Jews and Judaism in the Global Culture* (London: Hodder, 2010), 105.

45. Bernard Lewis, *Semites and Anti-Semites: An Inquiry into Conflict and Prejudice* (1986; repr., New York: Norton, 1999), 121–22.

46. The quotations in this paragraph, unless otherwise noted, are from Martin Gilbert, *In Ishmael's House: A History of Jews in Muslim Lands* (New Haven, CT: Yale University Press, 2010), 149, 181.

47. Elaine Sciolino, "Heroic Tale of Holocaust, with a Twist," *New York Times*, October 3, 2011.

48. Peter Novick, *The Holocaust in American Life* (Boston: Houghton Mifflin, 1999), 158.

49. Gilbert Achcar, *The Arabs and the Holocaust: The Arab-Israeli War of Narratives*, trans. G. M. Goshgarian (New York: Metropolitan Books, 2009), 164.

50. Josh Lanamelis, "Muslims, Jews Gather in Paris for Interfaith Parlay," *Jerusalem Post*, July 9, 2012, http://www.jpost.com/Jewish-World/Jewish-News/Muslims-Jews-gather-in-Paris-for-interfaith-parley.

51. Scott Sayare, "Bucking French Tradition, City Sets Up a Kind of Holy Quarter," *New York Times*, April 2, 2013.

52. Robert Leiken, *Europe's Angry Muslims: The Revolt of the Second Generation* (New York: Oxford University Press, 2011).

53. Jonathan Laurence, *The Emancipation of Europe's Muslims: The State's Role in Minority Integration* (Princeton, NJ: Princeton University Press, 2012), 268–69.

54. Robin Shepherd, *A State Beyond the Pale: Europe's Problem with Israel* (London: Phoenix, 2009), 105.

55. Robert S. Wistrich, *A Fatal Obsession: Anti-Semitism from Antiquity to the Global Jihad* (New York: Random House, 2010), 542.

56. Both the Wiesenthal listing and the quotations from Broder can be found in "2012 Top Ten Anti-Semitic/Anti-Israel Slurs," Simon Wiesenthal Center website, http://www.wiesenthal.com/2012slurs.

57. The quotations in this paragraph and the next are in Shepherd, *State Beyond the Pale*, 170, 176–77, 145.

58. Jonathan Freedland, "What U.S. Jews Don't Get about European Anti-Semitism," *Daily Beast*, February 14, 2013, http://www.thedailybeast.com/articles/2013/01/14/what-u-s-jews-don-t-get-about-european-anti-semitism.html.

59. For some examples, see Adam Levick, "Jonathan Freedland's Illusions about the Nature of Modern Antisemitism," *Algemeiner*, January 18, 2013, http://www.algemeiner.com/2013/01/18/jonathan-freedland%E2%80%99s-illusions-about-the-nature-of-modern-antisemitism/; and Liam Hoare, "Downplaying Western European Anti-Semitism," *Daily Beast*, January 29, 2013, http://www.thedailybeast.com/articles/2013/01/29/anti-semitism-is-alive-and-well-in-western-europe.html.

60. Jonathan Freedland, "The Living Lie," review of *Trials of the Disapora*, by Anthony Julius, *New Republic*, September 23, 2010, http://www.newrepublic.com/article/books-and-arts/magazine/77373/the-living-lie-antisemitism-england.

61. "Working Definition of Antisemitism," European Forum on Antisemitism,

http://www.european-forum-on-antisemitism.org/working-definition-of
-antisemitism/english/.

62. University and College Union (UCU), "EUMC Working Definition of
Anti-Semitism," http://www.ucu.org.uk/index.cfm?articleid=5540.

63. The letter can be found at the Academic Friends of Israel website, http://
www.academics-for-israel.org/Mishcon_letter_to_UCU_010711.pdf.

64. Cited in Anshel Pfeffer, "British Jewry in Turmoil after Tribunal Blasts
Pro-Israel Activist for Bringing Harassment Case," *Ha'aretz* (Israel), April 10, 2013,
http://www.haaretz.com/jewish-world/jewish-world-news/british-jewry-in
-turmoil-after-tribunal-blasts-pro-israel-activist-for-bringing-harassment-case
.premium-1.514173#.

65. Julius, *Trials of the Diaspora*, 16.

CHAPTER 7. THE END OF EXILIC HISTORY?

1. Lagodinsky's letter of resignation can be found on *Jüdische Allgemeine*, April
23, 2011, http://www.juedische-allgemeine.de/article/view/id/10256/highlight/
lagodinsky. See also Tony Patterson, "Return of Anti-Muslim Author Leaves
German Left Wing in Crisis," *Independent* (UK), April 27, 2011, http://www
.independent.co.uk/news/world/europe/return-of-antimuslim-author-leaves
-german-left-wing-in-crisis-2275228.html.

2. Serge Lagodinsky, "Wir müssen mit anpacken" (We must lend a hand),
Deutschlandradio Kultur, October 20, 2012, http://www.deutschlandradiokultur
.de/wir-muessen-mit-anpacken.990.de.html?dram:article_id=224941.

3. Sandra Lustig and Ian Leveson, eds., introduction to *Turning the Kaleidoscope: Perspectives on European Jewry* (New York: Berghan Books, 2006), 2.

4. Bernard Wasserstein, *Vanishing Diaspora: The Jews in Europe Since 1945*
(London: Penguin Books, 1997), 289–90.

5. Figures calculated from "Judaism: Jewish Population of the World," Jewish
Virtual Library, http://www.jewishvirtuallibrary.org/jsource/Judaism/jewpop
.html. These figures do not include the former East Germany, as it was no longer
a country in 2012. Using self-reporting as its methodology, which in secular France
most likely results in fewer individuals identifying with any religion, another count
produces only 310,000 Jews, fewer than in Canada. Pew Research Center's Forum
on Religion and Public Life, *The Global Religious Landscape: A Report on the Size
and Distribution of the World's Major Religious Groups as of 2010* (Washington, DC:
Pew Research Center, December 2012), 46.

6. Todd M. Endelman, *The Jews of Britain: 1656 to 2000* (Berkeley: University
of California Press, 2002), 256.

7. Lars Dencik, "The Dialectics of the Diaspora: On the Art of Being Jewish in

Swedish Modernity," in *A Road to Nowhere? Jewish Experiences in Unifying Europe*, ed. Julius H. Schoeps and Olaf Glöckner (Leiden: Brill, 2011), 134.

8. Raanan Rein and Martina Weisz, "Ghosts of the Past, Challenges of the Present: New and Old 'Others' in Contemporary Spain," in Schoeps and Glöckner, *A Road to Nowhere?*, 104.

9. The quotations in this paragraph unless otherwise noted are from Y. Michal Bodemann, "A Cultural Renascence in Germany?" in *Turning the Kaleidoscope: Perspectives on European Jewry*, ed. Sandra Lustig and Ian Leveson (New York: Berghan Books, 2006), 166, 171.

10. Gabriel Sheffer, "The European Jewish Diaspora: The Third Pillar of World Jewry?" in Schoeps and Glöckner, *A Road to Nowhere?*, 37.

11. The quotations in this and the next paragraph come from Diana Pinto, "Towards a European Jewish Identity," *Golem: Europäisch-jüdisches Magazin*, n.d., http://www.hagalil.com/bet-debora/golem/europa.htm.

12. The quotations from Benima can be found in Nick Lambert, *Jews and Europe in the Twenty-First Century: Thinking Jewish* (London: Vallentine Mitchell, 2008), 104, 288.

13. E-mail communications to the author from Noa Hermele, deputy director and head of the One Year Program, June 2013.

14. Lars Dencik, "'Homo Zappiens': A European-Jewish Way of Life in the Era of Globalization," in Lustig and Leveson, *Turning the Kaleidoscope*, 93.

15. See "Barbara Spectre," *Metapedia*, http://en.metapedia.org/wiki/Barbara _Spectre; and Kevin MacDonald, "Jews Play a Role in Promoting Multiculturalism in Europe," *Occidental Observer*, September 16, 2010, http://www .theoccidentalobserver.net/2010/09/kevin-macdonald-jews-play-a-leading-role -in-promoting-multiculturalism-in-europe/.

16. Barbara Lerner Spectre, "Jewish Peoplehood," in United Jewish Communities, *The Peoplehood Papers* (Nashville: UJC General Assembly, 2007), 17, http://www.bh.org.il/Data/Uploads/Peoplehood%20Papers%201-%20 November%202007.pdf.

17. For a critical view of such organizations from the perspective of one who found himself increasingly alienated from them, see Antony Lerman, *The Making and Unmaking of a Zionist: A Personal and Political Journey* (London: Pluto Press, 2012).

18. Clive A. Lawton, "Great Britain Tackles 'Jewish Continuity,'" *AVAR ve'ATID: A Journal of Jewish Education, Culture, and Discourse*, Jewish Agency for Israel (JAFI) (December 1995): 19, http://www.bjpa.org/Publications/ downloadPublication.cfm?PublicationID=12842.

19. Cited in Keith Kahn-Harris and Ben Gidley, *Turbulent Times: The British Jewish Community Today* (London: Continuum, 2010), 75.

20. "Algemeiner Jewish 100: The Full List," *Algemeiner*, http://www.algemeiner
.com/2013/04/25/algemeiner-jewish-100-the-full-list/.

21. Clive Lawton, "The Jewish Community Called Limmud," *eJewish Philanthropy*, January 28, 2013, http://ejewishphilanthropy.com/the-jewish
-journey-called-limmud/.

22. Quoted in Daniel K. Eisenbud, "Limmud FSU Holds Jewish Conference in Belarus," *Jerusalem Post*, June 4, 2013, http://www.jpost.com/Jewish-World/
Jewish-Features/Limmud-FSU-holds-Jewish-conference-in-Belarus-315404.

23. Steven M. Cohen and Ezra Kopelowitz, *The Limmud International Study: Jewish Learning Communities on a Global Scale*, Research Success Technologies (London: Limmud International, December 2011), 20, 22, 23, 24, http://www.
bjpa.org.

24. Kahn-Harris and Gidley, *Turbulent Times*, 171–75.

25. Paula Hyman, *The Jews of Modern France* (Berkeley: University of California Press, 1998), 206. See also Dominique Goy-Blanquet, "In Memoriam: Les horizones immenses de Richard Marienstras," Archives Des Actualités, Société Française Shakespeare, http://www.societefrancaiseshakespeare.org/
document.php?id=1660; Philippe Lazar, "Richard Marienstras, *inoubliable pionnier du 'diasporisme,'*" *Diasporique*, no. 14 (June 2011), http://www
.diasporiques.org/Diaspo_14_Marienstras.pdf.; and Judith Friedlander, *Vilna on the Seine: Jewish Intellectuals in France Since 1968* (New Haven, CT: Yale University Press, 1990).

26. Benny Lévy, *Être Juif: Études lévinassiene* (Paris: Editions Verdier, 2003).

27. For a more polemical work dealing with the current political situation, see Shmuel Trigano, *Politique du peuple juif: Les Juifs, Israël, and le monde* (Paris: François Bourin Editeur, 2013).

28. This estimate comes from the Israeli Ministry of Immigrant Absorption, as cited by Gil Yaron, "Fears of Anti-Semitism: More and More French Jews Emigrating to Israel," *Spiegel Online*, March 22, 2012, http://www.spiegel.de/
international/world/jews-emigrating-from-france-to-israel-a-822928.html.

29. Diana Pinto, *Israel Has Moved* (Cambridge, MA: Harvard University Press, 2013), 159.

30. Anshel Pfeffer, "Aliyah Is an 'Insurance Policy' for Jews in Rome," *Ha'aretz* (Israel), March 23, 2013, http://www.haaretz.com/weekend/week-s-end/aliyah
-is-an-insurance-policy-for-jews-in-rome.premium-1.511296.

31. In order, Meryl Yourish, "Will the Last Jew Leaving Europe/South America/Turkey Please Turn Out the Lights?," Yourish.com, http://www.yourish
.com/2013/03/12/17620; Guilio Meotti, "A Jew-Free Europe," op-ed, Ynetnews
.com, March 22, 2012, http://www.ynetnews.com/articles/0,7340,L-4206110,00
.html; Guy Millière, "Europe: The Submission That Dare Not Speak Its Name,"

Gatestone Institute website, March 28, 2013, http://www.gatestoneinstitute
.org/3644/france-mohamed-merah-anniversary; Mike L., "The Decline of the
Jewish Presence in Europe" (a reprint of the Millière post), *Israel Thrives*, March
28, 2013, http://israel-thrives.blogspot.com/2013/03/the-decline-of-jewish
-presence-in-europe.html; Adam Turner, "Europe Acquiesces While Jews Are
Threatened, and Killed. Again," *American Thinker*, March 28, 2013, http://www
.americanthinker.com/2013/03/europe_acquiesces_while_jews_are_threatened_
and_killed_again.html; and Anshel Pfeffer, "A Jewish Exodus from Europe?,"
Ha'aretz, March 22, 2013, at http://www.haaretz.com/weekend/jerusalem
-babylon/a-jewish-exodus-from-europe.premium-1.511093.

32. Mark Tracy, "Op-Ed on Israeli Gay Rights Lifts Without Credit," *Tablet*,
May 16, 2012, http://www.tabletmag.com/scroll/99862/op-ed-about-israel-gays
-quotes-without-credit; and Max Blumenthal, "Guilio Meotti: Serial Plagiarist
or Common Hasbarist?," at http://maxblumenthal.com/2012/05/giulio-meotti
-serial-plagiarist-or-common-hasbarist/.

33. Cited in Ruth Ellen Gruber, *Virtually Jewish: Reinventing Jewish Culture in
Europe* (Berkeley: University of California Press, 1992), 42.

34. A YouTube video is available at http://www.democraticunderground
.com/discuss/duboard.php?az=view_all&address=385x116852.

35. Sheryl Nestel, "Universalism as a Basis for Ethical Particularism," *Outlook*,
January/February 2013, 5, http://www.vcn.bc.ca/outlook/current_issue/Outlook
%20website%2013/Jan-Feb%2013/Particularism%20&%20farmisht.pdf.

36. These figures are from Sharonne Cohen, "Canadian Jewry," *My Jewish
Learning*, n.d., http://www.myjewishlearning.com/history/Jewish_World_
Today/Jews_Around_the_Globe/Canada.shtml.

37. Quotations in this paragraph are from Abigail Pogrebin, "Immersion,"
Tablet, January 21, 2011, http://www.tabletmag.com/jewish-life-and-religion/
56589/immersion.

38. "Social Justice," Kehilat Hadar, http://www.kehilathadar.org/social
-justice.

39. Jack Wertheimer, "Mapping the Scene," in *The New Jewish Leaders:
Reshaping the American Jewish Landscape*, ed. Jack Wertheimer (Lebanon, NH:
Brandeis University Press, 2011), 13.

40. Peter Beinart, *The Crisis of Zionism* (New York: Henry Holt, 2012), 177.

41. Wertheimer, conclusion to *New Jewish Leaders*, 324.

42. Wertheimer, introduction to *New Jewish Leaders*, 17.

43. Encounter, http://www.encounterprograms.org/who-we-are/the
-purpose.

44. Wertheimer, conclusion to *New Jewish Leaders*, 323.

45. Ibid., 327.

46. Pew Research Center, *A Portrait of Jewish Americans: Findings from a Pew Research Survey of American Jews* (Washington, DC: Pew Research Center, 2013), 7.

47. Lynn Davidman, "The New Voluntarism and the Case of Unsynagogued Jews," in *Everyday Religion: Observing Modern Religious Lives*, ed. Nancy T. Ammerman (New York: Oxford University Press, 2007), 51–68.

48. Eric H. Yoffie, "The Self-Delusions of Secular Jews," *Huffington Post*, January 15, 2013, http://www.huffingtonpost.com/rabbi-eric-h-yoffie/the-self -delusions-of-secular-jews_b_2479888.html.

49. The quotations in this paragraph are from Leonard Fine and Steven M. Cohen, "Let Secular Jews Be Secular Jews," *Huffington Post*, January 28, 2013, http://www.huffingtonpost.com/leonard-fein/let-secular-jews-be-secular-jews _b_2567318.html.

50. Norman Podhoretz, *Why Are Jews Liberals?* (New York: Doubleday, 2009), 290.

51. The original article can be found at *Kropf's Poli Sci Grotto*, http://www .kropfpolisci.com/exceptionalism.fukuyama.pdf. The book is Francis Fukuyama, *The End of History and the Last Man* (New York: Free Press, 2006).

52. For examples of that debate, see Howard L. Williams, ed., *Francis Fukuyama and the End of History* (Cardiff: University of Wales Press, 1997); Chris Hughes, *Liberal Democracy as the End of History: Fukuyama and Postmodern Challenges* (New York: Routledge, 2012); and Christopher Bertram and Andrew Chitty, *Has History Ended? Fukuyama, Marx, Modernity* (Aldershot, UK: Avebury, 1994).

53. Cited in Lerman, *Making and Unmaking of a Zionist*, 124.

54. Michael Walzer, *Exodus and Revolution* (New York: Basic Books, 1985), 130.

55. Daniel Boyarin and Jonathan Boyarin, "Generation and the Ground of Jewish Identity," *Critical Inquiry* 19, no. 4 (Summer 1993): 712.

56. Gershom Gorenberg, *The Unmaking of Israel* (New York: Harper Collins, 2011), 236.

57. Shlomo Aveneri, "What's Happening to Diaspora Jews?," *Ha'aretz*, May 10, 2010, http://www.haaretz.com/print-edition/opinion/what-s-happening-to -diaspora-jews-1.289347.

58. Alex Sinclair, "Response to Shlomo Aveneri: Diaspora Jews Can and Should Have Their Say on Israel," *Ha'aretz*, May 13, 2010, http://www.haaretz .com/jewish-world/response-to-shlomo-avineri-diaspora-jews-can-and-should -have-their-say-on-israel-1.290167.

59. E-mail to the author, July 23, 2013.

60. Alex Sinclair, "Israeli Education Must Urge Diaspora Jews to Discuss Hot Topics," *Ha'aretz*, February 24, 2012, http://www.haaretz.com/print -edition/opinion/israel-education-must-urge-diaspora-jews-to-discuss-hot -topics-1.414483.

PERSONAL AFTERWORD

1. The results of our discussion can be found in Andrea Sterk, ed., *Religion, Scholarship, and Higher Education* (Notre Dame, IN: University of Notre Dame Press, 2002).

2. Alan Wolfe, "The Opening of the Evangelical Mind," *Atlantic Monthly*, October 2000, 55–76.

3. Judith Shulavitz, "Alan Wolfe Turns Evangelical," *Slate*, October 5, 2000, http://www.slate.com/articles/news_and_politics/culturebox/2000/10/alan _wolfe_turns_evangelical.html.

4. Alan Wolfe, *The Transformation of American Religion: How We Actually Live Our Faith* (New York: Free Press, 2003).

5. "RJN: 5.10.06, Alan Wolfe Is," *First Things*, http://www.firstthings.com/ onthesquare/2006/5/rjn-51006-alan-wolfe-is.

6. David J. Goldberg, *This Is Not the Way: Jews, Judaism, and Israel* (London: Faber and Faber, 2012), 184.

7. David Biale, *Not in the Heavens: The Tradition of Jewish Secular Thought* (Princeton, NJ: Princeton University Press, 2011).

8. Isaac Deutscher, *The Non-Jewish Jews, and Other Essays* (New York: Oxford University Press, 1968), 27.

9. Biale, *Not in the Heavens*, viii.

10. Yosef Haim Yerushalmi, *Zakhor: Jewish History and Jewish Memory* (Seattle: University of Washington Press, 1982). For a study of how memory can be shaped, see Yael Zerubavel, *Recovered Roots: Collective Memory and the Recovery of Israeli National Tradition* (Chicago: University of Chicago Press, 1995).

11. For Lord Snowdon, see Todd M. Endelman, *The Jews of Britain: 1656 to 2000* (Berkeley: University of California Press, 2002), 259; for Paltrow, see David Landau, "Alive and Well," *Economist*, July 28, 2012, http://www.economist .com/node/21559464.

12. Amos Elon, *The Pity of It All: A Portrait of Jews in Germany, 1743–1933* (New York: Penguin Books, 2004).

INDEX

Achcar, Gilbert, 182
ACJ. *See* American Council for Judaism
ACLU (American Civil Liberties Union), 81, 82
ADL (Anti-Defamation League), 78, 81, 82, 176
Adler, Joshua, 29–30
African Americans, 79
Ahmadinejad, Mahmoud, 30
AIPAC (American Israel Political Action Committee), 108
AJC. *See* American Jewish Committee
al-Banna, Hasan, 180
Albright, Madeleine, 196
Aleichem, Shalom, 50
al-Faisal, Abdullah, 178–79, 187
Algemeiner.com, 199
al-Husseini, Amin, 180, 181–82
Aloni, Shulamit, 56
American Civil Liberties Union (ACLU), 81, 82
American Council for Judaism (ACJ): anti-Zionist position of, 107–8, 119,

231n29; criticisms of, from Jews, 108; diminishing influence of, 111; establishment of, 25
American Friends of the Middle East, 109
American Israel Political Action Committee (AIPAC), 108
American Jewish Committee (AJC): General Jewish Council and, 76–77, 97; position on Israel, 231n29; *A Statement* and, 136; universalism and, 24–25, 81; willingness of, to disagree with Israel, 126
American Jewish Congress, 76, 78, 81, 231n29
American Jews: admonitions to from Zionists, 32–33; claiming space in communities, 145–46; communities in New York, 152–53; ethnic origins of, 151–52; evidence that Judaism is preserved in mixed-marriages of, 140–41; examples of movement toward a broad spatial outlook by, 147–49; generational

222–23; dislike of the idea of Jewishness as a fixed category, 224–25;
establishment of a center for study
of religion and public life, 219–21;
feeling of being Jewish without
being deeply Jewish, 224; interest
in and writings about evangelical
Protestantism, 217–20; pride taken
in accomplishments of other Jews,
224; status as a non-practicing Jew,
221–22; support of a future born of
Jewish universalism, 225–26
Woocher, Jonathan, 35–37, 146
Wright, Frank Lloyd, 146

Yale University: admissions policies, 167; alumni and funders'
opposition to admission of Jews,
169; basis of Jewish reluctance to
acknowledge help received, 172;
culture change facilitation, 168–69;
ideologues' opposition to admission of Jews, 169–70; Kamil's accusations against Clark, 171; result
of Brewster's efforts to improve
the sociology department, 167–68;
some Jews' lack of appreciation for
outreach efforts, 170–71
Yehoshua, A.B., 31, 32, 33, 35, 56, 213
Yellin College of Education, 197
the "Yid," 17–18
Yiddish, 20, 43, 49, 91, 94–95, 155, 158,
223
Yitzhaki, Shlomo (Rashi), 50
Ynet, 37

Yoffie, Eric, 150, 209, 210
Yom Ha'atzmaut (Israeli Indepen-
dence Day), 2
Yom HaShoah (Holocaust Memorial
Day), 2

Zakhor, 223
Zangwill, Israel, 152
Zionism: admonitions to American
Jews from Zionists, 32–33; anti-
Zionist position of the American Council for Judaism, 107–8,
119, 231n29; anti-Zionists and a
two-state solution, 128–29; belief
that Diasporic Jews will lose their
Jewishness, 132; Classical Reform
Judaism's view of, 106–7; contemporary anti-Zionist views, 119–21;
European's reasons for equating
anti-Zionism with anti-Semitism,
186; influences on Wise's view of,
113–14, 118; Labor Zionism, 14, 22,
114, 214; liberal views of Gorenberg
and Beinart, 124–26, 213; liberal
Zionists and a two-state solution,
129–30; negation of the Diaspora
and, 12; place in history, 212; political (see political Zionism); realities
facing progressive liberals, 126–27;
shared objective with Reform
Judaism, 60; universalism's view of,
104–6; Weiss's anti-Zionism, 112,
119–20
Zionist Federation, 198
Zipperstein, Steven, 48, 55